BOWLS
The Records

Patrick Sullivan

GUINNESS BOOKS

Editor: Beatrice Frei
Design and layout: Alan Hamp

© Patrick Sullivan
and Guinness Superlatives Ltd., 1986

Published in Great Britain by Guinness Superlatives
Ltd., 33 London Road, Enfield, Middlesex, EN2 6DJ

Phototypeset in 9/11pt. Times and 8pt. Univers
by Fakenham Photosetting Ltd., Fakenham,
Norfolk

Printed and bound in Great Britain by
R. J. Acford Ltd., Chichester, Sussex

British Library Cataloguing in Publication Data

Sullivan, Patrick
    Guinness bowls : the records.
    1. Bowling on the green – History
    I. Title
    796.31   GV909
    ISBN 0–85112–414–3

BOWLS
The Records

Dr W. G. Grace, founder and first president of the English Bowling Association.

Contents

Acknowledgements

I have received a tremendous amount of assistance in the preparation of this book and extend my gratitude to the secretaries of the various bowling associations world-wide who have responded so diligently to my promptings and queries. I also thank for their invaluable co-operation, Eric Bloor (Douglas Kenn Ltd.), Geoffrey Browne (*World Bowls*), Ferrell Burton (*ALBA Bowls*), Peter Clare (E. A. Clare & Sons Ltd.), John Cooper (*Bowls In Victoria*), Dave Crocker (EBPA), Eric Crosbie (EBC), Duncan Cubitt (*Bowls International*), Jimmy Davidson (WIBC), Eddie Elson, Frank Fullijames, C. M. Jones, E. Jenkins (Cardiff BC), David Marshall (IBB), Don McCosh, Albert Neill, D. S. Norman (Wisden-Edwards), Alan North, Garry Pearson (*Bowlers World*), Harry Rigby, Jack Scrimgeour (*Scots Bowler*), Noel Taylor (Thomas Taylor Bowls Ltd.), Syd Thompson, Bob Warters (*Bowls International*) and Tom Yeoman. To the above and the many others who have given of their time and knowledge, my grateful appreciation. To my wife Sheila, who has deciphered my handwriting, corrected my English and my spelling in the course of typing the manuscript . . . where would I be without you?

Patrick Sullivan

'You should have consulted the committee before you accepted the Snugfit Truss sponsorship, Major.' (*Punch*).

Gateway Building Society is currently the world's largest sponsor of outdoor bowls. At a national level, sponsorships include the Home International Series, the EBA National Championships, the British Isles Championships and the Gateway Masters, which is featured in the BBC Television series *Jack High*. Bowls sponsorship has allowed Gateway to promote itself via its nationwide network of branches and agents to an increasingly widening audience of players and followers alike.

The association between Gateway Building Society and bowls started in 1981. Since then, Gateway's involvement has grown rapidly. Why should a major national building society wish to support the game? In Gateway's case, the fact that its headquarters are situated in Worthing gave one significant reason. As well as being known as a sunny, south coast seaside resort, Worthing is equally famous for the quality of its bowling facilities. Gateway quickly recognized the game's growing popularity and saw great potential for the future, particularly as increasing numbers of younger players were being attracted. Even after a relatively short involvement, Gateway's name has already become more widely known and the game of bowls has benefited equally from Gateway's sponsorship.

It is an enormous pleasure for Gateway Building Society to extend its involvement with the continuing growth in the popularity of bowls through this excellent detailed work of reference from Guinness Books. Whether you are a player, spectator or new to the game, reading this can only add to the pleasure you derive from bowls.

Introduction

UNLIKE the majority of outdoor sports bowls requires no superhuman display of strength or explosion of energy to separate winner from loser. It is a game of finesse in which skill, judgement, a will to win and no more than the normal endowment of stamina are the prime requisites of both enjoyment and success. These qualities are not the sole prerogative of youth however and it is hardly surprising if people looking back on middle age revel in a game which, although conducted at a deceptively sedate pace, can prove to be taxing, exciting and, above all, satisfying.

The advent of televised tournaments has introduced bowls to a growing and increasingly enthusiastic audience. This exposure, long overdue all bowlers will agree, is now helping to draw fresh blood into the game with teenagers turning to a sport they may have spurned just a few years ago. Television, together with sponsorship and the introduction of professionalism, has at last given bowls the opportunity to throw off the sobriquet 'an old man's game' as it enters one of the most vigorous periods in its long and chequered history.

This book is intended as a guide to the game. It is not an instructional tome, there are plenty of those around for those who feel the need. I hope it will tell the reader, bowler or not, something about the game he did not already know. Above all it is intended to give pleasure and to act as a browser's reference book. I have done my best to ensure that the facts given are correct.

1 Early History

THE PRECISE origins of bowls lie back in dark and distant pre-history. Aiming a missile at a target with some degree of accuracy, whether for recreation or more serious endeavour, must have been a fairly basic, even a required skill when one's next meal was not only still breathing but often still mobile.

The first documented evidence of a game at least akin to bowls, was unearthed, literally, by Sir Flinders Petrie, Professor of Egyptology at University College, London from 1893 to 1935. Excavating the grave of an Egyptian child dating back some 7000 years to 5200 BC, he discovered a set of skittles or ninepins buried along with the remains. Even more precise data was to be found in the excavations at Thebes, the ancient capital of Upper Egypt, carried out by Sir John Gardner Wilkinson. Among the artefacts recovered were vases, dishes and wallhangings clearly showing people of the period 3000 BC involved in bowling games which closely parallel the game we play today.

The early Chinese bowled carefully selected stones towards a hole in the ground with the object, unlike that of golf, of getting the stone as close to the edge of the hole without it falling in.

The Polynesians developed Ula Maika, a game in which pieces of whetstone, 3 to 4 inches in diameter and painstakingly shaped into an oval, were rolled at pins set at a distance of 60 feet (18·3 m), the exact regulation length incidentally of today's ten-pin bowling lane. Different versions of this game filtered down to Polynesian descendant groups including those in Hawaii, Samoa, Fiji and New Zealand where a set of ten stone bowls of Maori origin are on display in the Auckland War Memorial Museum. Similar stone bowls were used in religious ceremony by the Red Indian tribes of North America and a set of these can be seen in the Vancouver Museum.

In the past, bowling games have taken on a mystical significance for many peoples including the Kiwais tribe of New Guinea. Much closer to home, in Germany, the *Encyclopaedia Britannica* tells of a custom practised by some God-fearing German folk in the 3rd and 4th century AD, in which the clubs, or kegels, carried by them for protection, were placed on end in church cloisters and bowled at with stones. Toppling the kegel cleansed the bowler of sin while those missing the mark were advised by their priest to repent and to lead a better life.

Bowling games were popular in both ancient Greece and Rome and it is believed that the Romans refined a game played by inhabitants of the Italian Alps region some 2000 years ago, into the game of *boccie*, a version still enjoyed in Italy and by people of Italian extraction all over the world.

In *boccie*, stones were tossed underhand at a target, but stones gradually gave way to wooden balls and then to the all-metal ball used today. From the unusual delivery and metal ball used, it is not difficult to make the connection with the popular French game of *boule* and there can be little doubt that this variation was introduced by the Romans. The spread of bowling games to the rest of Europe was due in no small part to the Roman urge for territorial acquisition and there is evidence to suggest that this dissemination took place prior to the 10th century as, by then, forms of bowls were popular in Germany and France.

The game enters England

Although the first stirrings of the game in England are believed to date from around the time of the Norman Conquest, one of the earliest references is to be found in the works of William Fitzstephen (or Stephanides), a close friend of Thomas à Becket and a valuable observer of the manners of his age. In the prologue to his biography of the martyr published in AD 1174, Fitzstephen tells how the young men of the day would spend their holidays 'at the bow, running, leaping and throwing of stones'. The work however was written in Latin and this last activity appears as *jactus lapidum*, a phrase which has suffered various translations. It is possible to deduce, however, whether one chooses 'casting', 'putting' or 'throwing the stones' from the three most popular interpretations, that the sport was more a feat of sheer strength rather than one of pure skill, having little in common with the game we know today.

By the 13th century, however, bowls in this country had developed into a more recognizable pattern. Evidence of this comes from drawings in a manuscript of the period once lodged in the Royal Library at Windsor but now housed in the British Library. This drawing shows two men, one having delivered his bowl at a cone-shaped marker and the other crouched, bowl in hand, ready to send his on its way. Two 14th-century drawings in the same manuscript reveal that the cone targets had by then disappeared and, in one case at least, had been replaced by a smaller bowl or jack.

Tradition rather than hard fact tells us that The Old Green at Southampton was laid prior to 1299 during the reign of Edward I but, truth or wishful thinking, that venerable turf is generally regarded as being the oldest bowling venue in existence. The first documentary evidence of the green dates from 1550 when an unfortunate was fined for the misdeed of 'keeping common playinge with bowles, tabylles and other unlawful games against the King's Statute'.

During this period bowling games, in one form or another, figured prominently among the common man's prime means of recreation, pastimes which, to the dismay of successive monarchs, began to distract attention from the archery butts. The skills with which the English archers handled the longbow reached a peak during the reign of Edward I (1272–1307) with the finest bowmen having the ability to unleash up to 12 arrows a minute at their luckless targets. Small wonder then that any games which seduced the male population away from practice at the butts, should be viewed as a threat to the very heart of this country's fighting capabilities.

In an attempt to redress matters, Edward compelled all men with an annual income of less than 100d (42p) (the vast majority) to own 'bow, arrows and other arms'. For those residing within the royal forests arrows were to be of a round-headed variety while for those living outside of the forests, the normal, short arrow was deemed suitable. This legislation proved something of a failure, however, and a number of statutes were passed over the following years with the object of eradicating all such dangerous pastimes. Edward III in his English Statute of Labourers passed in 1350, decreed that 'every man must work six days each week, attend church service on Sunday mornings under penalty of a fine and to assemble at the archery butts in the afternoon to practise and to pass on their knowledge and skills to their sons'. Various games, including *gettre de pere* (*jeter de pierre* or throwing of stones) were banned within the walls of the City of London under the act which heralded a series of punitive measures by successive monarchs all aimed at forcing the yeomen and commoners of England back to the butts. Richard II kept up the pressure by declaring in 1388 that all such games were unlawful, while Henry IV followed with a measure passed in 1409 which found anyone playing the forbidden games liable to six days imprisonment.

The game of bowls enjoyed a brief respite in 1455 when Henry VI lifted the ban on games within the City walls. That same year the capital saw the construction of the first bowling alley and the first bowls explosion with greens and alleys springing up with almost indecent haste. The alleys were of two kinds, one simply a narrow single lane affair, situated at a convenient and suitable spot, often between

Illustrations of bowling from an early manuscript of the 14th century redrawn in *Sports & Pastimes of the English People* by Joseph Strutt, 2nd ed 1810. (BBC Hulton Picture Library).

hedges of yew or rows of trees. The other, found mainly in London and used more often than not for skittle type games, was a covered alley with a laid wooden floor.

Although greens were now being laid at many of the large country estates, the majority, like the alleys, were constructed adjacent to inns and taverns, a custom which was to give cause for even stricter controls upon the already embattled game. Alleys, perhaps because of their siting, were to become the stamping grounds of the gambling fraternity, drunks and low-life characters of the day and these tawdry associations were to remain an unwelcome feature of bowls for many years. The outdoor game, while carrying on much as it had done over the years, tended to be tarred with the same brush as the alley game as bowls in general fell into disrepute and eventually paid the consequence.

The year 1477 saw Parliament under Edward IV reinstating the ban on certain games to commoners and introducing new and harsher measures to punish the transgressor. Under the new laws the prison term was raised from 6 months to 2 years while the fine rose steeply to £10. Anyone allowing such games to be played in his 'gardens or other place shall be Three Years imprisoned and forfeit £20', the ruling continued. But even these penalties were to prove unsuccessful and almost impossible to enforce.

Henry bans bowls

Like many other Royal figures, Henry VIII, a keen sportsman, embraced the game of bowls with great enthusiasm. *Strutt's Sports and Pastimes of the People of England* (Methuen & Co) credits that somewhat forbidding roisterer with the laying of greens at Whitehall Palace and reveals that the King's privy purse expenses show that he lost £4 10s (£4.50) at bowls to Mr Fitzwilliam, the treasurer, on 29 January 1530. Another entry, two years later, finds Henry on the wrong end of a pairs match in which he and a Mr Baynton lost £9.00 to Lord Wiltshire and Lord Rocheford who were able to add a further £35 5s (£35.25) to their winnings a few days later. The King's obvious enjoyment of the game, not to mention the added spice of a wager on the outcome, failed to temper his view of the common man's shared enthusiasm for it.

In 1511 Henry won the dubious distinction of becoming the first monarch actually to mention the game of bowls by name (rather than the all-embracing 'bowling games') in a statute confirming existing laws. 'The game of bowls,' he declared, 'is an evil because the alleys are in operation in conjunction with saloons or dissolute places, and bowling has ceased to be a sport, and rather a form of vicious gambling'.

Thirty years on Henry was to frame the infamous statute which Strutt termed 'a curious kind of class legislation'. Reacting (or perhaps over-reacting) to complaints by representatives of the Bowyers, Fletchers (arrow-makers), Stringers, and Arrowhead makers that the neglect of archery practice was a threat to their livelihoods, the King made his heavy-handed move to put matters right once and for all. With bowls once more given the role of main offender, all games devised by 'many subtil inventive and crafty Persons' were deemed unlawful. Anyone keeping an alley or 'Place of Bowling for Gain, Lucre or Living' was liable to a fine of £2 for every day of operation while the players were 'to forfeit for every Time so doing, 6s 8d (33p)'. Local magistrates were duty bound to seek out and bring any lawbreakers to book with the town mayors and their officers adding their weight by searching out any likely meeting places each week. However, it was sections 16 and 23 in a long and involved statute which made Henry's ruling so unjust. Section 16 banned all 'Manner of Artificer or Craftsman of any Handicraft or Occupation, Husbandman, Apprentice, Labourer, Servant at Husbandry, Journeyman or Servant of Articifer, Mariners, Fishermen, Watermen or any Serving Man' from playing bowls or any of the other forbidden games 'out of Christmas under pain of 20s (£1) to be forfeit for every Time'. Hence, a huge slice of the population of England found its bowling time restricted to the Christmas period and even then play was only possible 'in their Masters' Houses and in their Masters' Presence'.

The injustice of this wretched shackle on the leisure time of the common man is revealed in the last few words and sure enough, Henry had provided a convenient escape clause for the ruling classes. Section 23 allowed 'every Nobleman and other having Manors, Lands, Tenements or other yearly Profits for Term of Life in his own Right or in his Wifes Right to the yearly value of an Hundred Pounds or above' to play bowls 'within the Precinct of his or their House, Garden or Orchards' under licence. Surprising as it may seem this inequitable piece of legislation remained on the Statute Book until 1845 when it was repealed. Perhaps not so surprising is that it was to prove no more successful than any previous rulings.

Some eight years following the death of Henry VIII in 1547, Mary I deprived even those of noble birth the right to play bowls with

17th-century bowls on the terrace, Bramshill House, Hants. The seated figure is considered to bear a close resemblance to Charles I, a bowler of some prowess. (BBC Hulton Picture Library).

an act passed at Westminster in 1555. A staunch Catholic, Mary, the daughter of Henry and Catherine of Aragon, had married Phillip of Spain in 1554 and completely turned the religious order of England on its head. Not without some cause, Mary saw the bowling alleys and greens as being ideally suited as meeting places for men of influence opposed to her views and beliefs. Unlike her father, Mary aimed her act at some of the highest and mightiest in the land rather than the commoner. After the Christmas of 1555, licences for bowling granted under Henry were declared 'utterly void and of none effect' while the greens and alleys of which Mary had become so suspicious were seen as attracting 'idle and misruled persons' who held 'divers and many unlawful Assemblies, Conventicles, Seditions and Conspiricies' whereby 'Robberies and many other Misdemeanours' ensued to the breach of their Highnesses peace. Yet another stick had been found to wave in the face of bowlers, religious and political intrigue.

It was, however, gambling which bedevilled the game throughout the 17th and 18th centuries and many writers of the day contributed damning evidence of the fall from grace of a once harmless pastime. In his book *The Compleat Gamester* first published in 1674, Charles Cotton tells of the 'swarms of Rooks which so pester bowling-greens, bares and bowling-alleys where any such places are to be found, some making so small a spot of ground yield them more annually than fifty acres of land shall do elsewhere about the city, and this done cunning, betting, crafty matching, and basely playing booty'.

The majority of greens at this time were

anything but the smooth running surfaces we are used to today and this is illustrated as Cotton continues: 'In bowling there is a great art in chusing out his ground, and preventing the windings, hanging, and many turning advantages of the same, whether it be in open wide places, as bares (a bare strip of ground) and bowling greens, or in close bowling alleys'.

John Earle, who in 1662 was to become Bishop of Worcester and one year later Bishop of Salisbury, was another observer with strong views on the alleys, describing them in his book of essays *Microcosmographie*, first published in 1628, as 'the place where three things are thrown away besides Bowles, that is Time, Money and Curses and the last ten for one. . . . It is the Schoole of wrangling, and worse than Schooles for men will cavill here for an hairs breadth and make a stir when a straw would end the controversie'.*

Taking an altogether more moral stance was Kent-born writer, Stephen Gosson. Previously an actor and playwright, Gosson, who was to end his days as Rector of St Botolph's church, Bishopsgate, attacked the stage, poetry, music and other pastimes in his book, *The School of Abuse* (1579). Of bowls he was scathing, describing the alleys as 'Privy moths that eat up the credit of many idle citizens; whose gains at home are not able to weigh down their losses abroad; whose shops are so far from maintaining their play, that their wives and children cry out for bread and go to bed supperless often in the year'. Quite an indictment but, bearing in mind the reputation the game had earned for itself, not altogether an unfair one.

Bowls however had its champions as well as detractors. Sir Francis Bacon declared it 'Good for the stones and the reines (kidneys)'; William Shakespeare refers to the game in *The Taming of the Shrew* where Petruchio exclaims: 'Well forward, forward! thus the bowl should run, And not unluckily against the bias'. (*Act IV Scene V*). While in *King Richard II*, Queen Isabella in some despair, enquires of a Lady: ' "What sport shall we devise here in this garden, To drive away the heavy thought of care?" Lady: "Madam we'll play at bowls." Queen Isabella: " 'Twill make me think the

* The 1969 edition of *Strutt's Sports and Pastimes of the people of England* attributes an almost identical passage to Cotton's *The Compleat Gamester*. Earle's *Microcosmographie* was published 46 years prior to Cotton's book and, although the passage does indeed appear in Cotton's work, one must conclude that Earle's was the original. Further, I have studied a copy of the third edition of Strutt's book, published in 1830, and there appears to be no trace of the passage and it is possible that it was added at a later date in error.

world is full of rubs and that my fortune runs against the bias." ' (*Act III Scene IV*). Samuel Pepys was another who obviously viewed the game with some affection, recording in his Diary for 1 May 1661 the following: 'Up early and bated at Petersfield. Here very merry and played with our wives at bowles.' A further entry dated 26 July 1662 reads: 'To Whitehall gardens and the Bowling Alley, where lords and ladies are now at bowles in brave condition'.

Drake – Legend or myth

Every sport has its legends, many undoubtedly verging on the apocryphal and bowls is certainly no different in this respect to any other. One of the most enduring and widespread of all sporting tales is that of Sir Francis Drake and his famous roll-up on Plymouth Hoe. Whether this comes under the banner of fact or fiction is difficult to say although on available evidence it would seem likely that such a match did indeed take place but not at the spot indicated by Charles Kingsley in his *Westward Ho!* or by the famous Seymour Lucas painting which must grace the walls of countless bowling clubhouses all over the world. E. J. Linney, Official Press Representative of the English Bowling Association during the early thirties, carried out considerable research with regard to the authenticity of the legend for his book *A History of the Game of Bowls* (T. Werner Laurie 1933) but was unable to unearth any hard evidence of the game being played at all.

A Mr R. J. Tittall, Town Clerk of Plymouth in 1932, informed him that the City's records contained no mention of the game and C. W. Bracken, author of *A History of Plymouth*, insisted in a letter that 'any attempt to connect the site of the present bowling green on the Hoe with the historic one is absurd. Plymouth in Drake's day was bounded by the shores of Sutton Port on the one side and the Wall, which ran from the Castle in a circle, enclosing St Andrew's Church and the adjacent buildings to the head of Old Town, and so back to the Pool. Any bowling green on the Hoe, therefore, would necessarily have been on the lower eastern landward slopes.' Plymouth archives contain no record of any Pelican Inn, the hostelry behind which the game was supposed to have taken place and there is general agreement that the true site of the green was in an area close by the town's Citadel, a fortification constructed shortly after the engagement with the Spanish fleet.

Whatever the achievements of Howard and Drake in routing Phillip II's Armada they, like all bowlers at that time, were openly flouting the law of the land. No doubt they would have been forgiven by a grateful Monarch but commoners were still braving fine and imprisonment in pursuit of their favourite pastime.

While the game remained one of ill repute, a true 'pot house recreation' as it was termed, it continued to hold a fascination for Royalty. That doomed Monarch Charles I was an enthusiastic bowler but, by all accounts, not a lucky one. One of his favourite greens was at Barking

The White Fryers in Gloucester, 18th century. (BBC Hulton Picture Library).

Hall in Essex, the estate of Richard Shute, a turkey merchant, where playing for large stakes was clearly the order of the day. Following a particularly unfortunate run of games Charles found himself £1000 in debt to Shute who suggested that one more game may see the King's fortune change for the better: 'No, Shute,' replied Charles, 'thou hast won the day, and much good may it do thee; but I must remember I have a wife and children'. Charles' love of the game survived his misfortunes and led him to have a green laid at Spring Gardens (Charing Cross) and during the period of his imprisonment at Carisbrooke Castle on the Isle of Wight, he passed much of his time on a green constructed within the ramparts. Charles and his love of bowls were commemorated on an inn sign at Collins End, near Goring in Oxfordshire, where he occasionally bowled. The sign carried a portrait of the King and a verse which reads:

> Stop traveller, stop! In yonder peaceful glade
> His favourite game the royal martyr played;
> Here, stripped of honours, children, freedom, rank,
> Drank from the bowl, and bowl'd for what he drank;
> Sought in a cheerful glass his cares to drown
> And changed his guinea ere he lost his Crown.

Charles' favourite game however was to bring tragedy to his life when his deformed daughter, Princess Elizabeth, died from an illness contracted after playing bowls in the pouring rain at Carisbrooke Castle.

Charles II, the son of Charles I, shared his father's passion for the game and paid for a green to be laid at Windsor Castle for his private use. Bearing in mind the huge costs involved today for such an undertaking, the bill or this task makes interesting reading. Dated 11 May 1663, the bill states:

	£	s	d
To W. Herbert for making ye bowling green and walkes	10	0	0
For cutting turfe for green	3	12	0
For 8 Pairs of Bowles and Carriage and Lamps	4	5	6
Iron work for ye Bowling-green door	1	17	11
Will Tonks, 4 days and W. Herbert, 3 days @ 1/6 per day, for making ye walke		10	6
Francis Goodall, for 2 days work in ye walkes		2	0
	£20	7	11

The building of bowling greens and alleys was at full spate in the 17th century both in London and at estates around the country. Many London streets bear witness to the popularity of the game among our ancestors. In Putney, close to the Heath, we find Bowling Green Close, an area which probably boasted the notorious green and Bowling Green House, once used as a clubhouse by the shady people who frequented it. Off the Kennington Oval lies Bowling Green Street while near the junction of City Road and Old Street we find Bowling Green Walk. At Clerkenwell's Bowling Green Lane there were no fewer than 31 rinks in 1674, both open and covered. Piccadilly Hall, at the top of Haymarket was, in the words of Lord Clarendon, 'a fair house for entertainment and gaming, with handsome gravel walks with shade and there was an upper and lower Bowling green, wither very many of the nobility and gentry of the best quality resorted both for exercise and conversation'. Marylebone's greens were popular with the gentry and their ladies as were those at Southwark and Blackheath.

Charles II lays down the law of bowls

No doubt at the urging of their masters, greenkeepers during the reign of Charles II began to get to grips with the task of providing a well grassed and level bowling surface which would be easy to control. This period also saw the King, together with his brother, James, Duke of York and George, Duke of Buckingham, attempt to formalize the game with a set of rules to replace the rag bag of 'local' rulings usually designed to cheat the unwary visitor out of his meagre savings. A

Bowls in the Tudor period. (BBC Hulton Picture Library).

preface to this innovatory document stated that the game should consist of five or seven points as might be agreed upon, four or six bowlers to constitute a set and from that we can deduce that the game had moved, or was about to move, away from the single confrontation into a team game.

This first attempt at controlling the game, while no doubt finding favour with the more genteel upper classes, appeared to have little effect on the rough and ready masses. The sullied reputation of bowls and bowlers alike hardly became shining bright overnight and the game drifted on, despised by those good people who resisted its temptations and still a pastime outside the law. In Scotland however it was a different matter entirely. North of the border the game was never proscribed but

---

Rules for the game of bowls as settled by His Most Excellent Majesty King Charles II, His Royal Highness James, Duke of York, and His Grace George, Duke of Buckingham in the year 1670.

1 The party who hath the highest die shall lead the Jack, keeping his foot on the trig, which must be placed at least one yard from the verge of the green. No cast shall be less than 30 yards.

2 Whoever shall once throw the Jack off the green, shall lose the leading of the Jack to their opponents, and shall be obliged to follow the Jack so led by their opponents, or adverse party.

3 At the commencement of every end, the trig shall be played where the Jack was taken up, or three strides wide of it, in any direction before the Jack be thrown; provided by so doing, the cast be not less than 30 yards.

4 If the Jack be bowled off the green, there shall be a fresh cast, and the same party again lead.

5 If a bowl, whilst running, be stopped by the adverse party it shall be laid close behind the Jack.

6 If any bowler do take up the Jack before the cast or casts won be granted, he shall lose the cast to the adverse party.

7 If any bowler who lieth all, i.e. who is nearest the Jack do take the Jack up, or cause the same to be taken up, before his opponent has thrown the last bowl, his side shall lose the cast and the lead shall begin again.

8 If any bowler who lieth all do take up the Jack or cause the same to be taken up before his own partner has thrown his last bowl, he shall lose the benifit of that bowl.

9 If any bowl do lie between the Jack and that Bowl that is to be measured, or the Jack leanith upon the Bowl, or the Bowl upon the Jack, it shall be lawful to bolster up the Bowl or Jack, and to take away the Bowl which hindered the measuring; provided it doth not prejudice the adverse party in so doing. If it shall appear to the spectators (being no bettor), the adverse party was prejudiced thereby, although the Bowl did not win, yet the benifit thereof shall be lost.

10 If in measuring it shall appear that the Bowl or the Jack was removed, or made worse by the measurer, the cast so measured shall be allowed to the adverse party.

11 If any bowler bowl out of turn, his bowl may be stopped by the adverse party, but not by him who delivered the same.

12 If any bowl be stopped whilst running, or touched by its own party, it shall then be taken away.

13 If any bowler deliver his bowl or bowls not touching the trig with his foot, it shall be lawful for the adverse party to stop the same whilst running, and make him bowl it again; but it shall not be lawful for him that bowls to do it.

14 If any bowler who lieth all do take up a bowl or bowls before the adverse party hath granted them the cast shall be lost, and the Jack shall be thrown again.

15 Bowlers nor bettors shall do anything to prejudice or favour a bowl by wind, hat, foot, or otherwise, and if done the cast shall be lost.

16 No cast shall be measured before all bowls are bowled.

17 If he that is to throw the last bowl do take up the trig or cause it to be taken up, supposing the game to be won, or that he shall do some hurt, the same bowls shall not be bowled that cast, or end, for the trig once taken up shall not be set again.

18 If any running bowl be stopped, or touched by a spectator, nor being a bettor, whether it be to the benifit or hinderence to the caster, the same bowl shall take its chance and lie.

19 If a bowl be removed out of its place by the party that bowled the same at any time before the cast be ended the same may be cleared away by the adverse party.

20 Keep your temper! and remember he who plays at bowls must take the Rubbers!

Village Bowlers (1852) from the painting by Sir George Harvey. (BBC Hulton Picture Library).

neither did it fall into disrepute by the activities of its players and bowls flourished in an altogether more healthy environment. It is to the Scots that all bowlers owe a debt of gratitude for rescuing their game and its revival, which led to the modern game we play today, stems from their influence and the discipline they brought to bowls. While in England the game continued its headlong rush into ignominy, the Scots assumed an altogether more civilized approach towards bowling and bowlers alike. Although records in Glasgow dating back to 1595 reveal that play was forbidden on the Sabbath, the game was never in any danger of being outlawed nor ever

regarded as a threat to the general well-being of the country. In his book, *The Complete Bowler* (Adam & Charles Black 1912), Charles A. Manson (Jack High) credits Glasgow as being the birthplace of the game north of the border but, with James IV known to have enjoyed the occasional roll-up at Holyrood Palace, surely Edinburgh must also have a claim in that direction. One fact we can be certain of is that bowls took very firm root in Scotland and was nurtured there as it never was in England. The contrasting atmosphere in which the game was played in the two countries is perfectly exemplified by Dr Thomas Somerville of Jedburgh in his book *My Own*

A Game of Bowls, a drawing dating from 1870. (BBC Hulton Picture Library).

Life and Times. Dealing with a period commencing around 1741, Somerville recalled, 'Bowls were then a common amusement. Every country town was provided with a bowling green for the diversion of the inhabitants in the summer evenings. All classes were represented among the players, and it was usual for players of different ranks to take part in the same game'.

While the early outdoor game in England continued to be played over rough ground, the Scots began to experiment with sea-washed turf in place of the seed-grown grass during the 19th century. The turf, collected mainly from the coasts of Cumberland and Lancashire, contains a high proportion of the best fescue grasses and has a root system more vigorous than that of turf from inland areas. The density of its root fibres reduces the chances of breakage during transit, makes it easier to handle and, with a uniform consistency, provides a true and level surface. This last virtue was to change the very nature of a game in which success was often due to pure chance into one in which skill proved the dominant factor.

'News of the Armada' – Drake's interrupted match on Plymouth Hoe. (from a drawing by Allan Stewart)

2 The Organizers

In 1848 REPRESENTATIVES of some 200 Scottish bowling clubs met in Glasgow's Town Hall in an attempt to form a national body which would exercise some control over the game as a whole. Not surprisingly perhaps, with so many points of view struggling to be heard, they failed to reach agreement and a later meeting confirmed that such a lofty ideal was 'impracticable' at the time. This second meeting, held one year after the first abortive attempt, resulted in the momentous decision of appointing a committee to draft a set of laws by which play should be governed. Honorary Secretary of the committee was William W. Mitchell, a Glasgow solicitor and a bowler since the age of 11. To his everlasting credit he accomplished this task virtually single handed and the results were immediately adopted by bowlers in the West of Scotland. Sixteen years later Mitchell included the laws in his *Manual of Bowls Playing*, thought to be the first instructional volume on the game published.

The need for one body to unite the bowlers of East and West Scotland became once again a matter of great urgency and, following a letter to *The Scotsman* newspaper in 1889 from James Brown of Sanquhar, further meetings were arranged to thrash out remaining differences. The success of these led directly to the formation, in 1892, of The Scottish Bowling Association, the first national body in bowls history. The instigator of these fruitful deliberations, James Brown, was appointed honorary secretary and Dr James Clark (Partick) the first president. Mitchell's laws were, with certain revisions and additions, adopted as the official code of play by the fledgling body and the game of bowls had taken the first step towards recognition as a major sport.

The Imperial Bowling Association

Despite the many obvious advantages enjoyed by having a game controlled by a single unifying body, the other home countries showed a curious reluctance to follow Scotland's trail-blazing example. England's laggardly approach to the organization of the game is apparent in the fact that ten long years were to elapse between the formation, in 1882, of the country's first regional body, the Northumberland and Durham Bowling Association and the second such organization, the Border City Bowling Association. 1895 saw the founding of both the Midland Counties and the London and Southern Counties Bowling Associations but, although successful in their limited capacity, all of these bodies were essentially regional in nature and made no claim to speak on behalf of English bowlers as a whole.

The first serious attempt to provide something other than merely a parochial voice in the English game was made as late in the day as 1899 with the founding of the Imperial (originally International) Bowling Association. Even then the promptings came not from within but from Australia, or at least from two of that country's most prominent bowlers, Alderman John Young, president of the New South Wales Bowling Association and Charles Wood, holder of the same position in the Victoria Bowling Association. Visiting the country to watch the progress of the Australian cricket team led by Joe Darling in the 1899 Test series, the two men met S. E. Yelland of Hove at the Kennington Oval and, perhaps inspired by the series, explored the possibility of arranging matches of a similar nature between teams of Australian and English bowlers. In turn Yelland enlisted the aid of E. C. Price of the London based Brownswood BC, a leading figure and past president of the London and Southern Counties Bowling Association (1896–7) and subsequently Mayor of Stoke Newington. Price quickly canvassed a number of English bowling clubs and convened a meeting which resulted in the formation of the IBA with the Earl of Jersey as the association's first president and Price as secretary.

The aims of the new body were simply to encourage and arrange matches with bowlers from other countries which, in those days, home countries apart, meant the

Commonwealth and the Dominion of Canada. Price applied to the Scottish Bowling Association for permission to adopt their laws but found that the SBA had not only copyrighted the laws but were loth to part with permission for their use elsewhere. Having achieved the formation of at least a kind of National Association, the officers of the IBA were not about to see their efforts lain to waste and promptly formulated laws of their own to govern their 'international' matches. The first official match between England and Australia on 6 June 1901 took place, fittingly, at Brownswood BC, the club of E. C. Price, with the home team coming good in the latter half of that historic game to win by 22 shots. The 24-man Australian contingent had originally been teamed with 8 bowlers from New Zealand but, due to some unidentified dispute, the party split with the Kiwis playing as a separate, if minute, national touring team. Although exact details of their matches are not available, it is known that the New Zealand party completed 19 matches, winning 9 which, for so small a squad playing abroad, was a very creditable achievement. The Australians also proved hardy travellers and, having followed their initial loss with another, to Bounds Green by 97 shots to 69, they then reeled off 5 wins in a row and ended their tour winning 11 of their 22 matches, with one drawn.

1901 Australian Touring Party Match Record

Australian Tourists	89	Brownswood 111
Australian Tourists	69	Bounds Green 97
Australian Tourists	80	Brighton 76
Australian Tourists	127	Chichester 93
Australian Tourists	87	Southampton County 73
Australian Tourists	109	Reading 79
Australian Tourists	130	Cheltenham 50
Australian Tourists	91	Leicester 97
Australian Tourists	76	Newcastle 102
Australian Tourists	97	Hawick 76
Australian Tourists	61	Galashiels 91
Australian Tourists	89	Braid BC (Edinburgh) 75
Australian Tourists	74	Lutton Place BC (Edinburgh) 90
Australian Tourists	77	Perth 76
Australian Tourists	70	Bellahouston (Glasgow) 96
Australian Tourists	62	Wellcroft 83
Australian Tourists	82	Kilmarnock 74
Australian Tourists	79	Ayr 108
Australian Tourists	76	Maxwelltown 86
Australian Tourists	82	Ormeau (Belfast) 68
Australian Tourists	94	Ulster (Belfast) 94
Australian Tourists	89	Bromley (Kent) 61

Enter W. G. Grace

Despite the obvious success of the tour and its impact on the game as a whole, the somewhat limited activities of the IBA offered no solution to the lack of cohesion in English bowls at grass roots level. This situation however was due to undergo a radical change in 1903 when a group of farsighted and determined men, led by the legendary W. G. Grace, took matters into their own hands by forming the English Bowling Association. On his retirement from the international cricket scene and Gloucestershire in 1899, Grace was appointed manager of cricket and other sports at Crystal Palace, captaining the London County cricket team and becoming sufficiently entranced by bowls to replace tennis courts in his charge with bowling greens. Although holding no office in the association, Grace nevertheless played a role in the formation of the IBA and assisted in arrangements for the Australian tour. Back seats were not however built to fit the character of a man such as Grace and, in 1901, he formed the London County Bowling Association and, in an astute move, applied for and was granted affiliation to the Scottish Bowling Association. This gave Grace

The magnificent Eglinton 'Joog'. (Jack Scrimgeour).

and the London County BA a certain advantage over the IBA in that permission to use the Scottish laws came gift wrapped with affiliation, permission that was denied the older body. At the invitation of Grace, A. H. Hamilton, secretary of the Scottish BA, brought a two-rink team to the Crystal Palace to meet and play against members of the London County Bowling Club. The next year, 1902, following visits to Crystal Palace by the Scots as well as teams from Ireland and Wales, Grace himself led a team north of the border, playing matches in Glasgow, Edinburgh and Ayr and, as Hamilton has recorded, the visit by the great man found several hundreds of bowlers and cricketers crowding around the greens whenever he appeared.

At the time the SBA boasted some 400 clubs in its ranks, a true association and one which obviously worked for the good of all Scottish bowlers. In England the London and Southern Counties BA was clearly the best organized and influential of the regional bowling bodies. Beginning in the October of 1895 with six clubs, Brownswood, Bounds Green, Bromley, Lewisham, North London and Southampton 1299, the L and SCBA soon added Southampton County, Mansfield (London), and Upton Park to its list of associated clubs and has played an annual match against the Midland Counties BA since 1897.

No doubt inspired by the sheer scope of the Scottish example, however, Grace's ideas went far beyond the handful of clubs involved in regional associations and the 18 which came under the wing of the IBA. As captain and hon. secretary to the London County BA, Grace, together with his associates Stanley Fortescue and Walter Stonehewer, contacted every bowls club in England to explain their ideas for a single governing body for bowls. An added incentive was the prospect of international matches between the home countries and to achieve this end, Grace rightly insisted, the new association would have to adopt the laws of the Scottish Bowling Association otherwise the Scots could not take part.

The response was large, favourable and immediate and on 8 June 1903 the English Bowling Association was duly formed, with Grace as its first president, Walter Stonehewer as hon. secretary and Stephen Fortescue hon. treasurer. Amalgamation with the IBA was an obvious objective for the new association and, after some initial hostility towards the EBA, a conference between the two bodies was held on 9 January 1904. E. C. Price, hon. secretary of the IBA was unable to attend, but made his views known to the delegates of both sides by letter: 'In all but name,' he wrote, 'the duties of an English Bowling Association are, at present, discharged by the Imperial BA. It would be unfortunate if there were two organizations discharging similar functions, and the reasonable course would appear to be to join hands in what might be regarded either as a reorganization of the IBA, or as an amalgamation of that body with the new EBA. I regard it as essential to the best interests of the game in this country that all our clubs should act unitedly together and in harmony with those with whom we are allied. The very root basis of an association is

A bygone elegance: the greens at Alexander Gardens, Scarborough at the turn of the century. (BBC Hulton Picture Library).

mutual action for the common interest.' Honest words and wise counsel which was taken to heart at once, at least by the members of the IBA. On 3 February they passed a resolution calling for amalgamation and recommended that a general meeting of representatives from all clubs associated with the two bodies be held, with the objects of framing a new constitution and appointing officers to run the new association. Oddly enough however it was the younger, seemingly more dynamic body which then played hard to get. At its first general meeting on 10 February, the EBA delegates voted to leave the whole question of amalgamation in the hands of its newly appointed committee, which then promptly deferred the matter.

This apparent vacillation on the part of the EBA can be viewed in retrospect as nothing more than strategic manoeuvring as it sought to strengthen its position in the game. With affiliation to the Scottish Bowling Association safely in the bag, Dr Grace and his committee were quick to see the value of similar ties to any organizing bodies which might be formed by bowlers in Ireland and Wales. With the SBA and EBA already operating it was only a matter of time before the remaining home countries followed suit and it was Grace who was to prove the catalyst in each case.

In Ireland bowls has been traced back to the 17th century when the game, according to records, was played on greens at Belfast Castle. A plan of Belfast dated 1790 and reproduced in *Benn's History* shows the site of a bowling green close to the Academy, but it was not until 1842 that Ireland had its first bowls club, Belfast BC which, despite being forced to move its premises and lay new greens on no less than four occasions, remained the sole Irish bowling club for 30 years. It is interesting to note that the costs involved in building the clubhouse and laying the green for its final home amounted to something in the region of £800.

The bowlers of Belfast were the cream of the Irish game with skips such as John Rose, Joe McCready, Robert Andrews and expatriate Scots, Andrew Gibson and John C. Hunter setting and maintaining standards to a high level. Hunter, a native of Kilbarchan in Renfrewshire, took up bowls at the age of 13 and although spending much of his bowling life in Ireland, often enjoyed matches against teams from his home country and eventually returned there in 1910 having been a member of the Belfast BC for 32 years. Between them Hunter and Andrew Gibson were the bedrock upon which Irish bowling was built and, in 1903, in response to an invitation by Dr Grace, Hunter took a party of Irish bowlers to England. On their return to Ireland, Hunter, after consultations with other leading figures in the Irish game, called a meeting with the express purpose of forming the Irish Bowling Association.

Not surprisingly, perhaps, bearing in mind his unstinting work on behalf of Ireland's bowling fraternity, J. C. Hunter was elected to the office of president at the meeting held on 20 January 1904, with D. McLaughlin (Coleraine) as vice president and J. Boyd (Belmont) hon. secretary and treasurer. At the outset the Irish Bowling Association consisted of just five

W. G. Grace looks on approvingly as John Young (president of the New South Wales BA) demonstrates his skill. Photographed 8 June 1901. (*Illustrated London News* Picture Library).

clubs, Belfast, Ulster, Coleraine, Belmont and Ormeau and operated exclusively in Northern Ireland until 1906 when the Dublin-based Kenilworth Bowling Club became affiliated.

Wales now stood alone as the sole Home Country without an official representative body to care for the interests of its bowlers on a national scale. In the North the crown green code held sway as it does to this day, but in the South of Wales it was the flat green game which flourished with Cardiff as the natural focal point.

Within the city, bowlers pursued their friendly games on any convenient grassed piece of land, but among these itinerate bowlers were men of ambition and enterprise who sought a permanent home, a base for bowls in the city. Fortunately, among these was Andrew Pettigrew, head gardener to the Marquess of Bute who, with the support of John Boyle, Trustee to the Bute family, pleaded the cause of his friends and their game with his employer with such conviction that the Marquess offered to pay for the laying of a three-rink green in the city's beautiful Sophia Gardens. This welcome news was conveyed to a meeting held at Castle Gardens, Cardiff which resulted in the formation of Cardiff Bowling Club on 5 March 1878. No doubt in recognition of his services and his rank in society, John Boyle was voted in as president of the club, with Andrew Pettigrew, treasurer; Peter Whyte, hon. secretary and Archibald Hood as vice president. The green, constructed under the supervision of Pettigrew, was opened by Boyle and handed over to the club for its exclu-

The founders of the Home International series. W. A. Morgan (Wales), Dr W. G. Grace (England), J. C. Hunter (Ireland), A. H. Hamilton (Scotland).

sive use, exactly three months to the day following the historic inaugural meeting which saw the birth of organized bowls in Cardiff.

Thirteen years later, in 1891, Cardiff bowlers formed a second club within the city, The Mackintosh. This club had its green and clubhouse at the Mackintosh Institute on land leased at a peppercorn rent from the owner, Mackintosh of Mackintosh, a Scot who had married into Welsh Society. While the two Cardiff-based clubs were among the earliest to be founded in Wales, the honour of being the first belongs to Abergavenny which was formed in, or around, 1860 and is one of only two private green clubs in Monmouthshire. However it was to be the Cardiff and Mackintosh Bowling Clubs, together with Pontypool, which were to exert the biggest influence on the Welsh game. Bowlers from these clubs formed the Welsh contingent to the 1901 International Meeting at Crystal Palace organized by W. G. Grace. At the time, Cardiff was a member of the Imperial Bowling Association and played host to the visiting Australian side on 14 August 1901 in what was probably an 'unofficial' match. No records appear to have survived however and the result of the club's first encounter with visiting tourists is unknown. The Cardiff track record in succeeding matches against teams from Australia, New Zealand and Canada between the years 1904 and 1936 shows a creditable six wins against only three losses. Cardiff Bowling Club made its final contribution to IBA funds in 1904, subsequently withdrawing its support from that association.

Personalities involved in the first national singles championship of the English Bowling Association in 1905. Left to right: James Telford (runner-up), Dr W. G. Grace (marker) and Jimmy Carruthers (England's first champion).

Following the international meetings of 1902 Grace moved with commendable speed and single-mindedness of purpose to arrange the first series of matches between the Home Counties. These took place on the greens of Crystal Palace and South London over 13–15 July 1903 ending with victory for England. More important than the result however was that their success prompted the formation of the Welsh Bowling Association at the Park Hotel, Cardiff nine months later with W. A. Morgan (Cardiff) appointed chairman of committee, H. A. Keenor (Cardiff) hon. secretary and the Earl of Plymouth elected to the office of president.

The International Bowling Board

With the formation of the WBA, the circuit that was to electrify the game in the British Isles was now complete. The links formed between the four new associations and the institution of the international series were to prove punishing blows to the old Imperial Bowling Association. The final knock-out however was to be delivered by the newest and smallest body, the Welsh when, at the 1905 series in Cardiff, following a proposal by John Thomas of the Mackintosh club, a meeting at the Park Hotel on 11 July saw the formation of the International Bowling Board. Charged with the task of forming the rules and the

arrangements of international matches, tours by overseas teams of the UK and by British bowlers abroad, the new body was to become the most important and influential in the game and one which rendered the IBA virtually superfluous. The meeting from which the IBB emerged found the representatives of each country: J. C. Hunter and D. McLaughlin (Ireland), J. T. Morrison and A. H. Hamilton (Scotland), W. A. Morgan and J. Thomas (Wales) and, inevitably, W. G. Grace and Walter Stonehewer (England) all agreed on the adoption of the Scottish laws. J. T. Morrison was appointed chairman of the new board and A. H. Hamilton, secretary.

On 7 March 1904 Walter Stonehewer conveyed an EBA resolution to the secretary of the IBA, E. C. Price, which read: 'That this Association cannot entertain the question of dissolution, but if your Association will recommend their constituent clubs to join this Association (the EBA), a fair and just representation will be given to them on the Committee.' Grace, his power-base growing stronger by the day, had made his move, beautifully worded perhaps but an ultimatum whichever way one looks at it. Price, perhaps unwilling to enter into the cut and thrust which would come with defiance, resigned his position and was succeeded by James Manson. The IBA, with its member clubs deserting to join the better organized and more egalitarian English Bowling Association, tottered on for a

The bowl arriving at the head is the. . . . Bowlers at the London & N. W. Railway Athletic Grounds, Wembley, Middlesex 1912. (BBC Hulton Picture Library).

few months before finally capitulating on 13 November 1905, a brave and innovative body overtaken by events.

The Associations
Scotland

Bowls in the British Isles was at last functioning in an organized manner. Certainly some areas found early progress difficult to achieve, but a general climate which encouraged growth had been created from the chaos prevailing in the game during the early 19th century and the way forward was clear.

In Scotland the ideals of association were readily embraced by bowlers and in 1893, with the Scottish Bowling Association barely one year old, 173 clubs were affiliated under its banner. The same year saw the institution of the Scottish National Rinks (Fours) Championships (The McKewan Trophy) and this was followed in 1894 by the Single-Handed Championship (The Rosebery Trophy). Predating these and indeed the Scottish BA itself is the 'grand match', a mammoth annual contest between the clubs of Glasgow and those of Ayrshire. This one-day affair for the Eglinton Trophy has been an important date in the bowling calendar since 1855 when the first match took place on the greens of Ayrshire following a meeting at the Eglinton Arms Hotel in Ardrossan on 2 August of that year, with the return at Glasgow two days later. For this initial confrontation play was governed by a three-hour time limit but this was subsequently changed to a limit of 31 ends. In 1857 the 13th Earl of Eglinton presented the official trophy, affectionately known as the Eglinton Jug, and battling it out on that occasion were no less than 86 rinks comprising 344 bowlers! Since then the number of competitors has risen steadily, 135 rinks per side in 1900 (1080 bowlers), 308 per side in 1955 (2464 bowlers) and in 1984 the number of participants had risen with 315 fours per side to a total of 1260. Matches are played to 31 ends with the home or host clubs providing their guests with breakfast, lunch and tea plus a generous and ready supply of 'the Spirit'. Winners of the trophy which is insured for £2000 must undertake to deposit it in a bank vault for safety.

Unlike the English and Welsh Associations, power in the SBA lies, as it always has done, with the clubs. It was not until 1934 that, following a proposal by the Hamilton BC, the various county and city bodies were admitted on an associate basis but with representation at all General Meetings and full rights of membership.

Killwinning BC became the first holders of the McKewan Trophy (fours), defeating the quartet from Carluke in the inaugural final. The entry of the Single-handed Championship in 1894 also signalled the arrival of the Sprot family of Wishaw onto the Scottish bowling scene. George Sprot won the first national singles title to collect the Rosebery Trophy and made it a double, two years later, no mean feat but one that was to be bettered by his own son Robert. The younger Sprot won his first national singles title in 1910, equalled his father's record ten years later and surpassed it in 1929 with his third victory after being runner-up in 1927. In a long career at the top level of Scottish bowling, Robert Sprot's crowning achievement was to come in the 1934 Empire Games when he took the singles gold medal with an undefeated run and a shot advantage of +62.

Abbotsford became the first holders of the *Evening Times* Trophy, defeating Lilybank in the 1933 Pairs Championship final but it was not until 1971 that a triples competition entered the Scottish National arena with Dalmellington beating Blackland Mill to take the Cockburn Trophy and the title. The J. B. Richardson Trophy was originally presented to the winners of an additional fours competition first held in 1900 and open to all 'male members over the age of 18'. Belvidere (Glasgow) were the first holders of the trophy which, in 1966 was reallocated to a new competition, the senior fours which is restricted to bowlers 'not less than 60 years of age' with Hamilton Caledonian taking the initial honours.

The Scottish Bowling Association and the game in general owe a debt of gratitude to Andrew H. Hamilton who succeeded James Brown as hon. secretary of the SBA in 1895 and held that position for a staggering 41 years. Hamilton had learned the finer skills of bowls from James Telford, an Anglo-Scot and losing finalist in the first ever singles championship of the English Bowling Association. Moving to Edinburgh from Moffat in 1889, Hamilton joined the Lutton Place BC, winning that club's singles title in his first year. As if to prove that administrative duties had not dulled his appetite for success on the greens, he repeated that singles victory in 1892, 1895 and 1899 and was also Champion of City Champions on three occasions. On the formation of the International Bowling Board in 1905 he was elected as its first hon. secretary and, after retiring from the post in 1907, emerged to take up the same office in 1913. In a formidable career Hamilton served as hon. secretary of the Royal Caledonian Curling Club and was High Constable of his adopted home city. In 1939 he presented the A. H. Hamilton Trophy to be played for by teams representing county and city associations and this has become one of the most sought-after trophies in the Scottish bowling programme. Originally devised as a knock-out competition, games are now played on a league basis with 23 associations taking part. Following Ayrshire's victory in the 1939 inaugural tournament there came a seven-year break when the Second World War intervened, and it was Glasgow who were the first winners on resumption in 1947.

With 34 victories, Scotland lead the international table by a healthy margin, proving just

Eglinton Trophy

Year	Winner/Club
1855	Glasgow *Wellcroft*
1856	Glasgow *Wellcroft*
1857	Glasgow *Wellcroft*
1858	Glasgow *Hillhead*
1859	Glasgow *Kingston*
1860	Ayrshire *Ardeer*
1861	Glasgow *Kingston*
1862	Ayrshire *Girvan Victoria*
1863	Glasgow *St Rollox*
1864	Ayrshire *Ardeer*
1865	Glasgow *Calton*
1866	Glasgow *Kingston*
1867	Glasgow *Govan*
1868	Ayrshire *Kerelaw*
1869	Glasgow *Pollokshields*
1870	Ayrshire *Ladeside Kilbirnie*
1871	Glasgow *Whitevale*
1872	Ayrshire *Ardeer*
1873	Glasgow *Hillhead*
1874	Ayrshire *Largs*
1875	Glasgow *Queen's Park*
1876	Ayrshire *Girvan Victoria*
1877	Glasgow *Albany*
1878	Ayrshire *Dalry*
1879	Glasgow *Partick*
1880	Ayrshire *Dalmellington*
1881	Glasgow *Govan*
1882	Ayrshire *Ardeer*
1883	Glasgow *Queen's Park*
1884	Ayrshire *Galston Loudoun Working Men's*
1885	Glasgow *Bellahouston*
1886	Ayrshire *Girvan Victoria*
1887	Ayrshire *Kilmarnock West Netherton*
1888	Ayrshire *Saltcoats*
1889	Ayrshire *Kilmarnock* and *Cumnock (Equal)*
1890	Ayrshire *Cumnock*
1891	Glasgow *Albany*
1892	Ayrshire *Dalry*
1893	Ayrshire *Troon*
1894	Ayrshire *Dalry*
1895	Glasgow *Maryhill*
1896	Ayrshire *Dreghorn*
1897	Glasgow *Wellcroft*
1898	Ayrshire *Troon*
1899	Glasgow *Wellcroft*
1900	Ayrshire *Galston Loudoun Working Men's*
1901	Glasgow *Whitevale*
1902	Ayrshire *Dalry*
1903	Glasgow *Springburn*
1904	Ayrshire *Dreghorn*
1905	Glasgow *Camphill*
1906	Ayrshire *Kilmaurs*
1907	Ayrshire *Dalry*
1908	Ayrshire *Kilmaurs*
1909	Ayrshire *Prestwick*
1910	Ayrshire *Newmills*
1911	Glasgow *Burnbank*
1912	Ayrshire *Dairy*
1913	Ayrshire *Auchinleck*

Year	Winner/Club
1914	Ayrshire *New Cumnock*
1915–8	No play
1919	Glasgow *Burnbank*
1920	Ayrshire *Saltcoats*
1921	Glasgow *Cathcart*
1922	Ayrshire *Dreghorn*
1923	Glasgow *Mount Florida*
1924	Ayrshire *Beith*
1925	Glasgow *St Rollox*
1926	Ayrshire *Darvel*
1927	Glasgow *Tollcross*
1928	Ayrshire *Dreghorn*
1929	Glasgow *Victoria Park*
1930	Ayrshire *Dreghorn*
1931	Glasgow *Kingston*
1932	Ayrshire *Crosshouse*
1933	Glasgow *Kirkhill*
1934	Ayrshire *Kilmaurs*
1935	Glasgow *Titwood*
1936	Ayrshire *Dreghorn*
1937	Glasgow *Hyndland*
1938	Ayrshire *Newmilns*
1939	Glasgow *Weir's Rec.*
1940–5	No play
1946	Ayrshire *Auchinleck*
1947	Glasgow *Springburn*
1948	Ayrshire *Auchinleck*
1949	Glasgow *Hutchesontown*
1950	Ayrshire *Dalry*
1951	Glasgow *Pollokshaws*
1952	Ayrshire *Cumnock*
1953	Glasgow *Cardonald*
1954	Ayrshire *Dailly*
1955	Ayrshire *Hurlford*
1956	Ayrshire *Darvel*
1957	Glasgow *Foxley*
1958	Ayrshire *Dailly*
1959	Ayrshire *Dailly*
1960	Ayrshire *Mauchline*
1961	Ayrshire *Kilmaurs*
1962	Ayrshire *Cumnock*
1963	Ayrshire *Dailly*
1964	Ayrshire *Mauchline*
1965	Ayrshire *Dreghorn*
1966	Ayrshire *Kilmaurs*
1967	Ayrshire *Drongan*
1968	Ayrshire *Coylton*
1969	Glasgow *Croftfoot*
1970	Ayrshire *Kilwinning*
1971	Glasgow *Busby*
1972	Ayrshire *Dalry*
1973	Ayrshire *Ayr Craigie*
1974	Ayrshire *Dreghorn*
1975	Glasgow *Rutherglen*
1976	Ayrshire *Girvan*
1977	Ayrshire *Patna Miners Welfare*
1978	Ayrshire *Kilwinning*
1979	Glasgow *Mount Vernon*
1980	Ayrshire *New Cumnock*
1981	Ayrshire *Stewarton*
1982	Ayrshire *Cumnock*
1983	Glasgow *Burnbank*
1984	Ayrshire *Rankinston*
1985	Glasgow *Linthouse*

Youngest competitor in an EBA tournament
Ian Mayne, Heaton Hall BC, Manchester.
Entrant in 1985 Kodak-EBA Under-25
National Championship at 11 years 4 months.

Scenes from the 1914 International between England and Scotland played at the Bellingham Club. (*Illustrated London News* Picture Library).

about invincible between the mid sixties and late seventies when they won the tournament 12 years in succession. In the British Isles Championships Scottish club bowlers have won the fours on five occasions, the triples on three, pairs on four and the singles on eight but these doughty performances in the British Isles were, for many years, poorly reflected on the wider stage of world bowls. Sprot's 1934 Empire Games gold medal stood in splendid isolation amid a welter of silver and bronze awards for 40 years until it was joined at last by the Commonwealth Games pairs gold medal won in 1974 by Alex McIntosh and John Christie at Christchurch, New Zealand.

After taking a breather in 1978, Scotland struck Commonwealth Games gold again in 1982 with Willie Wood of Gifford emulating Sprot's feat by winning the singles, while John Watson, world indoor champion at the time, teamed up with David Gourlay and made it a great year for the Scots by winning the pairs event. In the World Championships, Scotland has twice won the W. M. Leonard Trophy for best team performance but has yet to win an event gold medal in the world's most prestigious bowls tourney although Willie Wood came within a fraction of an inch of taking the singles title in the 1984 Championships when he was beaten, on a measure, by Peter Belliss

of New Zealand at Aberdeen. The 1984 Championships, which saw the host country winning the Leonard Trophy for the second time, proved to be a smoothly-run event and much credit for this must go to David Marshall, the organizer and his willing committee men who all burned the midnight oil to ensure that the logistics were right. Credit and admiration must also go to the 87 500 bowlers of Scotland who helped to fund the championships by means of a £2 per man levy, and to the 868 affiliated Scottish clubs, many of whom played hosts to the 132 visiting bowlers from 22 countries who descended upon Aberdeen in July 1984.

Scottish National Championships

Singles

1894 G. Sprot *Wishaw*
1895 J. S. Henderson *Dollar*
1896 G. Sprot *Wishaw*
1897 A. Johnston *Troon*
1898 W. Blackwood *New Cumnock*
1899 T. Dickie *Hutchesontown*
1900 Thos. Allan *Kelso*
1901 W. Law *Kilbirnie*
1902 A. Wilson *Rock, Dumbarton*
1903 Jas. Brown, jun. *Blantyre*
1904 J. McNaughton *Camelon*
1905 Jas. Aitken *West End Edinburgh*
1906 Thos. Logan *Whitevale Glasgow*
1907 Dr Robson *Maxwelltown*
1908 W. Blackwood *New Cumnock*
1909 Tom Wilson *Pollokshaws*
1910 R. Sprot *Wishaw*
1911 A. Goldie *Hurlford*
1912 John Dunsire *Buckhaven*
1913 John McGee *Coatbridge*
1914 D. Park *New Cumnock*
195–18 – No Competition
1919 M. Hannah *Lady Alice, Greenock*
1920 R. Sprot *Wishaw*
1921 Jas. Brown, jun. *Hamilton*
1922 W. H. Scouller *Corstorphine*
1923 W. H. Scouller *Corstorphine*
1924 W. Hunter *Leven*
1925 T. Duff *Airdrie*
1926 W. Blue *Caledonia, Paisley*
1927 R. H. Jamieson *Marchmount, Dumfries*
1928 Peter Craig *West End, Edinburgh*
1929 Robert Sprot *Wishaw*
1930 J. Cowie *Carron and Carronshore*
1931 Peter R. Brown *Udston*
1932 Walter J. Wilson *Scotstounhill*
1933 R. Banks *Winton, Irvine*
1934 J. Kyle *Strathaven*
1935 A. Clark *Dumbarton*
1936 T. Agnew *Ayr Hawkhill*
1937 A. Stewart *Lilybank, Johnstone*
1938 J. C. Irving *Lockerbie*
1939 D. Miller *Leven*
1940 John Young *Weir's Recreation*
1941 Adam Dougall *Kirkhill*
1942 W. Cunningham *Dreghorn, Ayrshire*
1943 D. Dall *Blantyre Welfare*
1944 D. Dall *Blantyre Welfare*
1945 J. C. Irving *Lockerbie*
1946 Adam Dougall *Kirkhill*

1947 W. Cunningham *Dreghorn*
1948 James Barclay *Strathmore–Coupar Angus*
1949 D. Dall *Blantyre Welfare*
1950 J. C. Irving *Lockerbie*
1951 N. Campbell *Spittalmyre*
1952 J. C. Irving *Lockerbie*
1953 R. Kissach *Burnbank*
1954 R. Crombie *Leslie*
1955 M. Allan *Hamilton Caledonian*
1956 C. Grant *Bridgeness and Carriden*
1957 W. D. Jones *Ardrossan*
1958 J. W. Black *Sanquhar*
1959 J. W. Black *Sanquhar*
1960 A. Brown *Tulliallan*
1961 E. M. Johnson *Dumbarton*
1962 J. W. Black *Sanquhar*
1963 A. Adrain *Dreghorn*
1964 W. Gibb *Bothwell*
1965 J. Hershaw *Ardeer Rec.*
1966 J. Hershaw *Ardeer Rec.*
1967 W. E. Wood *Gifford*
1968 J. Lamont *Kirn*
1969 R. Motroni *Dumfries*
1970 R. Bernard *Gorebridge*
1971 J. McAra *Wishaw South*
1972 A. Binnie *Mayfield*
1973 R. D. White *Sanquhar*
1974 J. Fleming *Mauchline*
1975 J. McLagan *Methil*
1976 D. McGill, jnr. *Sighthill*
1977 J. Milgrew *Springhill*
1978 H. Reston *Deans*
1979 N. Amos *Hawick Buccleuch*
1980 J. Farrow *Cumnock*
1981 F. Muirhead *Uphall Station*
1982 B. Rattray *Alva*
1983 J. Campbell *Alloa*
1984 W. Paul *Tanfield*
1985 W. McLaughlin *Lesmahagow*

Pairs

1933 Abbotsford
1934 Juniper Green
1935 Gourock
1936 Lenzie
1937 New Cumnock
1938 Balerno
1939 Cumnock
1940 Lochwinnoch
1941 Halfway and District Cambuslang
1942 Linthouse *Glasgow*
1943 Forth and Wilsontown
1944 Maxwelltown
1945 Sanquhar
1946 Hamilton
1947 Auchengeich Welfare
1948 Catrine
1949 Sanquhar
1950 Catrine
1951 Wattfield *Ayr*
1952 Maitland
1953 Udston
1954 Glasgow Transport
1955 Burnbank *Glasgow*

Continued

1956 Merchiston
1957 Kilmarnock
1958 Rosslyn
1959 Denny
1960 Rankin Park
1961 Houston (J. G.
     Fleming)
1962 Lesmahagow
1963 Errol
1964 Lenzie
1965 Dumfries
1966 Campsie
1967 Gala Abbotsford
1968 Craigentinny
1969 Dreghorn
1970 Abergeldie
1971 Dalmuir
1972 Balerno
1973 Newbattle
1974 Foxley
1975 Elderslie Wallace
1976 Bellahouston
1977 Lockerbie
1978 Rothesay
1979 Annan
1980 Coldstream
1981 Bogleha
1982 Thornliebank
1983 Wellington Park
1984 Oakley
1985 Newbattle

Triples
1971 Dalmellington
1972 Linthouse
1973 Blackburn
1974 Dreghorn
1975 Brechin
1976 Whitburn
1977 Meikleriggs
1978 Foxley
1979 Foxley
1980 Kingswood
1981 Overtown and
     Waterloo
1982 Overtown and
     Waterloo
1983 Turriff
1984 Glenrothes
1985 Catrine

Fours
1893 Kilwinning
1894 Kilmarnock
1895 Kilmarnock
1896 Carluke
1897 Rosslyn *Roslin*
1898 Uddingston
1899 Abbotsford *Galashiels*
1900 New Cumnock
1901 Stenhousemuir
1902 Queen's Park *Glasgow*
1903 Dumbarton
1904 Springburn
1905 Larbert
1906 Gala *Galashiels*
1907 Stewarton
1908 West End *Edinburgh*
1909 Wellington Park
     Greenock
1910 Stonehouse
1911 Titwood *Glasgow*
1912 Springhill *Kilmarnock*
1913 Auchinleck
1914 Camelon
1915–18 – No Competition

1919 Musselburgh
1920 Thornhill
     Dumfriesshire
1921 Halfway and District
     Cambuslang
1922 Beith
1923 Saltcoats
1924 Dalzell *Motherwell*
1925 Duns
1926 Wellcroft *Glasgow*
1927 Shettleston
1928 Rock *Dumbarton*
1929 Wishaw
1930 Bishopbriggs
1931 East Calder
1932 Larkhall Miners'
     Welfare
1933 New Cumnock
1934 Victoria *Coatbridge*
1935 Fauldhouse
1936 Fauldhouse
1937 Cumnock
1938 Caledonian *Hamilton*
1939 Kilmarnock
1940 Alva South
1941 Abbotsford *Galashiels*
1942 Kinnoull *Perth*
1943 Lockerbie
1944 Lockerbie
1945 Strathaven
1946 Lundin Links
1947 Juniper Green
1948 Crossgates Miners'
     Welfare
1949 Darvel
1950 Crosshouse
1951 Twechar
1952 Udston
1953 Galashiels
1954 Larkhall Welfare
1955 Cumnock
1956 West Netherton
     Kilmarnock
1957 Ayr Craigie
1958 Lesmahagow
1959 Lochgelly
1960 Dreghorn
1961 Bishopbriggs
1962 Dalry
1963 Croy
1964 Balerno
1965 Tulliallan
1966 Denny
1967 Mount Florida
1968 Newbattle
1969 Cardonald
1970 Chirnside
1971 Balerno
1972 Bellahouston
1973 Creetown
1974 Kittybrewster and
     Wooside
1975 Balerno
1976 Ladybank
1977 Prestwick
1978 Springhill
1979 East Linton
1980 Gifford
1981 Singer
1982 Abercorn
1983 Mount Florida
1984 West Barns
1985 Nethertown

Seniors' Fours
1966 Hamilton Caledonian
1967 Greenock Victoria
1968 Balgonie
1969 Victoria Coatbridge
1970 Tillicoultry
1971 Dalmellington
1972 Mosspark
1973 Methven
1974 Cathcart
1975 Cathcart
1976 Cardonald
1977 Motherwell M.W.
1978 Vale of Leven
1979 Wishaw
1980 Prestongrange
1981 Abbeyview
1982 Riverside
1983 Methilhill
1984 Wishaw
1985 Erskins

Junior Singles
1977 D. Clelland *Colinton*
1978 B. Stillie *Borestone*
1979 R. Whannel *Kirkcolm*
1980 J. Pryde *Denny*
1981 M. Graham *Linlithgow*
1982 S. Forrest *Overtown
     and Waterloo*
1983 R. Corsie *Craigentinny*
1984 S. Davidson *Longside*
1985 A. Poole *Pilrig*

**C.I.S. Insurance
Scottish Counties
Championship
A. H. Hamilton Trophy**
1947 Glasgow
1948 Edinburgh and Leith
1949 Edinburgh and Leith
1950 Lanarkshire
1951 Linlithgowshire
1952 Edinburgh and Leith
1953 Angus
1954 Edinburgh and Leith
1955 Lanarkshire
1956 Linlithgowshire
1957 East Lothian
1958 Edinburgh and Leith
1959 Lanarkshire
1960 Lanarkshire
1961 Linlithgowshire
1962 Lanarkshire
1963 Lanarkshire
1964 Ayrshire
1965 Linlithgowshire
1966 Ayrshire
1967 Ayrshire
1968 Ayrshire
1969 Dumfriesshire
1970 Linlithgowshire
1971 Edinburgh and Leith
1972 Midlothian
1973 Dunbartonshire
1974 Glasgow
1975 Midlothian
1976 Lanarkshire
1977 Clackmannan &
     Kinross
1978 Linlithgowshire
1979 Ayrshire
1980 Ayrshire
1981 Dunbartonshire
1982 East Lothian
1983 Ayrshire
1984 East Lothian
1985 Ayrshire

Biggest winning margin in Scottish National Championships Willie McLaughlin (Lesmahagow) beat Tommy Trotter (Colinton) 21–0 SBA Championships 1985 (first ever whitewash in championships).

Below Peter Line of Hampshire – England's most experienced skip. (S. J. Line)

Russ Morgan (Hampshire) *above*, Steve Halmai (Middlesex) *above right* and Martyn Sekjer (Kent) *below*, three of England's brilliant young bowlers. (S. J. Line)

'Joy and Pride', Ollie Jones (left) and Len Haynes of Lenham BC, Kent, EBA national pairs winners 1984. (S. J. Line).

Above Norfolk's England international skip, David Ward. (S. J. Line).

Below Left to right (standing): England's Russ Morgan, Julian Haines (hidden), Tony Allcock and Andy Thomson look sympathetic as their Irish opponents collapse, left to right: Rodney McCutcheon (crouching), R. McCune (bending), and M. McKeown (back view), Gateway Home Internationals, Worthing, 1985. (S. J. Line).

England

Under the firm leadership of W. G. Grace, the progress enjoyed by the English Bowling Association in its early years was steady rather than spectacular. Membership was channelled through individual clubs, with the country divided into 16 districts which collectively held the power to elect the EBA Council. After one year of operation the roll call of affiliated clubs stood at 44, but amalgamation with the Imperial Bowling Association in 1905 added a further 25 and by 1906 the number had risen to 90.

This period however also saw the formation of the first county associations beginning with Northants in 1904. This movement, once under way, was to prove a powerful and influential force in the game and by 1921 there were no less than 21 county bodies. Significantly not all of these were affiliated to the EBA and the pressure exerted by this new grouping was sufficient to prompt a hasty reappraisal by that organization of its position and its constitution. Sensing the danger posed by the counties, a three-man EBA committee comprising E. M. Vigers (hon. sec.), W. J. Thomas and G. T. Burrows drafted a new constitution in 1921 based, in part at least, on a far-sighted scheme outlined some years before by E. J. Linney (Herne Hill BC). Under the 1921 Constitution, control of the EBA passed from the districts, which were abolished, to the county associations. This new ruling however did not meet with universal approval and the sticking point for many was the clause which determined that entry to the English Bowling Association henceforth would be solely through the county associations. Dissatisfaction with this ruling was voiced at a meeting called by the Crouch End BC, presided over by Felix Hotchkiss and held, for space reasons, at the North London Club. The result was a resolution calling upon the EBA to reconsider the decision regarding entry, a request which was to prove unsuccessful. Subsequently 20 London-based clubs refused to affiliate with their county organizations in protest but this minor insurrection was to prove a short-lived affair with the most vocal and influential of the protesting group, Felix Hotchkiss, actually becoming president of the EBA nine years later.

The decision by the Vigers Committee to embrace the county associations, to work through them rather than against them, was an astute move and signalled a distinct rise in the fortunes and membership of the EBA. From 222 registered clubs enjoying individual membership in 1919, the figure rose, through the county associations, to 599 in 1922 just one year after the rewritten constitution was introduced. Twenty-five years later, with 31 county associations flying the EBA colours, there were no less than 1810 clubs represented and this figure topped the 2000 mark during the early fifties with 34 county bodies in affiliation. The latest (1984) count of clubs affiliated to the EBA through 35 county associations is 2656 with the total number of bowling members rapidly approaching the 120 000 mark. Minor alterations apart, the 1921 version of the EBA constitution remained virtually unchanged until the introduction of 'open' bowls in 1982.

Most venerable of the EBA national competitions are the rinks (fours) and the single-handed championships, both of which date back to 1905. The successful rink holds the Wood Cup, a trophy presented to the old Imperial Bowling Association by Charles Wood of Melbourne to commemorate the 1901 tour of the UK by Australian bowlers and subsequently known as the Australian Cup. Under IBA rules competing clubs each entered four rinks, the winner being the club with the highest agregate score and the first holders were Valentines Park of Ilford, Essex in 1902. The Wood Cup passed into the keeping of the EBA on the amalgamation of the two associations and, with clubs then restricted to a single rink, the first champions under EBA rules were Carlisle Subscription in 1905.

The Lipton Cup was presented to the English Bowling Association by Sir Thomas Lipton and is held by the winner of the national singles championships. J. G. Carruthers, a Scots-born bowler of outstanding ability, became the first EBA singles champion in 1905. His opponent in the final, James Telford, also came from north of the Tweed. On his way to that historic match Jimmy Carruthers, as good a skip as he was a singles player and, like many Scots at the time, a stalwart in the English International team, rather outclassed Grace beating him 21–9. He then allowed a luckless James Thompson the dubious luxury of just a single shot before taking on Telford and, with his appetite as sharp as ever, overcame the ferocious 'drive' game of his fellow countryman to win the first EBA singles title 21–11.

Clarence Park, Somerset were the first winners of the national pairs competition which got under way in 1912 with a trophy presented by Sir Thomas Dewar – the Dewar Cup – and 1945 saw the national competitions in England nicely rounded off by the institution of the triples championships, played for the Burrows Cup and the first to hold this trophy were Penzance, Cornwall. Despite the obvious importance and prestige of the four major EBA competitions it is perhaps the Middleton Cup which most arouses the passions and fervour of England's bowlers. The final stages of this inter-county competition are played in an atmosphere more akin to a soccer cup tie than a bowls match, but one in which good humour and sportsmanship are clearly among the natural order of things. Although dating from 1911 when Middlesex emerged as the top county, the competition only received its present title in 1922 when, in memory of his son who died in the First World War, P. C. Middleton, president of Norwood BC, presented a trophy to the EBA. The Middleton Cup was then allocated to the inter-county competition, replacing the John Bull Cup which had been donated by the notorious Horatio Bottomley. The competition is open to all affiliated county associations, each represented by a full complement of six rinks. Until 1959, play was on a simple knock-out basis but is now run almost entirely on a league system with only the final rounds reverting to the sudden death formula.

For many years Paddington BC was regarded as the unofficial headquarters of the English Bowling Association. The magnificent facilities available proved an ideal setting for the bowls matches of the Commonwealth Games of 1934 and that year also saw the club's two greens used for the national championships for the first time. In 1958 these championships were moved to the greens owned by Watney's Brewery at Mortlake where they were successfully staged until 1973, when they were moved to their present venue at Beach House Park, Worthing.

With 21 victories in the Home International series, England lags 13 behind the Scots but more than compensates for this lapse by a superior record in both the Commonwealth Games and World Championships. Much credit for recent English successes must go to David Bryant, CBE, of Clevedon, Somerset, easily the most revered bowler the game has ever known. Highlights of Bryant's extraordinary career include six national singles titles, four British Isles singles titles plus four Commonwealth Games and two World Championship gold medals.

The EBA took the decision to embrace 'Open' bowls at a special council meeting on 22 March 1980.

Other Associations

The London and Southern Counties Bowling Association is generally considered to be the oldest remaining grouping of private clubs in the country and is certainly the largest of its kind. Founded in 1895, the Association was the result of efforts to bring some form of regularization to the game in Southern England. The 11 founder clubs, Bounds Green, Bromley, Brownswood, Ilford, Lewisham, North London, Mansfield, Reading, Southampton Bowling Green, Southampton County and Green Man, and Upton Park, formed a tight-knit and almost

W. R. Arey of the New Zealand bowling team pictured at High Wycombe, Buckinghamshire, 1928. (BBC Hulton Picture Library).

Far left Tony Allcock.
(*World Bowls*).
Left Mal Hughes.
(Sporting Pictures).
Below Terry Sullivan
(left) and Cecil Bransky
with the Embassy
World Indoor Singles
Trophy. (*World Bowls*).

Above David Bryant. (*World Bowls*). *Below* John Bell. (*World Bowls*).

Above Robert Weale (Wales). (Stephen Goodger).
Above left John Leeman (England). (*Bowls International*).
Left Richard Corsie (Scotland). (*Bowls International*).

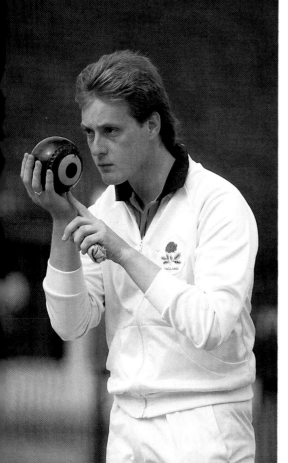

Far left Brett Morley (England). (*Bowls International*).
Below Russ Morgan (England). (*World Bowls*).

Above Arms and the men. (*World Bowls*).

Martyn Sekjer (Kent and England). *(World Bowls).*

Michael Dunlop (Ireland). (*World Bowls*).

Left Bill Hobart (Lincolnshire and England). (S. J. Line). *Above* Mr Bowls – David Bryant, the most successful bowler in the game. (S. J. Line). *Below left* Tony Allcock (Gloucestershire and England). (S. J. Line). *Below* Pip Branfield (Somerset and England). (S. J. Line).

Tic Tac from left to right: Tony Allcock, Andy Thomson and Julian Haines (England). (S. J. Line).

Alan Windsor, left, makes a point to David Cutler during the 1985 Gateway Home International championships at Beach House Park, Worthing. (Alan North, Gateway Building Society).

self-sufficient organization. The Association has its own competitions such as the inter-club Challenge Shield and the Gold Badge for singles play, both much sought-after trophies, and the annual match against the Midland Counties BA is one of the oldest fixtures in the bowling calendar dating from 1897. Similar organizations in other parts of the country either divided and collapsed, like the Northumberland and Durham BA (founded in 1892) or, as with the Midland Counties BA, immediately affiliated with the EBA. Not so the London and Southern Counties which stubbornly resisted every advance from the game's major governing body until 1932, when the long awaited affiliation took place. From the original 11 clubs, the membership of the London and Southern Counties BA has risen, in 1984 to 168.

EBA National Championships

Singles

1905 J. G. Carruthers *Muswell Hill, Middlesex*
1906 C. L. Cummings *Sunderland, Durham*
1907 J. S. Emmerson *Edenside, Carlisle, Cumberland*
1908 R. Knights *Hero of Switzerland, Surrey*
1909 J. W. Dick *Gosforth, Northumb*
1910 F. Shatford *Kettering, Northants*
1911 J. J. Postlethwaite *Carlisle Courtfield, Cumberland*
1912 W. J. Jones *Crouch Hill, Middlesex*
1913 C. Gibb *Sunderland, Durham*
1914 D. Irvine Watson *Malden, Surrey*
1915–18 Not played during war period
1919 E. E. Moore *Bellingham, Kent*
1920 A. E. Godsall *Forest Hill, Kent*
1921 A. F. Warner *Belmont, Surrey*
1922 W. F. Hamilton *Hexham, Northumb*
1923 W. F. Wade *Hinckley, Leics*
1924 R. Hodge *Torrington, Devon*
1925 H. P. Webber *Plymouth, Devon*
1926 R. Jack *Plymouth, Devon*
1927 T. Tickle *Park Institute, Reading, Berks*
1928 G. Wright *Southern Railway, Eastleigh, Hants*
1929 Capt R. G. Colquhoun *Bromley, Kent*
1930 W. F. Wade *Hinckley, Leics*
1931 E. P. Topp *Ryde, Isle of Wight*
1932 E. P. Baker *Poole Park, Dorset*
1933 J. M. McKinlay *Paddington, Middlesex*
1934 A. K. Cochrane *Southampton, Hants*
1935 W. Linton *Smith's Docks, Yorks*
1936 G. D. Goodson *Chesham, Bucks*
1937 W. Prentice *Redcar, Zetland, Yorks*
1938 K. I. Cross *Cosham, Hants*
1939 J. J. Laws *Summerhill, Northumb*
1940–44 Not played during war period
1945 A. A. Keech *Bootham, Yorks*
1946 E. P. Baker *Poole Park, Dorset*
1947 P. P. Mercer *Worthing, Sussex*
1948 E. Newton *Windsor & Eton, Berks*
1949 A. R. Allen *City & County, Oxford*
1950 J. Thompson *N. Shields, West End, Northumb*
1951 A. Pikesley *St Albans, Herts*
1952 E. P. Baker *Poole Park, Dorset*
1953 R. G. W. Cramp *Clay Hall, Essex*
1954 J. W. Griffiths *Wallsend Boro', Northumb*
1955 E. P. Baker *Poole Park, Dorset*
1956 N. C. Butler *Windsor & Eton, Berks*
1957 N. King *Parliament Hill, Middlesex*
1958 H. Powell *Farnborough Brit. Legion, Hants*
1959 K. Coulson *Croydon, Surrey*
1960 D. J. Bryant *Clevedon, Somerset*
1961 P. A. Line *Banister Park, Hants*
1962 C. Mercer *Lyme Regis, Dorset*
1963 C. S. Graham *Edenside, Cumbria*
1964 P. A. Line *Banister Park, Hants*
1965 R. E. Lewis *Preston, Sussex*
1966 D. J. Bryant *Clevedon, Somerset*
1967 W. C. Irish *Droitwich, Vines Park, Worcs*
1968 N. R. Groves *Witham, Essex*
1969 J. Davidson *Boscombe Cliff, Hants*
1970 H. Kershaw *Heaton Vic, Northumb*
1971 D. J. Bryant, MBE *Clevedon, Somerset*
1972 D. J. Bryant, MBE *Clevedon, Somerset*
1973 D. J. Bryant, MBE *Clevedon, Somerset*
1974 W. C. Irish *Vines Park, Worcs*
1975 D. J. Bryant, MBE *Clevedon, Somerset*
1976 A. O'Connell *Wimbledon Durnsford, Surrey*
1977 C. C. Ward *Cromer, Norfolk*
1978 C. Burch *Taunton, Somerset*
1979 D. J. Cutler *St Austell, Cornwall*
1980 T. Buller *View Lane Park, Durham*
1981 A. Thomson *Blackheath & Greenwich, Kent*
1982 C. C. Ward *Norfolk*
1983 J. N. Bell *Cumbria*
1984 W. Richards *M&O Surrey*
1985 R. Keating *Devon*

Pairs

1912 Clarence Park *Somerset*
1913 Forest Hill *Kent*
1914 Bristol *Somerset*
1915–18 Not played during war period
1919 Beech Hill *Beds*
1920 Taunton *Somerset*
1921 Preston *Sussex*
1922 Roker Park *Durham*
1923 Gosforth *Northumb*
1924 Taunton *Somerset*
1925 Abbey Park *Leics*
1926 Poole Park *Dorset*
1927 Poole Park *Dorset*
1928 Wellingborough *Northants*
1929 Carlisle Subscription *Cumberland*
1930 Frome Selwood *Somerset*
1931 St George's *Somerset*
1932 Wellingborough *Northants*
1933 Callenders *Kent*
1934 Callenders *Kent*
1935 Saltburn-by-Sea *Yorks*
1936 White Rock, Hastings *Sussex*
1937 Worthing *Sussex*
1938 Worthing *Sussex*
1939 Durham City *Durham*
1940–4 Not played during war period
1945 Bellingham *Kent*
1946 Penzance *Cornwall*
1947 County Ground *Worcs*
1948 Tiverton Boro *Devon*
1949 Darlington R.A. *Durham*
1950 Poole Park *Dorset*
1951 South Oxford *Oxford*
1952 Torquay *Devon*
1953 Bootham *Yorks*
1954 Dean and Chapter *Durham*
1955 Worthing *Sussex*
1956 Darlington East Park *Durham*
1957 Worthing *Sussex*
1958 Mid-Surrey *Surrey*
1959 Paddington *Middlesex*
1960 Aylesbury Boro *Bucks*
1961 Marlborough *Suffolk*
1962 Poole Park *Dorset*
1963 Greenhill *Dorset*
1964 MEB *Worcs*
1965 Clevedon *Somerset*
1966 Worthing *Sussex*
1967 County Ground *Northants*
1968 Dulwich *Surrey*
1969 Clevedon *Somerset*
1970 Pennywell *Durham*
1971 Livesey Memorial *Kent*
1972 Greenhill *Dorset*
1973 Penrith Castle Pk *Cumberland*
1974 Clevedon BC *Somerset*
1975 N. Shields West End *Northumb*
1976 Plessey BC *Notts*
1977 Brotherhood *Worcs*
1978 Angus *Northumb*
1979 Wymondham Dell BC *Norfolk*
1980 Framlingham Castle BC *Suffolk*
1981 Burton House *Lincs*
1982 Bedford Borough *Beds*
1983 Eldon Grove *Durham*
1984 Lenham *Kent*
1985 Haxby Road *Yorks*

EBA NATIONAL CHAMPIONSHIPS – Continued

Triples

1945 Penzance *Cornwall*
1946 Saltburn *Yorks*
1947 Redhill *Surrey*
1948 Faversham *Kent*
1949 Worthing Pavilion *Sussex*
1950 Hereford *Hereford*
1951 North Oxford *Oxford*
1952 Reading *Berks*
1953 Darlington Woodland *Durham*
1954 Rookery *Suffolk*
1955 Southbourne *Hants*
1956 Avenue, Leamington *Warks*
1957 Redbourn *Lincs*
1958 Blackpool *Lancs*
1959 Hatfield *Herts*
1960 Poole Park *Dorset*
1961 Stroud *Glos*
1962 Leamington Spa *Warks*
1963 Paddington *Middlesex*
1964 Forest Hill *Kent*
1965 Kettering Lodge *Northants*
1966 Clevedon *Somerset*
1967 Summerhill *Northumb*
1968 Wellingboro' Town *Northants*
1969 Rushden Town *Northants*
1970 George Kent *Beds*
1971 Marlow *Bucks*
1972 St Austell *Cornwall*

1973 Swan Hunter and W. R. Ltd. *Northumb*
1974 English Electric *Warks*
1975 British Legion, Farnborough *Hants*
1976 Wigton *Cumberland*
1977 Clevedon *Somerset*
1978 Rainworth *Notts*
1979 Bristol BC *Somerset*
1980 Heaton Hall BC *Lancs*
1981 St Peters *Hunts*
1982 Lenham BC *Kent*
1983 Marlborough BC *Suffolk*
1984 Clevedon *Somerset*
1985 Clevedon *Somerset*

Fours

1905 Carlisle Subscription *Cumberland*
1906 Newcastle West End *Northumb*
1907 Carlisle West End *Cumberland*
1908 Carlisle Edenside *Cumberland*
1909 Wellingborough *Northants*
1910 Victoria *Somerset*
1911 Banbury *Oxford*
1912 Wellingborough *Northants*
1913 Dulwich *Surrey*
1914 Reading *Berks*
1915–18 Not played during war period

1919 Belgrave *Leics*
1920 Sunderland *Durham*
1921 Belgrave *Northumb*
1922 Belgrave *Leics*
1923 Alnwick *Northumb*
1924 Southend-on-Sea *Essex*
1925 Belgrave *Northumb*
1926 Preston *Sussex*
1927 Margate *Kent*
1928 Luton Town *Beds*
1929 Basingstoke Town *Hants*
1930 Lammas *Middlesex*
1931 Kingston Canbury *Surrey*
1932 Atherley *Hants*
1933 Southsea Waverley *Hants*
1934 Worthing *Sussex*
1935 Sunderland *Durham*
1936 Boscombe Cliff *Hants*
1937 Sheen Common *Surrey*
1938 Paddington *Middlesex*
1939 High Wycombe *Bucks*
1940–4 Not played during war period
1945 Ilford *Essex*
1946 Faversham *Kent*
1947 Redhill *Surrey*
1948 Oxford City & County *Oxford*
1949 Skefko *Beds*
1950 Richmond Park *Hants*
1951 Oxford City & County *Oxford*
1952 Prospect Park *Berks*
1953 Poole Park *Dorset*

1954 Belgrave *Leics*
1955 Wootton Basset *Wilts*
1956 Fleet United *Hants*
1957 Clevedon *Somerset*
1958 Morton *Cumberland*
1959 Princes Risborough *Bucks*
1960 Essex County *Essex*
1961 Worthing *Sussex*
1962 Slough ICI *Bucks*
1963 Wellingboro' Town *Northants*
1964 Preston *Sussex*
1965 Bournemouth Electric *Hants*
1966 Summerhill *Northumb*
1967 Sandwich *Kent*
1968 Clevedon *Somerset*
1969 Clevedon *Somerset*
1970 Blackhall CW *Durham*
1971 Clevedon *Somerset*
1972 Burton House *Lincs*
1973 Poole Park *Dorset*
1974 Brotherhood *Worcs*
1975 Cromer *Norfolk*
1976 Baldock Town *Herts*
1977 Aveley *Essex*
1978 Erdington Court *Warwick*
1979 Carlisle Subscription *Cumbria*
1980 Cromer & District (EBA) *Norfolk*
1981 Owton Lodge *Durham*
1982 Castle BC *Notts*
1983 Bolton *Lancs*
1984 Boscombe Cliff *Hants*
1985 Aldersbrooke *Essex*

'Ooh its a toucher'. The London Scottish take on Scotland at Ilford, Essex, August 1923. (BBC Hulton Picture Library).

David Cutler with the *News of the World* Home International trophy after the 1985 series at Beach House Park, Worthing. (Alan North, Gateway Building Society).

Willie Wood (Scotland). (*Bowls International*).

Len Bowden (England). (S. J. Line).

England's Peter McCall, an ex-Bristol City soccer star, won EBA Invitation Singles (128) in 1984. (S. J. Line).

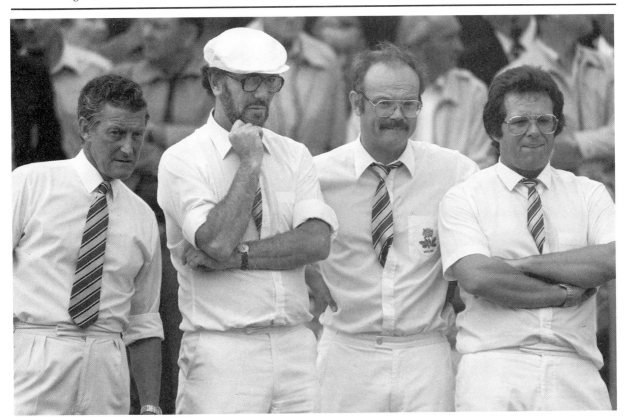

Anxious moments in the 1984 Middleton Cup for the Sussex rink of (left to right) Frank Armstrong (Southbourne BC), Ivan Orchin (Lindfield), Paul Lewis (Preston) and Dave Ovett (Preston). (S. J. Line).

The Middleton Cup – a flavour all of its own. Sussex have just scored three against Somerset in the 1984 semi-finals but went down overall by 131 shots to 91. (S. J. Line).

Middleton Cup

1911 Middlesex
1912 Kent
1913 Middlesex
1914 Surrey
1915–18 Not played during war period
1919 Bedfordshire
1920 Surrey
1921 Surrey
1922 Bedfordshire
1923 Surrey
1924 Surrey
1925 Middlesex
1926 Northumberland
1927 Surrey
1928 Surrey
1929 Kent
1930 Northumberland
1931 Surrey
1932 Northamptonshire
1933 Surrey
1934 Northamptonshire
1935 Hampshire
1936 Gloucestershire
1937 Surrey
1938 Dorset
1939 Surrey
1940–4 Not played during war period
1945 Northumberland
1946 Yorkshire
1947 Yorkshire
1948 Devonshire
1949 Devonshire
1950 Devonshire
1951 Northumberland
1952 Middlesex
1953 Yorkshire
1954 Middlesex
1955 Surrey
1956 Sussex
1957 Surrey
1958 Surrey
1959 Devonshire
1960 Surrey
1961 Nottinghamshire
1962 Middlesex
1963 Hampshire
1964 Leicestershire
1965 Middlesex
1966 Norfolk
1967 Hampshire
1968 Hampshire
1969 Middlesex
1970 Warwickshire
1971 Hampshire
1972 Surrey
1973 Yorkshire
1974 Kent
1975 Surrey
1976 Lincolnshire
1977 Somerset
1978 Yorkshire
1979 Somerset
1980 Northamptonshire
1981 Somerset
1982 Berkshire
1983 Surrey
1984 Somerset
1985 Northumberland

'Nat West' national club two fours

1973 Angus BC *Northumb*
1974 Brotherhood BC *Worcs*
1975 Guisborough KGV *Yorks*
1976 Malmesbury BC *Wilts*
1977 Exonia BC *Devon*
1978 Plymouth Hoe *Devon*
1979 Eldon Grove *Durham*
1980 Chesham *Bucks*
1981 Banister Park *Hants*
1982 Burnham on Sea *Somerset*
1983 GEC Willans *Warks*
1984 View Lane *Durham*
1985 Wymondham *Norfolk*

SAGA National 60's & over singles and pairs

Singles
1974 V. E. Bullock *Hants*
1975 E. Wood *Berks*
1976 W. S. Andrews *Herts*
1977 H. V. Wisdom *Norfolk*
1978 F. T. Summers *Worcs*
1979 F. James *Northumb*
1980 B. Walker *Devon*
1981 H. W. J. Clarke *Wilts*
1982 C. Bussey *Northants*
1983 E. R. Bundy *Hants*
1984 R. Theobald *Middx*
1985 R. Theobald *Middx*

Pairs
1974 F. Forey, A. Parkin *Middlesex*
1975 W. Stower, F. Jenkins *Warks*
1976 I. Boys, L. Traves *Middlesex*
1977 E. Rayner, F. Summers *Worcs*
1978 F. Ash, H. Stevenson *Surrey*
1979 E. C. Weston, E. C. Websell *Hants*
1980 G. C. Collinson, W. Hughes *Glos*
1981 J. Adams, A. Whitehead *Bucks*
1982 J. Grigor, B. Read *Lincs*
1983 T. S. Fenn, A. P. Lucas *Suffolk*
1984 H. Wadham, W. Firby *Somerset*
1985 B. Walker, R. Kivell *Devon*

National junior singles

1974 D. J. Cutler *Cornwall*
1975 A. Allcock *Leics*
1976 J. Hobday *Hants*
1977 A. Allcock *Leics*
1978 N. A. Atkinson *Yorks*
1979 P. Mattravers *Somerset*
1980 G. W. Spencer *Surrey*
1981 A. Allcock *Glos*
1982 I. Grady *Norfolk*
1983 A. Irons *Leics*
1984 B. Morley *Notts*
1985 J. Bates *Essex*

National county top four

1982 Gloucestershire
1983 Cumbria
1984 Middlesex
1985 Surrey

National invitation singles

1981 W. J. Hobart *Lincs*
1982 G. Standley *Hants*
1983 D. J. Cutler *Yorks*
1984 P. McCall *Bristol*
1985 D. Cutler *Plymouth*

DRG Croxley Script Champion of Champions

1984 D. Cutler *Devon*
1985 D. Denison *Devon*

Most titles: English and British David John Bryant (Clevedon) holds the record number of EBA titles with 16 victories. He won the EBA singles in 1960, 1966, 1971–3 and 1975; pairs in 1965, 1969 and 1974; triples in 1966, 1977 and 1985; fours in 1957, 1968, 1969 and 1971. He has also won six British Isles titles including the singles in 1960, 1971–3.

Youngest winner of an EBA title David J. Cutler, St Austell. Won the triples 1972 aged 18 years 18 days with C. J. Yelland and W. E. Oliver.

David J. Cutler (born 1 August 1954) became the youngest-ever winner of the EBA singles championships in 1979 at 25 years 16 days.

The Gateway Masters

Since its inception in 1978 the annual invitation Masters tournament held at Worthing's Beach House Park has played a significant role in making bowls one of the fastest growing sports in England. Screened each year by BBC Television under the programme title of *Jack High*, the Masters has proved an invaluable shop window for the attractions of a game which, while retaining all the qualities fast disappearing from other sporting events, boasts its own brand of excitement.

Appearing in 1978, the 75th anniversary year of the EBA, were David Bryant of England, John Russell Evans of Wales, Ireland's Willie Watson, David McGill the young star from Scotland, Dick Folkins from America, South Africa's Bill Moseley, Bob Middleton of Australia and New Zealander John Malcolm. The winner of that inaugural tournament sponsored by Kodak Ltd was David Bryant who also took the honours in 1979. South African Bill Moseley then showed his class by winning the 1980 tournament and made it a double in the following year. In 1982 Moseley threatened again, winning all of his section A matches while Bryant, in section B, only squeezed into the final rounds on shot average after losing two of his three matches. By the time the semi-finals arrived, however,

Bryant's form had returned with a vengeance and the South African reeled to a 21–11 defeat. In the final against Australia's John Snell, Bryant recovered from a 6–2 deficit to draw level at 7–7 on the eighth end. Snell then managed two singles to lead 9–7 before the Clevedon man launched his match winning onslaught scoring 4–3–1–2–2 to lead 19–9. A three on the 16th end by Snell delayed matters hardly at all and Bryant finished off the match with a two one end later.

The EBA policy on sporting links with South Africa led to the exclusion of Moseley from the 1983 Masters but anyone who imagined this would leave a free run for Bryant were proved wildly wrong. Appearing for the first time in England, George Souza, Hong Kong's leading bowler, began his challenge by defeating the defending champion 21–18 in the opening match and endorsed his obvious merit by accounting for Commonwealth Games champion Willie Wood 21–10, Burnie Gill of Canada 21–15 and John Snell 21–13 in the semi-final.

Weather conditions at Worthing deteriorated alarmingly immediately prior to the final, with an avalanche of giant hailstones completely covering the greens. To the everlasting credit of greenkeeper Jock Munro, play was delayed no more than an hour as he swept, squeegeed and prayed. After the hail,

Gateway/EBA national pairs final 1985. Keith Renwick (left) and Ken Briscoe (right) of Durham look wary while winning skip Frank Maxwell (centre) of Yorkshire gives his full attention to his partner, Peter Richardson (out of shot). (Author).

came the rain and the waterproofs as Souza and Bryant took to the green. A close and enthralling match was eventually halted when the bowlers had difficulty in reaching even a short jack and scores locked at 18 all. With the agreement of the EBA the players decided to share the prize money whatever the outcome but the struggle for the title of Masters Champion resumed after a half-hour break and a new Master eventually emerged as Souza registered his second victory over Bryant in beating him 21–19.

The Gateway Building Society entered as sponsors for the Masters in 1984 following Kodak's decision to review their promotional activities. Making their debuts in the tournament were John Bell, the EBA singles champion, Darby Ross, the Australian state singles champion of champions, and Dan Milligan from Canada. Old hands Peter Belliss of New Zealand, Willie Wood, Frank Souza from the USA, David Bryant and the defending champion George Souza made up a strong field. In the event Bryant, despite a close shave against Bell in the opening match and a 21–16 loss to Belliss on the second day, reached the semi-finals where he met the surprise of the tournament, Dan Milligan, who had earlier ruined things for the defending champion, George Souza beating him 21–12 in the first round, and edged out Willie Wood by

the odd shot. Against Bryant's experience and range of shot, however, the Canadian found things tough from the outset and did well to reach 13. Belliss, whose form had been impressive throughout, reached the final with a 21–10 victory over a sad George Souza but in the final confrontation with Bryant the big New Zealander's game wilted at the crucial point. Forced in the latter stages to rely on his trusty high-speed drive, Belliss found that his normal accuracy had taken wing and with it went the match as Bryant, emerging from a slight trough at 15–13 down, powered his way to a hard-earned 21–16 victory and his fourth Masters title.

The appearance of Tony Allcock, fresh from his National Indoor Singles success at Hartlepool, was the main talking point at Worthing in 1985 but an unkind draw found him up against John Bell, Peter Belliss and Canada's pocket battleship, Ronnie Jones. Bryant was in with Cecil Bransky of Israel, George Souza and new boy, Dennis Katunarich from Australia, on the face of it an easier grouping. Nevertheless Allcock began his challenge brightly enough beating Belliss 21–15 thanks to a dogged rearguard battle after seeming dead and buried at one stage. For the New Zealander, now World Singles champion, that defeat was the start of a very unhappy tournament which saw him successful on only one occasion, a 21–15 win over

Ian Murray and George Adrain of Scotland seem delighted, Robbie Price (right) of Wales less so. 1984 Gateway Home Internationals, Larne, N. Ireland. (Author).

Below South Africa's Bill Moseley won the Kodak Masters twice before his exclusion in 1983. (S. J. Line).

The champion! David Bryant flanked by runner-up Peter Belliss of New Zealand and third-placed Dan Milligan of Canada, Worthing 1984. (Author).

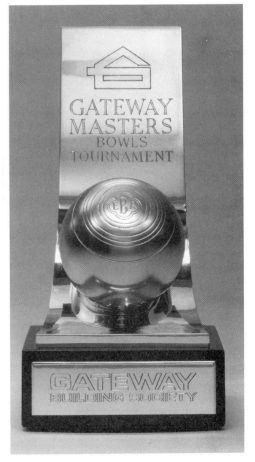

The Gateway Masters tournament trophy. (Gateway Building Society).

John Bell when the Cumbrian was already through to the semi-finals. Bell and Allcock staged a remarkable game in their encounter, full of excitement and superb bowling skills. Bell came out on top, but only just as Allcock fought to sustain his challenge. The score of 21–20 is an accurate reflection of a superb match but Allcock's loss to Jones by the same score proved a catalogue of missed chances and poor bowling. While all this was going on Bryant was striding through his matches, reaching the semi-finals undefeated. There he met Jones, victor over Allcock and Belliss. Bryant then showed precisely how to deal with the Canadian's capers by the application of sound tactics and naggingly accurate bowling; good basic stuff but so effective against the inspirational play of Jones. To the surprise of the bowls buffs, the supposedly stronger A section players were up against it. Not so surprising was the fact that they had fought each other to a collective standstill. John Bell, the sole survivor, staggered into the semi-finals where he met the South African-born Israeli, Cecil Bransky and promptly staggered out on the wrong end of a 21–11 scoreline. Bransky had already lost 21–11 to Bryant on the opening day and we waited to see whether he had learned from the experience. The Israeli can be a very tough competitor, always steady, normally accurate and never ruffled. Bryant however has the uncanny ability to raise his

Beach House Park, Worthing at the start of the 1984 Gateway/EBA national championships. (S. J. Line).

game when the occasion demands and, obviously deciding that here was just the occasion, played too many good bowls for Bransky to match or better with any regularity, allowing his opponent just twelve shots, one better than in their first-round meeting. The victory brought David Bryant his fifth Masters title and the satisfaction of winning from the strongest field yet assembled for a Masters tournament.

EBA Competitions
The Kodak Masters

1978 David Bryant *England*
1979 David Bryant *England*
1980 Bill Moseley *South Africa*
1981 Bill Moseley *South Africa*
1982 David Bryant *England*
1983 George Souza *Hong Kong*

The Gateway Masters

1984 David Bryant *England*
1985 David Bryant *England*

The Irish bowling team in London, August 1931. (BBC Hulton Picture Library).

Ireland

Bowls gained a foothold in Northern Ireland during the 17th century when, under the 'plantation' policy of James I, the counties of Armagh, Fermanagh, Londonderry, Tyrone, Cavan and Donnegal received an unwelcome influx of Scottish and English 'settlers'. It wasn't until the affiliation of the Dublin-based Kenilworth Bowling Club to the Irish Bowling Association in 1906 that bowlers in the South began to organize and, to this day, it is still the North East which remains as the stronghold of the game in that divided land.

Following the example set by the Kenilworth BC, many greens were laid throughout the south but it was not until 1944, when the Herbert Park Green at Ballsbridge, Dublin was opened, that Eire had its first public bowling green.

The Irish Bowling Association is made up of the Northern Ireland Region, with three subsidiary associations, and the Bowling League of Ireland which represents bowlers in Eire. League play is an important component of the structure of all four associations which also have their own competitions plus the usual fours, triples, pairs and singles championships. In addition to these, the inter-association matches for the Major Sir William Baird Cup are regarded as unofficial trials for entry to a truly representative Irish international team.

First among the sub-associations is the Northern Ireland Bowling Association founded in 1910 and firmly committed to the encouragement of the game among the Public Greens clubs. From an initial roll call of just four clubs (Ballynafeigh, Ormeau, Shaftsbury and Woodvale), membership in 1984 stands at 60. The Northern Ireland Private Greens Bowling League, formed in 1917, has a rota of 38 clubs and, apart from the usual league and championship matches, its bowlers also play for The Richard Minnis Trophy, presented to the Kenilworth Bowling Club and the Private Greens League in 1943 by Richard Minnis of Larne and competed for annually with all proceeds going to assist 'Institutions or hospitals which have for their object the preserving of sight and relief for the blind'. The last of the Northern Ireland Region associations to be formed was the Northern Ireland Provincial Bowling Association which was founded in 1925 as the representative body of five clubs, Coleraine, Ballymena, Ballymoney, Portrush and Limvady, all based in north Antrim and north Londonderry. There are now 14 clubs in membership and, although small in number, the NIPBA has proved a vigorous and influential body in the Irish game.

A measure of Northern dominance of bowls in Ireland is the startling fact that of the 126

clubs in the four Associations, the Bowling League of Ireland (Eire) can muster only a total of 14 and has yet to succeed in the inter Association tournament. Founded in 1927, the Bowling League of Ireland (formerly the Irish Free State Bowwling League) operates on similar lines to those associations in the North but in its early days at least displayed remarkable ambition by instituting its own 'International' competition in 1932, The Baird Cup, open to English, Scottish and Irish members of clubs affiliated to the League. The first winner of this competition was an Englishman, F. G. West but, in these internationals at least, Ireland emerged as top dogs with 11 wins in the 19 years during which the competition was played. In 1952 The Baird Cup became a club, two wood, triples competition with Kenilworth BC the first winners.

All four associations are represented on the ruling Council of the Irish Bowling Association with the Northern Ireland BA and Private Greens Association each having six delegates while the NI Provincial BA and Bowling League of Ireland have three apiece.

Of the 126 clubs which comprise the four Irish sub-Associations, 108 are in direct membership of the overall governing body, the Irish Bowling Association, which thus represents some 7000 bowlers. The fours, triples, pairs and singles championships of each sub-association act as qualifying tournaments for the national competitions although bowlers winning titles at clubs not in full membership of the IBA are required to stand down. The single-handed and fours (rinks), both instituted in 1908, hold pride of place as the oldest national competitions in the Irish bowling calendar. Kenilworth BC were the first winners of the fours while R. Archer of Ormeau took the singles title.

Dr John Rusk, then a member of the Belfast BC, was president of the IBA in 1912 but represented Cavehill 20 years later when he won the national singles trophy which now bears his name. In 1934 he was Ireland's choice in the singles at the Empire Games held in London but will perhaps be best remembered as the author of the *Bowlers Ten Commandments*. The fours trophy was donated by C. L. MacKean JP of Larne who held the office of president of the IBA in 1914. C. Curran and C. Clawson (Shaftesbury) were the first winners of the pairs competition in 1932, taking the trophy which bears the name of the 1922 president, T. W. McMullen. Lastly, the triples entered the national field as late as 1970, with Coleraine becoming the first holders of the Annie R. Thompson Cup.

Ireland has a poor record in the Home International Championships with just three

A scene from the England v Ireland match in the Home International series 1939. (BBC Hulton Picture Library).

successes, 1905, 1951 and 1981, but can boast a more than decent one against visiting teams from abroad. They gained second place in the rinks at the 1934 Empire Games when they were represented by C. Curran, C. Clawson, G. Watson and P. Watson and took the pairs title with W. Rosbotham and P. Watson at the 1954 Commonwealth Games held in Vancouver, and the same players were fourth in 1958 at Cardiff. More recently Ireland won the triples gold medal at the 5th World Bowls Championships held at Aberdeen in 1984 thanks to superb play by Stan Espie, Sammy Allen and Jim Baker (skip).

Major Sir William Baird, who had the singular distinction of holding office as president of the IBA for 28 years following his election in 1928, also played a tremendous role on the international scene when, with the assistance of T. H. Barr and T. McCrindle, he successfully moved for a change in the constitution of the International Bowling Board in 1928 to allow entry to the four dominions – Australia, Canada, New Zealand and South Africa. In 1937 he inaugurated the Irish Inter-Association Championship to which he donated the winner's trophy.

Irish National Championships

Singles

1908 R. Archer *Ormeau*
1909 D. W. Barnett *Belmont*
1910 A. Cherry *Ormeau*
1911 J. Coulter *Ormeau*
1912 G. W. Cooper *Kenilworth* and R. Archer *Ormeau* joint holders
1913 G. W. Cooper *Kenilworth*
1914 W. McLetchie *Belmont*
1915 J. Coulter *Ormeau*
1916 G. W. Cooper *Kenilworth*
1917 S. Windrum *Shaftesbury*
1918 W. Dougal *N. Belfast*
1919 J. B. Teuton *Shaftesbury*
1920 W. R. Forsythe *Ulster*
1921 S. Boyd *North Belfast*
1922 J. B. Teuton *Shaftesbury*
1923 J. Fitzpatrick *Falls*
1924 D. W. Barnett *Belmont*
1925 T. T. Kearney *Larne*
1926 C. Park *Ormo Bakery*
1927 T. McCrea *Ulster*
1928 J. Park *Forth River*
1929 J. Park *Forth River*
1930 J. Landon *Castleton*
1931 G. W. Cooper *Kenilworth*
1932 Dr J. Rusk *Cavehill*
1933 P. T. Watson *Cavehill*
1934 J. Park *Forth River*
1935 T. B. Molyneux *Ballynafeigh*
1936 W. Brown *Knock*
1937 A. B. MacLaughlin *Alexandra*
1938 P. T. Watson *Cavehill*
1939 J. Baker *Forth River*
1940 J. Baker *Forth River*
1941–45 No Competition
1946 B. Fitzmaurice *Cliftonville*
1947 Wm. Barr *Londonderry*
1948 F. J. Wright *Cliftonville*
1949 R. Miller *Bangor*
1950 S. J. Thompson *W'field*
1951 G. Anderson *Coleraine*
1952 T. L. Henry *Londonderry*
1953 W. Christie *Victoria*
1954 S. H. Park *Cliftonville*
1955 J. Webb *Musgrave*
1956 R. Fulton *Coleraine*
1957 R. Fulton *Coleraine*
1958 J. Webb *Musgrave*
1959 J. Connolly *Leinster*
1960 J. Hood *Cavehill*
1961 T. Kennedy *Lisnagarvey*
1962 R. Fulton *Coleraine*
1963 W. Tate *Bangor*
1964 R. Fulton *Coleraine*
1965 R. Fulton *Coleraine*
1966 D. McEnaney *Leinster*
1967 R. Fulton *Coleraine*
1968 T. Sutton *Cavehill*
1969 J. Higgins *YRCD*
1970 D. Laverty *Woodvale*
1971 R. Fulton *Coleraine*
1972 D. Marchant *Leinster*
1973 W. Curragh *Ards*
1974 S. Ashwood *Balmoral*
1975 W. Murray *Portrush*
1976 H. Wallace *Carrickfergus*
1977 D. Darcy *Crumlin*
1978 J. McCraig *Cliftonville*
1979 S. Allen *Ballymena*
1980 D. Corkhill, Jnr *Knock*
1981 W. Loughrey *Portrush*
1982 P. McVeigh *Falls*
1983 G. Woods *Ballymoney*
1984 I. Gillen *Blackrock*
1985 M. Horner *Belmont*

Under-25 Singles J. W. S. Barr Cup

1973 W. Murray *Portrush*
1974 C. Worthington *N. Down*
1975 M. Meown *Bangor*
1976 W. Begley *Coleraine*
1977 P. Smyth *Leinster*
1978 T. Porter *Donaghadee*
1979 D. Livingstone *Ewarts*
1980 C. Worthington *Knock*
1981 R. McCutcheon *Bangor*
1982 S. Brewster *Ballymoney*
1983 J. McGuinness *Limavady*
1984 R. McCutcheon *Bangor*
1985 J. McGuinness *Limavady*

Pairs

1932 C. Curran and C. Clawson *Shaftesbury*
1933 W. Andrews and S. Bradley *Forth River*
1934 F. J. Bestall and G. W. Cooper *Kenilworth*
1935 J. Kernohan and W. J. Irwin *Castleton*
1936 J. Patterson and J. Wilkin *Alexandra*
1937 H. Jones and W. J. Thompson *Belfast*
1938 F. G. Bestall and E. A. Ingram *Kenilworth*
1939 C. Curran and C. Clawson *Shaftesbury*
1940 Wat Robinson and J. A. Boyd *Clontarf*
1941–45 No Competition
1946 W. J. Flook and W. L. Bowie *Kenilworth*
1947 R. Miller and S. Mulholland *Bangor*
1948 R. McCartney and J. Leadbetter *Castleton*
1949 G. Best and S. J. Thompson *Willowfield*
1950 J. Webb and A. Carr *Musgrave*
1951 G. Anderson and R. Fulton *Coleraine*
1952 R. M. Watson and T. L. Henry *Londonderry*
1953 J. McPherson and C. Fox *Willowfield*
1954 J. J. Burns and G. Crossey *Falls*
1955 S. H. Park and W. J. McDonald *Cliftonville*
1956 R. Sterling and J. Boyd *Shaftesbury*
1957 G. Best and S. J. Thompson *Willowfield*
1958 A. G. Elder and J. A. Gault *Woodvale*
1959 R. Dunn and H. Stevenson *Donaghadee*
1960 J. Kelso and T. L. Henry *Londonderry*
1961 H. Watterson and G. Crossey *Falls*
1962 J. Connolly and P. McGuirk *Leinster*
1963 C. Taylor and R. Fulton *Coleraine*
1964 C. Taylor and R. Fulton *Coleraine*
1965 C. Park and T. Russell *Belmont*
1966 C. Taylor and R. Fulton *Coleraine*
1967 C. Taylor and R. Fulton *Coleraine*
1968 T. Kennedy and D. McEnaney *Leinster*
1969 G. McDowell and W. Furongel *Holywood*
1970 L. Fisher and J. Ringland *Lisnagarvey*
1971 L. Byrne and D. Mellor *Leinster*
1972 D. Marchant and T. Kennedy *Leinster*
1973 G. R. Anderson and R. Fulton *Leinster*
1974 D. Marchant and T. Kennedy *Leinster*
1975 D. Marchant and T. Kennedy *Leinster*
1976 A. Keegan and L. Halpin *CYM*
1977 J. Gallagher and C. Beck *Banbridge*
1978 P. Moorehead and P. McGuirk *Leinster*
1979 J. Rogan and J. J. Donnelly *Falls*
1980 A. Murray and T. Kennedy *Herbert Park*
1981 R. McCutcheon and K. Herron *Bangor*
1982 N. Lambe and J. McMullan *Ormeau*
1983 L. Wilson and T. Porter *Bangor*
1984 H. Dunlop and K. Hogg *Ballymoney*
1985 W. Chambers and S. Hegan *Shaftesbury*

Triples

1970	Coleraine
1971	Leinster
1972	CYM
1973	Leinster
1974	Leinster
1975	Portrush
1976	Falls
1977	York Road CD
1978	Falls
1979	Cliftonville
1980	Knock
1981	Leinster
1982	North Belfast
1983	Ballymoney
1984	Ballymoney
1985	Crumlin Dublin

Fours

1908	Kenilworth
1909	Belfast
1910	Ballynafeigh
1911	Shaftesbury
1912	Belfast
1913	Cavehill
1914	Shaftesbury
1915	Ballynafeigh
1916	Larne
1917	Ulster
1918	Baird's
1919	Shaftesbury
1920	Coleraine
1921	Ulster
1922	North Belfast
1923	North Belfast
1924	Shaftesbury
1925	Ballymena
1926	Cavehill
1927	Ormeau
1928	Castleton
1929	Ballynafeigh
1930	Queen's Island
1931	Woodvale
1932	Ballynafeigh
1933	North Belfast
1934	Alexandra
1935	Belmont
1936	Strand
1937	Shaftesbury
1938	Woodvale
1939	Leinster
1940	Divis
1941–45	No Competition
1946	Alexandra
1947	Shaftesbury
1948	Cavehill
1949	St James' Gate
1950	Leinster
1951	Forth River
1952	Leinster
1953	Leinster
1954	Leinster
1955	Botanic
1956	Coleraine
1957	Kenilworth
1958	Portrush
1959	Bangor
1960	Willowfield
1961	Willowfield
1962	Falls
1963	Leinster
1964	Belmont
1965	Bangor
1966	Bangor
1967	Banbridge
1968	Falls
1969	Bangor
1970	Woodvale
1971	Balmoral
1972	Falls
1973	Ballymoney
1974	Portrush
1975	Lisnagarvey
1976	Leinster
1977	Knock
1978	Musgrave
1979	Whitehead
1980	Portrush
1981	Leinster
1982	Belmont
1983	Herbert Park
1984	Crumlin Dublin
1985	Coleraine

Inter-Association Championship
Major Sir William Baird, DL Cup

1937	Northern Ireland Private Greens League
1938	Northern Ireland Private Greens League
1939	Northern Ireland Private Bowling Association
1940	Northern Ireland Private Greens League
1941	No Competition
1942	Northern Ireland Private Bowling Association
1943	Northern Ireland Private Bowling Association
1944	Northern Ireland Private Bowling Association
1945	Northern Ireland Private Bowling Association
1946	Northern Ireland Private Greens League
1947	Northern Ireland Private Greens League
1948	Northern Ireland Private Greens League
1949	Northern Ireland Bowling Association
1950	Northern Ireland Bowling Association
1951	Northern Ireland Private Greens League
1952	Northern Ireland Private Greens League
1953	Northern Ireland Bowling Association
1954	Northern Ireland Private Greens League
1955	Northern Ireland Private Greens League
1956	Northern Ireland Private Greens League
1957	Northern Ireland Bowling Association
1958	Northern Ireland Private Greens League
1959	Northern Ireland Private Greens League
1960	Northern Ireland Private Greens League
1961	Northern Ireland Private Greens League
1962	Northern Ireland Private Greens League
1963	Northern Ireland Private Greens League
1964	Northern Ireland Private Greens League
1965	Northern Ireland Bowling Association
1966	Northern Ireland Bowling Association
1967	Northern Ireland Private Greens League
1968	Northern Ireland Bowling Association
1969	Northern Ireland Private Greens League
1970	Northern Ireland Private Greens League
1971	Northern Ireland Bowling Association
1972	Northern Ireland Private Greens League
1973	Northern Ireland Private Greens League
1974	Northern Ireland Provincial Bowling Association
1975	Northern Ireland Bowling Association
1976	Northern Ireland Provincial Bowling Association
1977	Northern Ireland Private Greens League
1978	Northern Ireland Private Greens League
1979	Northern Ireland Private Greens League
1980	Northern Ireland Provincial Bowling Association
1981	Northern Ireland Bowling Association
1982	Northern Ireland Provincial Bowling Association
1983	Northern Ireland Private Greens League
1984	Northern Ireland Bowling Association
1985	Northern Ireland Private Greens League

Wales

In the ten years immediiately following the formation of the Welsh Bowling Association in 1904, any hopes of speedy progress withered on the vine as a mere 19 clubs sought and were granted affiliation. By 1924 the situation had improved only marginally with the figure struggling to 43, but a dramatic change for the better was close at hand. A government levy of one half-penny on each ton of coal produced in Great Britain was earmarked to provide recreational facilities for miners and steelworkers. Part of this fund was used to form the Miners Welfare Associations which, in turn, financed the laying of bowling greens in various areas of South Wales and by 1932 the number of affiliated clubs had risen to 152. The large industrial concerns also played a part in the growth of the flat-green game in Wales with company-owned sporting facilities, and a change in the rules of the WBA, allowing the entry of public park clubs in 1906, confirmed the Association's function as the sole representative and governing body of the flat-green game in Wales. While there were rules of affiliation in existence, an official constitution of the Welsh Bowling Association was not adopted until 1908.

The first tournament of any note in the Welsh bowling calendar was the Open Singles

On the green at Paddington BC, for many years the unofficial headquarters of the EBA, the Irish International team take on Paddington's bowlers in a match played on 11 July 1931. (BBC Hulton Picture Library).

Championships, held by the Dinas Powis club each year since 1908. The fully ratified championships were instituted in 1919. Initially these championships comprised only singles, fours and pairs competitions with the triples added only from 1970. Among the most coveted of Welsh bowling trophies is The Carruthers Shield, presented to the Association by Sir William Carruthers in 1918 and allocated to the Club Championships one year later, with Cardiff defeating Newport Athletic to become the first holders. The Cadle Cup, held by the winners of the singles championship, was presented to the WBA in 1919 by P. C. Cadle. J. P. Williams of the Grange BC was the first winner, beating W. Tucker (Splott) in the final. Arthur Hutchins carried out the task of hon. secretary to the Welsh Bowling Association for 19 years (1915–34) and a trophy, presented by his wife in his memory, is held by the winner of the rinks championship. Similarly, the pairs trophy, the Jack Anslow Shield, was given by Mrs Anslow in 1952 in memory of her husband who was president of the WBA in 1950. W. R. Evans and T. Taylor (Penarth) were the first pairs champions and the first winners of the rinks

were H. G. Hill, A. E. Fiddes, F. W. Alty and A. H. Emery (Windsor). R. T. B. Ebbw Vale, represented by R. Concreave, E. J. Jones and H. Nicholas became the first holders in 1970 of the A. T. Evans Shield as victors in the triples.

A distinct lack of clout on the greens during the early years saw the Welsh international squad taking the wooden spoon in each of the first three contests. Success continued to elude them in the series until 1920, when they confounded the rampant Scots, winners of the series on nine occasions between 1903 and 1919, beating them into second place on their own Glasgow greens. In their defence it must be said that in the early years of the championships the Welsh team was hardly a representative one. No less than 13 members of the 1903 Welsh International squad were drawn from the ranks of the Cardiff Bowling Club, with the Mackintosh supplying a further two and Pontypool represented only by the manager of the steelworks at Pontnewydd, the deliciously named Zacharia Onions.

Apart from being the year of the first success in the internationals, 1920 also saw a change in the rules of association of the WBA when the offices of president and chairman of committee were altered to that of patron and president respectively, with the Earl of Plymouth installed as the first patron and the 1920 chairman of committee, A. Edwards, taking over the presidency in the following year. Since their initial victory in the international series,

Welsh bowlers have managed to chalk up just 12 more winning score-lines from a total of 57 matches played, on the face of it a poor reflection on the pride and enthusiasm always present in the Welsh game. It is, however, only by comparing the 1984 membership of the WBA, like the EBA, a county-based organization – 8300 bowlers from 313 clubs – with those of the English and Scottish Associations – 115 169 from 2656 clubs and 87 000 from 868 clubs respectively – that Welsh performances in the international series is seen in true perspective. In the more individual, head-to-head confrontations the record is much more impressive with Welsh bowlers collecting three victories in the British Isles singles competition, nine in the pairs, four in the triples and five in the rinks (fours). In the second Empire Games held in 1934 at the Paddington and Temple greens in London, the Welsh pair of T. Davis and S. Weaver took third place behind the victorious English and second-placed Canadians. It was at Worthing in the 1972 World Championships, however, that Welsh bowls had its proudest moments with Mal Evans of Gelli Park, Glamorgan repeating a 1966 World Championship victory over the great David Bryant of England on his way to the singles gold medal, and the trio of J. Russell Evans, Hugh Andrews and Gareth Humphreys taking the bronze in the triples.

Sophia Park, The Mackintosh, Ebbw Vale and Dinas Powis apart, Llandrindod Wells must rank among the most famous of Welsh clubs. The international series were held there in 1925, 1929 and 1937, but it is the celebrated Gibson-Watt Singles Tournament, a three-week long affair of great character, for which the club will perhaps be most fondly remembered by many bowlers. The tournament, widely known as the 'Visitors Championship of Wales' began in 1913, the year in which the club itself was founded, and regularly attracts top-ranking bowlers to the club greens each August.

S. T. Smith of Kettering had his own method of keeping dry during the EBA national singles played at Denmark Hill in 1938. (BBC Hulton Picture Library).

WBA National Championships

Singles

1919 J. P. Williams *Grange*	1930 C. Cecil *Pontnewynydd*	1943 W. J. Bowen *Merthyr WE*	1954 A. T. Evans *Tonypandy*
1920 T. J. Jones *Llanbradach*	1931 A. Reynolds *Six Bells*	1944 R. Pettit *Bedwellty Park*	1955 W. Glyn John *Parc Weren*
1921 H. Burbridge *Cadoxton*	1932 S. Weaver *Swansea*	1945 Wilf John *Rhymney Gwent*	1956 C. Standfast *Newport Ath*
1922 E. Jones *Abertillery*	1933 Emrys Rees *Llwynypia*	1946 W. McCombe *Newbridge*	1957 A. B. Williams *Pontymister W*
1923 P. Holloway *Barry Ath.*	1934 P. Holloway *Bargoed*	1947 C. Weager *Oakdale*	1958 R. D. Roberts *RTB Landore*
1924 C. G. K. Penn *Penylan*	1935 Len Hill *GKB*	1948 J. Rodway *Ebbw Vale*	1959 Llew Rees *Tyrfran*
1925 W. McAllister *Bridgend*	1936 Edgar Thomas *Bargoed*	1949 Evan Rees *Brynhyfryd, Neath*	1960 R. D. Roberts *RTB Landore*
1926 J. F. Williams *Cadoxton*	1937 A. Thomas *Dafen*	1950 A. Thomas *Dafen*	1961 A. E. Evans *Abergavenny*
1927 W. H. Green *Belle Vue*	1938 E. Jones *Abertillery*	1951 A. E. Evans *Abergavenny*	1962 A. Thomas *Llanelli*
1928 H. R. Rees *Howad Gdns*	1939 W. Rees *Pontrhydyfen*	1952 Harry Pearson *Sketty*	1963 Lyn Probert *Abergavenny*
1929 H. R. Edwards *Rhiwbina*	1940 E. Jones *Abertillery*	1953 E. Jones *Abertillery*	
	1941 T. Williams *Tonypandy*		
	1942 T. Williams *Tonypandy*		

WBA NATIONAL CHAMPIONSHIPS – Cont.

1964 B. Roan *Penarth*
1965 Ron Smith *Aberkenfig*
1966 W. Brown *Sketty Church*
1967 J. Pipe *Panteg House*
1968 V. King *Aberdare Park*
1969 Des Morgan *Ammanford*
1970 P. Wright *Aberystwyth*
1971 D. Price *Ammanford*
1972 S. Evans *Brynhyfryd, Carms*
1973 Rod Hughes *Tyrfran*
1974 Les Hughes *Rhiwbina*
1975 R. B. Thomas *Cwmbran Park*

1976 J. Russell Evans *Barry Ath*
1977 J. Russell Evans *Barry Ath*
1978 S. Wiltshire *Tonypandy*
1979 D. Cook *Senghenydd*
1980 L. H. E. Thomas *Talgarth*
1981 J. Colwill *BF Combine*
1982 R. Price *Brynmawr*
1983 D. Wilkins *Pontrhydyfen*
1984 M. Goss *Ogmore Vale*
1985 A. Evans *Aberystwyth*

Under-35 Singles

1961 Malcolm James *Penylan*
1962 Raymond Hill *P. Talbot M*
1963 Gar. Humphreys *Barry Ath*
1964 Gar. Humphreys *Barry Ath*
1965 Russell Evans *Barry Ath*
1966 Mal Evans *Gelli Park*
1967 Gar. Humphreys *Barry Ath*
1968 J. Morgan *Barry Ath*
1969 I. Webley *Barry Ath*
1970 E. Hughes *Grange*
1971 P. Bailey *Brynhyfryd, Carms*
1972 L. Webley *Barry Ath*
1973 P. Santos *Gellifaelog*
1974 P. Webley *Cadoxton*

1975 Paul Wright *Aberystwyth*
1976 W. H. Thomas *Loughor*
1977 R. Davies *St Gabriels*
1978 R. Davies *St Gabriels*
1979 L. Webley *Dinas Powis*
1980 Lyn Perkins *Tonypandy*
1981 M. Bishop *Tick Tock*
1982 T. Mounty *Abertridwr*
1983 Phil Rowlands *Penhill*
1984 J. Davies *Abersytwyth*
1985 B. Powell *Pontrhydfen*

Under-25 Singles

1981 G. J. Hazell *Cardiff Ath*
1982 D. Vowles *Barry Central*
1983 John Price *Aberavon*
1984 R. Weale *Presteigne*
1985 S. Rees *Old Llandonians*

Pairs

1919 W. R. Evans, T. Taylor *Penarth*
1920 W. Rowe, F. E. Rees *St Julian*
1921 T. B. Gracie, W. McAllister *Bridgend*
1922 P. Driscoll, J. P. Williams *Grange*
1923 I. B. Thomas, R. Graham *Dinas Powis*
1924 W. Sargeant, H. J. Strong *Belle Vue*
1925 W. J. Dummer, J. Dummer *Melyn United*
1926 B. P. Evans, T. Evans *Penylan*
1927 T. Toms, E. Hill *Pantygwydr*
1928 W. Skym, A. J. Stacey *Llanelli*
1929 H. M. Chapman, G. A. Bullock *Newport Athletic*
1930 W. Edwards, S. H. Travers *Mackintosh*
1931 S. H. Travers, F. O'Donnell *Mackintosh*
1932 F. Prince, W. J. Treen *Abercam*
1933 H. Roper, W. Walters *Aberbargoed*
1934 T. R. Davies, S. Weaver *Swansea*
1935 C. Barker, Edgar Evans *Pontypool Park*
1936 J. Miles, Len Hill *Port Talbot Municipal*
1937 Meirion Jones, Amwel Jones *Bargoed*
1938 R. Williams, W. Howells *Gelli Park*
1939 L. Edwards, R. Bigs *Oakdale*
1940 D. John, A. J. Stacey *Parc Howard*
1941 J. Hillman, F. Pemberton *Lovell's Athletic*
1942 W. Gaskell, C. Knight *Roath Park*

1943 Evan Evans, Wilfred John *Rhymney Gwent*
1944 D. V. John, W. R. Davies *Gowerton*
1945 A. E. Evans, W. H. Evans *Bailey Park, Abergavenny*
1946 A. Rees, J. Dummer *Melyn United*
1947 D. Morgan, T. Beasley *Melyn United*
1948 Ken Rees, Evan Rees *Brynhyfryd (Neath)*
1949 F. Jones, W. Coop *Briton Ferry Steel*
1950 Ivor Davies, F. L. Cottle *Cardiff*
1951 Dr E. M. Jones, L. C. Williams *Penarth*
1952 J. M. Evans, Cliff Evans *Ocean Staff*
1953 C. Stephens, A. E. Evans *Abergavenny*
1954 E. Mullen, W. R. Evans *Ely Valley*
1955 J. Morgan, F. Hinders *Melyn United*
1956 J. H. Lewis, Wilfred John *Rhymney Royal*
1957 J. A. Griffiths, Len Hill *Port Talbot Municipal*
1958 T. Warren, T. R. Williams *Penygraig Belle Vue*
1959 B. Lewis, R. J. Yeo *Troedyrhiw*
1960 K. Holl, R. Bowen *Beaufort*
1961 W. Williams, R. Manfield *Mackintosh*
1962 E. Jenkins, A. Thomas *Llanelli*
1963 A. Rees, C. Rees *Gelli Park*
1964 Len Lloyd, R. Randall *Penarth*
1965 D. Hughes, M. Davies *Nantclydach*

1966 M. Evans, G. Evans *Gelli Park*
1967 Mal Evans, G. Evans *Gelli Park*
1968 G. Howells, G. L. Jenkins *Penclawdd*
1969 R. Jones, V. Hubbard *Aberaeron*
1970 I. Ivett, F. Bishop *RTB Landore*
1971 T. Daniel, I. Sutherland *Beaufort*
1972 L. H. E. Thomas, L. Moses *Talgarth*
1973 R. Evans, D. L. Jenkins *Tick Tock*
1974 E. Thomas, L. Moses *Talgarth*
1975 L. Perkins, S. Wiltshire *Tonypandy*
1976 N. Harris, R. Harris (Skip) *Kenfig Hill & Pyle*
1977 P. Cossins, L. Becker *Neath Town*
1978 L. Perkins, S. Wiltshire *Tonypandy*
1979 A. N. Tippett, D. Thomas *Rhymney Gwent*
1980 L. Perkins, S. Wiltshire *Tonypandy*
1981 J. Price, H. Price *Aberavon*
1982 P. D. Evans, J. D. H. Thomson *Rhiwbina*
1983 J. Wright, P. Webley *Cadoxton*
1984 G. Evans, M. Evans *Llanelli*
1985 A. Jones, P. Young *Pontardawe*

Triples

1970 R. Concreave, E. J. Jones, H. Nicholas *RTB Ebbw Vale*
1971 B. Seldon, L. Jeremiah, A. Ivett *RTB Landore*
1972 J. Preece, D. Astey, J. Astey *Bailey Park*
1973 W. Phillips, J. Adams, W. Setterfield *Milford Haven*
1974 L. Webley, W. Webber, G. Humphreys *Barry Athletic*
1975 E. Charles, W. R. Hart, D. Richards (Skip) *Brynhyfryd (Carms)*
1976 T. Mounty, G. Roberts, L. Jones (Skip) *Abertridwr*

1977 P. L. Harris, G. Thomas, I. Davies (Skip) *Haverfordwest*
1978 A. Calcombe, T. A. Jenkins, R. Walker *Builth Wells*
1979 J. King, G. James, J. Davies *Penylan*
1980 K. Bolton, J. E. Thomas, G. Williams *Tonypandy*
1981 B. Thomas, H. Jenkins, F. Brown *Girlings*
1982 J. Price, H. Price, R. Hill *Aberavon*
1983 P. Turton, D. Maundrell, C. Diamond *Wattstown*
1984 D. Pugh, P. Wright, A. Evans *Aberystwyth*
1985 G. Rees, I. Howells, M. Harris *Carmarthen*

Fours

1919 H. G. Hill, A. E. Fiddes, F. W. Alty, A. H. Emery *Windsor*
1920 W. H. Thomas, G. W. Smith, I. B. Thomas, R. Graham *Dinas Powis*
1921 A. T. Evans, H. Snell, T. Taylor, J. Rees *Penarth*
1922 H. M. Chapman, J. Whitehouse, W. Luke, G. A. Bullock *Newport Athletic*
1923 J. Pratt, T. Bowker, J. Morgan, W. Whitlock *Victoria Park*
1924 W. H. Jenkins, W. David, M. Wood, J. Batstone *Cardiff Athletic*

1925 J. Merriman, H. Williams, S. Weaver, D. J. Squires *Swansea*
1926 J. McGill, J. Duthie, T. Evans, L. Jones *Penylan*
1927 T. R. Davies, J. Merriman, S. Weaver, F. Taylor *Swansea*
1928 J. Davies, E. Holdsworth, D. Parry, E. Hill *Pantygwydr*
1929 D. J. Williams, P. E. Cadle, E. Parry, G. A. Chambers *Windsor*
1930 J. Thomas, G. Bishop, G. Whyte, C. C. Johnston *Roath Park*
1931 T. Toms, T. Howell, F. Reed, E. Hill *Pantygwydr*
1932 W. Abbott, G. E. Martin, E. Jones, E. Thompson *Barry Central*
1933 T. R. Davies, H. Williams, W. Mitchell, S. Weaver *Swansea*
1934 R. Williams, W. G. Kemp, M. Manweller, I. Rees *Wattstown*
1935 J. Maplestone, P. Lempiere, W. Davies, J. Maile *Grange*
1936 W. H. Harris, T. S. Foster, A. Jones, J. Fine *Trelyn Park*
1937 J. A. Griffiths, J. Miles, J. B. Davies, Len Hill *Port Talbot Municipal*
1938 E. Lewis, E. Evans, I. T. Jones, W. D. Jones *Dinam Park*
1939 J. A. Griffiths, J. Miles, J. B. Davies, Len Hill *Port Talbot Municipal*
1940 G. Davies, H. Hughes, L. Jones, J. Phillips *Abertridwr*
1941 J. A. Griffiths, A. Jenkins, T. W. Jones, Len Hill *Port Talbot Municipal*
1942 J. Millman, C. Toomer, S. Day, E. Jones *Abertillery*
1943 A. Jones, I. Thomas, Sgt J. Probert, B. A. Jones *Rhymney Royal*
1944 V. Thomas, D. H. Griffiths, G. Rees, D. Prosser *Pontrhydyfen*
1945 R. Cornwall, C. Toomer, S. Day, E. Jones *Abertillery*

1946 R. Cornwall, C. Toomer, S. Day, E. Jones *Abertillery*
1947 W. D. Ford, G. Morgan, P. D. Thomas, A. Thomas *Dafen*
1948 I. John, K. Rees, W. Powell, E. Rees *Brynhyfryd (Neath)*
1949 T. Griffiths, C. Vokes, B. Kingston, C. W. J. Watts *Victoria Park (Cardiff)*
1950 H. Ravalde, H. T. Ewings, A. Kirk, C. Standfast *Newport Athletic*
1951 Ivor Davies, J. Budd, T. King, F. L. Cottle *Cardiff*
1952 T. J. Bord, D. W. Davies, O. Thomas, H. Maylott *Merthyr West End*
1953 R. Williams, D. Morgan, W. B. Williams, T. R. Williams *Penygraig Belle Vue*
1954 A. H. Pearce, W. Preece, H. Edwards, W. McCombe *Newbridge*
1955 J. R. Davies, J. Baker, Ken Rees, A. Rees *Melyn United*
1956 J. M. Evans, M. Jenkins, M. Coleman, D. G. Coleman *Gelli Park*
1957 D. Prosser, Evan Jones, J. A. Griffiths, Len Hill *Port Talbot Municipal*
1958 F. Bishop, W. G. John, F. L. Taylor, S. J. Perman *Victoria (Swansea)*
1959 A. James, T. H. Griffiths, K. Rowlands, T. Rowlands *Llandaff Fields*
1960 C. Stephens, L. Proberts, T. Griffiths, A. E. Evans *Abergavenny*
1961 C. Evans, M. Jenkins, D. J. Mantle, J. M. Evans *Gelli Park*
1962 E. Jones, L. Hill, D. Prosser, Len Hill *Port Talbot Municipal*
1963 R. Evans, J. Morgan, Ron Thomas, G. Humphreys *Barry Athletic*

1964 R. J. Hudman, C. Misto, F. L. Williams, C. L. Jones *Brecon*
1965 T. Roberts, W. D. Jones, R. Bending, J. Thomson *Rhiwbina*
1966 C. Colwell, G. Tallamy, D. Reynolds, G. Cox *Llansawel*
1967 Gwyn Howells, E. J. Davies, D. Palmer, D. L. Jenkins *Penclawdd*
1968 F. Jones, E. Petty, F. Pipe, H. Baynton *Caerphilly*
1969 J. R. Evans, J. A. Morgan, R. Thomas, G. Humphreys *Barry Athletic*
1970 W. Richards, E. Spooner, J. Palmer, B. Maunder *Llandrindod*
1971 C. Rees, E. C. Oliver, H. S. Andrews, D. Richards *Brynhyfryd (Carms)*
1972 O. Rees, E. Oliver, J. Thomas, D. Richards *Brynhyfryd (Carms)*
1973 D. Price, P. Williams, R. John, G. Morris *Ammanford*
1974 A. Young, E. Stanbury, A. Marshall, R. Young *Llanbradach*
1975 R. A. Jones, R. J. Keeble, R. Williams, V. J. Porter (Skip) *Bryn Rd, Swansea*
1976 G. Storey, W. J. Webber, D. K. Williams, G. Humphreys (Skip) *Barry Athletic*
1977 J. Dally, G. E. Evans, G. Wiltshire, D. J. Evans (Skip) *Tonypandy*
1978 A. Jones, G. Evans, A. Galbraith, A. Evans *Aberystwyth*
1979 P. Fulilove, B. Lewis, C. Strange, R. Morgan *Troedyrhiw*
1980 H. Meddins, G. Bishop, A. R. Dibble, L. Webley *Dinas Powis*
1981 W. Plumley, C. Folkes, W. H. Thomas, W. E. Pugh *Abertridwr*
1982 G. Griffiths, G. Hopkins, P. Morgan, T. Mounty *Abertridwr*
1983 R. Bryant, D. Pritchard, K. Nash, J. Haddock *Caldicot*
1984 Weale D, B, W and R *Presteigne*
1985 M. Gillmore, D. Hazell, G. Hazell, R. Pullen *Cardiff Athletic*

Ireland's J. A. Boyd in action against the English during the 1939 Home International series at the Lensbury BC, Teddington. (BBC Hulton Picture Library).

Club Championship
Carruthers Shield

1919 Cardiff	1954 Victoria *Swansea*
1920 Barry General	1955 Llanbradach
1921 Grange	1956 Grange
1922 Newport Athletic	1957 Barry Athletic
1923 Roath Park	1958 Grange
1924 Newport Athletic	1959 Pontrhydyfen
1925 Cardiff	1960 Parc Howard *Llanelli*
1926 Newport Athletic	1961 Grange
1927 Mackintosh	1962 Caerphilly
1928 Parc Howard	1963 Gelli Park
1929 Victoria Park	1964 Llanbradach
1930 Newtown	1965 Gelli Park
1931 Pantygwydr	1966 Llanbradach
1932 Pantygwydr	1967 Melyn United
1933 Mackintosh	1968 Gelli Park
1934 Llanelli	1969 Llanbradach
1935 Dinam Park	1970 Gelli Park
1936 Barry Athletic	1971 Tonypandy
1937 Pantygwydr	1972 Penylan
1938 Abercarn	1973 Rhiwbina
1939 Victoria Park	1974 RTB Ebbw Vale
1940–5 Not Played	1975 Penylan
1946 Llanelli	1976 Llanbradach
1947 Pontymister Welfare	1977 Aberystwyth
1948 Skewen	1978 Tonypandy
1949 Pontypool Park	1979 Cwmbran Park
1950 Caerau Welfare	1980 Harlequins
1951 Penclawdd	1981 Tick Tock
1952 Victoria *Swansea*	1982 Aberystwyth
1953 Bridgend	1983 Old Landorians
	1984 Cardiff
	1985 Dinas Powis

Wales, seen here in their match against the Scots, ended as runners-up to England in the 1939 Home International championships played at the Lensbury BC, Teddington. (BBC Hulton Picture Library).

Open Bowling Championship of Wales

1908 John Pollock *Cardiff*	1951 T. R. Williams* *Penrhys*
1909 J. T. Shelton *Penhill*	1952 F. Groves *Cardiff Athletic*
1910 John Pillans *Carluke*	1953 Dr E. M. Jones *Penarth*
1911 D. Wilkinson *Dinas Powis*	1954 A. S. Gwilliam *Victoria Park*
1912 John Pillans *Carluke*	1955 Don Ashton *Cadoxton*
1913 John Pillans *Carluke*	1956 Ron Bennett *Cadoxton*
1914 J. Millar *Scotland*	1957 A. Spry *Hailey Park*
1915–19 War period	1958 A. R. Dibble *Penarth*
1920 Albie Brown *Victoria Park*	1959 Len Lloyd *Penarth*
1921 Windsor Thomas *Mackintosh*	1960 Ron Bennett *Barry Athletic*
1922 John Pollock *Cardiff*	1961 Doug Prince *Cardiff Athletic*
1923 Geo. A. Chambers *Penarth W.*	1962 K. Rowlands *Llandaff Fields*
1924 Percy Holloway *Barry*	1963 Ron Groves *Llanbradach*
1925 F. C. Parfitt *Newport Athletic*	1964 C. Williams *Penhill*
1926 Don H. Ross *Mackintosh*	1965 Ron Thomas *Barry Athletic*
1927 Tom Yeoman *Barry Athletic*	1966 A. R. Dibble *Penarth*
1928 Albie Brown *Penhill*	1967 J. L. Davies *GKB*
1929 John Pollock *Cardiff*	1968 E. Stanbury *Llanbradach*
1930 Tom Yeoman *Barry Athletic*	1969 Trevor Phillips *Cardiff Ath*
1931 W. H. Harris *Llandbradach*	1970 Bryn Hawkins *Cardiff Ath*
1932 C. Colley *Penarth Windsor*	1971 Viv Harris *Splott*
1933 Geo. Langford *Mackintosh*	1972 Ellis Stanbury *Llanbradach*
1934 Frank o'Donnell *Mackintosh*	1973 Gordon Crowther *Cardiff SG*
1935 J. L. Dalton *Barry Athletic*	1974 Ellis Stanbury *Llanbradach*
1936 E. Parry *Penarth Windsor*	1975 Les Durham *Dinas Powis*
1937 E. Parry *Penarth Windsor*	1976 P. Critcher *Penarth Windsor*
1938 A. J. Bibb *Newtown*	1977 P. Evans *Rhiwbina*
1939 H. Peach *Barry Central*	1978 G. R. Williams *Penygraig*
1940 Tom Yeoman *Barry Athletic*	1979 C. Watkins *Dinas Powis*
1941–46 War period	1980 C. Watkins *Dinas Powis*
1947 P. R. Morrish *Heath*	1981 P. Critcher *Dinas Powis*
1948 J. Cable *Barry Central*	1982 Ellis Stanbury *Llanbradach*
1949 D. Clarke *Penylan*	1983 Ellis Stanbury *Llanbradach*
1950 J. L. Dalton *Barry Athletic*	1984 C. Watkins *Dinas Powis*
	1985 P. Evans *Rhiwbina*

Scots born John Pollock skipped for Wales in every international match up to 1925, played in a total of 22 series and won the Cardiff championships eight times.

* T. R. Williams (1951) is the father of G. R. Williams (1978).

The Gibson-Watt Cup

1913 Henry Davies *Chester*
1914 Harry Williams *Swansea*
1915 D. A. Sutherland *Swansea*
1916 D. A. Sutherland *Swansea*
1917 A. Johnson *Manselton*
1918 Tom Evans *Llanelli*
1919 D. J. Squires *Swansea*
1920 W. G. Green *Newport*
1921 A. J. Stacey *Llanelli*
1922 Peter Snoddon *Cardiff*
1923 W. J. Treen *Abercarn*
1924 J. Swarbrick *Morriston*
1925 J. Swarbrick *Morriston*
1926 A. J. Stacey *Llanelli*
1927 R. Parsons *Bristol*
1928 J. Swarbrick *Morriston*
1929 H. G. Smith *Glasgow*
1930 Robert Lawson *Glasgow*
1931 J. Swarbrick *Morriston*
1932 D. J. Phillips *Llanelli*

1933 W. Morgan *Thomastown*
1934 Stan Weaver *Swansea*
1935 A. Treseder *St Fagans*
1936 J. Haddow *Sanquhar*
1937 W. J. Richards *Ross-on-Wye*
1938 Joe Graddon *Brynmill*
1939 S. McVie *Kilmarnock*
1940 G. Goldie *Kilmarnock*
1941 D. T. Williams *Sketty*
1942 G. Goldie *Kilmarnock*
1943 H. Pearsons *Manselton*
1944 G. Goldie *Kilmarnock*
1945 A. T. Evans *Tonypandy*
1946 D. S. Thomas *Llanelli*
1947 J. Haddow *Sanquhar*
1948 W. J. Richards *Hereford*
1949 W. J. Richards *Hereford*
1950 T. J. Morgan *Dafen*
1951 W. R. Thomas *Gorseinon*

1952 G. Goldie *Kilmarnock*
1953 L. C. Williams *Penarth*
1954 J. Evenson *Abergavenny*
1955 T. Humphries *Penrys Park*
1956 W. R. Thomas *Gorseinon*
1957 P. T. Watson *Cavehill, Belfast*
1958 P. T. Watson *Cavehill, Belfast*
1959 G. M. Adamson *Carluke*
1960 R. D. Adamson *Carluke*
1961 E. L. Probert *Abergavenny*
1962 A. J. Palmer *Wolverhampton*
1963 Fred Thomas *Dafen*
1964 M. L. Evans *Gelli Park*
1965 L. C. Williams *Belle Vue*
1966 M. L. Evans *Gelli Park*

1967 M. L. Evans *Gelli Park*
1968 L. C. Williams *Cardiff*
1969 J. E. Pugh *Knighton*
1970 R. Daniel *Llanelli*
1971 L. H. E. Thomas *Talgarth*
1972 D. R. Jones *Clevedon*
1973 L. Probert *Abergavenny*
1974 J. Haddow *Sanquhar*
1975 C. Williams *Clydach*
1976 A. I. Jones *Montgomery*
1977 J. S. T. Harries *Aberystwyth*
1978 B. Powell *Kington*
1979 D. Powell *Crickhowell*
1980 R. Owens *Aberystwyth*
1981 R. Weale *Presteigne*
1982 L. H. E. Thomas *Talgarth*
1983 M. Roberts *Barry Port*
1984 R. Weale *Presteigne*
1985 W. Price *Llandrindod Wells*

Gateway British Isles Championships

Singles
1959 K. Coulson *England*
1960 D. J. Bryant *England*
1961 E. M. Johnson *Scotland*
1962 C. Mercer *England*
1963 W. S. Tate *Ireland*
1964 W. Gibbs *Scotland*
1965 J. Hershaw *Scotland*
1966 L. Stanfield *Wales*
1967 R. Fulton *Ireland*
1968 J. Lamont *Scotland*
1969 R. Motroni *Scotland*
1970 P. Wright *Wales*
1971 D. J. Bryant *England*
1972 D. J. Bryant *England*
1973 D. J. Bryant *England*
1974 W. C. Irish *England*
1975 J. McLagan *Scotland*
1976 D. McGill Jnr *Scotland*
1977 J. Russell Evans *Wales*
1978 C. Burch *England*
1979 S. Allen *Ireland*
1980 D. S. Corkill *Ireland*

1981 F. Muirhead *Scotland*
1982 C. C. Ward *England*
1983 J. N. Bell *England*
1984 W. Richards *England*

Pairs
1959 England
1960 England
1961 Scotland
1962 England
1963 Scotland
1964 Ireland
1965 England
1966 Ireland
1967 Ireland
1968 Scotland
1969 Scotland
1970 Wales
1971 England
1972 Scotland
1973 England
1974 England
1975 Wales
1976 Wales
1977 Ireland
1978 Wales
1979 Ireland
1980 Wales
1981 Wales
1982 Wales
1983 Wales
1984 Ireland

Triples
1971 England
1972 England
1973 Scotland
1974 Scotland
1975 Ireland
1976 Scotland
1977 Ireland
1978 England
1979 Ireland
1980 England
1981 Ireland
1982 Wales
1983 England
1984 England

Fours
1959 Scotland
1960 Wales
1961 England
1962 Ireland
1963 Wales
1964 Ireland
1965 Wales
1966 Scotland
1967 Ireland
1968 Ireland
1969 England
1970 Ireland
1971 England
1972 Wales
1973 Ireland
1974 Ireland
1975 Scotland
1976 England
1977 Ireland
1978 Scotland
1979 Scotland
1980 Wales
1981 Ireland
1982 Ireland
1983 England
1984 England

Home International Championships

Venue/Winners
1903 London *England*
1904 Glasgow *Scotland*
1905 Cardiff *Ireland*
1906 Belfast *England*
1907 Newcastle *Scotland*
1908 Edinburgh *Scotland*
1909 Cardiff *Scotland*
1910 Belfast *Scotland*
1911 London *England*
1912 Glasgow *Scotland*
1913 Cardiff *Scotland*
1914 Belfast *Scotland*
1915–18 Not played owing to war
1919 Carlisle *Scotland*
1920 Glasgow *Wales*
1921 Cardiff *Scotland*
1922 Larne *Scotland*
1923 London *Scotland*
1924 Glasgow *England*

1925 Llandrindod Wells *Wales*
1926 Belfast *England*
1927 Southampton *England*
1928 Glasgow *Scotland*
1929 Llandrindod Wells *England*
1930 Dublin *Wales*
1931 Westcliff-on-Sea *Wales*
1932 Glasgow *Scotland*
1933 Cardiff *Wales*
1934 Belfast *Wales*
1935 Weston-super-Mare *Scotland*
1936 Glasgow *Scotland*
1937 Llandrindod Wells *Wales*
1938 Larne *Wales*
1939 London *England*
1940–45 Not played owing to war

1946 Glasgow *Wales*
1947 Newport *England*
1948 Bangor *Wales*
1949 Brighton *England*
1950 Glasgow *Scotland*
1951 Swansea *Ireland*
1952 Dublin *Scotland*
1953 Brighton *Scotland*
1954 Glasgow *England*
1955 Cardiff *England*
1956 Belfast *England*
1957 Bournemouth *Wales*
1958 Glasgow *England*
1959 Cardiff *England*
1960 Belfast *England*
1961 Eastbourne *England*
1962 Glasgow *England*
1963 Cardiff *Scotland*
1964 Belfast *England*
1965 London *Scotland*
1966 Glasgow *Scotland*

1967 Llandarcy *Scotland*
1968 Belfast *Scotland*
1969 London *Scotland*
1970 Glasgow *Scotland*
1971 Aberdare *Scotland*
1972 Bristol *Scotland*
1973 Bournemouth *Scotland*
1974 Edinburgh *Scotland*
1975 Llanelli *Scotland*
1976 Not played
1977 Worthing *Scotland*
1978 Uddington *Wales*
1979 Gwent *Scotland*
1980 Nottingham *Scotland*
1981 Worthing *Ireland*
1982 Ayr *Wales*
1983 Cardiff *England*
1984 Larne *England*
1985 Worthing *England*

Scotland has won the Championship 34 times, England 20, Wales 13 and Ireland 3.

The International Bowling Board

The objects of the International Bowling Board, the premier governing body of the game throughout the world, include: to promote, foster and safeguard the flat green game; to frame, alter and revise the laws of the game; to authorize all international games (and lay down the conditions); to approve all international visits; to control a uniform test for bowls and to maintain good relations with all affiliated national authorities.

Following a proposal by John Thomas of the Mackintosh BC, Cardiff in 1904, the Board was formed at a meeting held at the Park Hotel, Cardiff on 11 July 1905 on the occasion of the Home International Championships held that year in the city. Those in attendance were: Dr W. G. Grace and Walter Stonehewer (England); J. C. Hunter and D. McLaughlin (Ireland); J. T. Morrison and A. H. Hamilton (Scotland) and W. A. Morgan and J. Thomas (Wales). J. T. Morrison was elected chairman of the new body, A. H. Hamilton becoming its first hon. secretary and the laws of the Scottish Bowling Association were duly adopted as the official code of play. While the domestic responsibilities of the old Imperial Bowling Association had passed to the English Bowling Association, the new Board assumed control of all aspects of the international game, at that time confined almost exclusively to arrangements for touring sides from the Dominions.

In 1928 Australia, New Zealand, South Africa and Canada were admitted to membership and ten years later the American Lawn Bowling Association joined them after a series of unsuccessful applications. Despite the presence of the overseas contingent, the home countries jealously guarded their power on the ruling body. On the entry of the Dominions, home country representation was increased from two to three compared with the lone delegate allowed to each of the newcomers. In 1929 the grievance was made worse when, while giving the dominion associations one more representative apiece, the Board decreed that the extra delegates must be members of one of the home associations. In 1937 the Board increased home country representation to four and this manoeuvre prompted the Australian Bowling Council to move, unsuccessfully, that each member of the Board should have equal representation. Against a background of increasing resentment the situation smouldered on until 1952 when the Board relented and parity for full members was at last achieved.

The Imperial Bowling Association had arranged tours of the UK by Australia (1901), New Zealand (1901) and Canada (1904) but it was not until 1906 that a British party ventured abroad. Team captain for this ground-breaking, IBB arranged tour of Canada was Samuel Fingland of Glasgow with J. C. Hunter (Belfast) and James Telford (Newcastle) as vice-captains. Match statistics reveal a total of 23 matches played with 21 wins and 2 losses. Costs involved per man are recorded as: First class ocean passage Liverpool–Montreal return £25 14s 0d (£25.70); rail travel in Canada for 1200 miles £6 10s 0d (£6.50); hotels for five weeks £17 10s 0d (£17.50), a total of £49 14s 0d (£49.70).

The Board, which meets every two years, whenever and wherever the World Championships or Commonwealth Games are staged, made one of the most far-reaching decisions of its existence with the constitutional amendment of 1982 which allowed for the introduction of open bowls, a move which gave the official seal of approval to a decision taken by a number of its member bodies some two years before.

Today there are ten full members of the Board, each with two delegates, and 15 associate members with one apiece but, with Spain and Portugal filing their intentions to seek admittance and signs of interest filtering through from India, Pakistan and the Netherlands, the IBB list could be greatly extended in the near future.

Willie Wood (Scotland) – a disastrous Master's debut. (Author).

The British Isles Bowling Council

Formed in 1958, the BIBC arranges and controls not only the Home International Championships but also the British Isles Championships. All matches played under BIBC control are bound by The IBB Laws of the Game as adopted by the Council. All bowls manufactured for use in the British Isles and all bowls sent to Official Bowls Testers must bear either a BIBC or IBB stamp. In 1977 the Council approved a 15-year period between testing for domestic purposes, although for Internationals, Championships, Commonwealth Games and World Championships the period is ten years.

The English Bowls Council

The EBC was formed with Sports Council blessing in 1974 as a consultative body for the game, representing all seven bowling authorities in England – Men's Flat Green (EBA), Women's Flat Green (EWBA), Men's Indoor (EIBA), Women's Indoor (EWIBA), Men's Federation (EBF), Women's Federation (EWBF) and Crown Green (BCGBA). Council business concerns a wide range of topics within bowls including grant aid, advice to clubs on procedure and administration. More recently the question of European participation in bowls has come to the fore with the advances made in Spain due to the holiday trade and interest in Germany, Holland and Belgium.

The English Bowls Coaching Scheme

April 1984 saw the establishment of the English Bowls Coaching Scheme, an ambitious and far-sighted project largely funded by the Sports Council which, for the first time in history, found the seven national bodies in control of the game in England, united in a single cause. Objects of the EBCS include: (a) to promote, foster, develop and implement bowls coaching in England for men, women and young persons, and to encourage the growth of the sport through instruction of beginners and coaching of bowlers; and (b) to be responsible for the setting of standards for bowls coaching and instruction and to be responsible for the assessment and certification of instructors, coaches and advanced coaches approved by the scheme.

For the purposes of administration the country is divided on a regional basis, the flat green codes areas defined as North, Midlands, East Anglia, Central, South Western and Southern. The crown green structure is based on the counties represented by the BCGBA and divided into North Western, Pennines, Midland and West Central.

The scheme is staffed, part-time by a director of coaching, national development officer and national coaches for each of the ten areas. A syllabus and guidelines for the instruction of beginners has been produced and issued to all level green clubs and a similar work was prepared and distributed to the crown green regions in 1984.

Left The Souzas – Frank (USA) left and George (Hong Kong) right – watch play at the Masters. (Author).

Right The smooth delivery of George Souza (Hong Kong) in action at the 1984 Gateway Masters. (Author).

Beach House Park greenkeeper, Jock (King Canute) Munro tackles the results of the 1983 hailstorm. (Duncan Cubitt, *Bowls International*).

Through the scheme courses in coaching and instruction are held at selected venues in each of the regions and this policy has already paid dividends with a significant advance not merely in the numbers of instructors and coaches available but in the quality of advice being proffered.

Figures released by the administrators of the scheme reveal that at 20 May 1985, 2000 instructors had been nationally certificated while the number of fully qualified coaches stood at 427. Courses and seminars had been held around the country and these included such topics as team coaching, youth coaching and a standard course entitled 'Improve your Bowling'.

English Bowls Players Association

National coach and 1969 EBA singles champion Jimmy Davidson was a prime mover in the founding of the English Bowls Players and Coaches Association at a meeting attended by 37 top players at Worthing on 22 August 1980. The new body was formally constituted on 6 November 1980 at the Paddington BC, London with David Bryant elected as president.

The expressed purpose of the Association was 'to protect the interests of coaches and players' in the new climate created in the game by the acceptance by the flat green bodies of 'open' bowls. A press release from the new body stated 'In many other sports the top performers are fairly limited in number and stand well ahead of "the pack". In bowls, one of the recognized top flight is always liable to be beaten "on the day by one of the following pack" of several hundred equally competitive bowlers. In recruiting membership and associate membership, the Association will make it clear that they are encouraging every competitive bowler to reach the top flight, by increased competitive opportunity and advanced coaching, thereby helping to improve the standards of English bowls at every level.'

Despite early opposition by some members of the established English Bowling Association who saw the BP and CA as a threat to the major body's authority, a spirit of guarded give-and-take eventually developed into one of cooperation. The new Association responded to a point made by the EBA that the interests of coaches were already catered for by the English Bowls Coaching Scheme, by dropping the word coaches from their title in 1981. The EBA in turn have acted on a number of suggestions regarding expenses for players in Middleton Cup matches and the institution of new tournaments such as the Top Fours Competition, and the National Invitation Singles Championship both introduced in 1982.

Prevented by the rules of the EBA from becoming associate members of that body, the EBPA found no such barrier in the indoor game and is an associate member of the EIBA eligible, under licence, to organize its own championships. The first of these took place at Wellingborough IBC on 3 March 1985 with a trophy presented by Max Engel, chairman of the EBA Charity Trust and legal adviser to the EBPA since its formation. Jim Hobday of East Dorset won the inaugural title in a tournament sponsored in the latter stages by Croft Original and attracting 160 players.

3 Women's Bowls

THE INVOLVEMENT of women in bowls has been well documented throughout the game's history but the associations necessary for successful organization arrived relatively late on the scene. For many years women were allowed on the green under sufferance rather than as a right, a situation which, while persisting in some clubs to this very day, has undergone a radical change as the women's associations have gained in strength and authority.

The first stirrings of organized women's bowls surfaced in Australia with the formation of the Victorian Ladies Bowling Association in 1907. This landmark in the game was however to prove no harbinger of any significant improvement in the fortunes of women bowlers. Twelve years were to pass before the example set by the ladies of Victoria was followed by the establishment in South Africa of the Western Provinces Women's Bowling Association in 1919.

England

A real competitive spirit breathed life into the women's game in England around the turn of the century. Certainly, records show that ladies in the Midlands and further North had begun to view the game as something more demanding than simply a gentle way of passing time on both crown and flat greens as early as 1902. In 1906 the London County Council endorsed that view by setting aside one rink on every park green under its jurisdiction for women's play and the momentum was continued in the South by the institution, in 1908, of a tournament for the wives of members of the Southey BC, Wimbledon, Surrey.

The giant leap forward came with the formation of the Kingston Canbury Ladies Bowling Club, Surrey in 1910, and one of the earliest recorded matches between ladies' clubs was played on the Kingston green against bowlers from the Wimbledon Corporation-owned Dundonald Recreation Ground sometime prior to the First World War.

Despite this flurry of activity in the Surrey area it was Somerset which was to produce the first English Women's County Association in 1928. Leicestershire followed suit two years later and, with enthusiasm now apparent in a more tangible form, ladies sections and clubs began to proliferate throughout England.

The Sussex seaside resort of Eastbourne earned its place in bowls history as the scene of the first national tournament for women in September 1931. A group of lady enthusiasts, led by the petite but redoubtable Mrs Clara E. Johns, organized the open competition which ran over four days, attracted 243 entries and brought the outstanding skills of Mrs E. S. Tigg to wider notice. Mrs Tigg ('Tiggie') proved a bowler of supreme accuracy, winning the singles and joining clubmate Mrs W. Privett, who later became President of the EWBA, to take the pairs title. The enthusiasm generated among the growing ranks of women bowlers by the success of the tournament underlined the need for a national association to control and unify their efforts.

A meeting held during the Eastbourne week confirmed support for such a body and a further meeting was set up to discuss the issue at The York Hotel, Berners St, London on 7 October 1931. This latent urge to organize drew some 200 women bowlers to the York Hotel from Essex, Kent, Leicestershire, Middlesex, Somerset, Surrey, Sussex and the triumvirate of Berks, Bucks and Herts. The meeting, following some early skirmishes, was quickly to suffer its first casualty and discover its first heroine. Mrs Greenwood of Leicestershire, elected chairman of this historic gathering, advocated an association comprising, at the outset at least, only the three existing organized county bodies, Essex, Somerset and Leicestershire. A counter proposal by Mrs Johns of Sussex that an association be formed with its officers elected from among the bowlers present was rejected out of hand by the chair, a decision which backfired with a vengeance when Mrs Greenwood found herself promptly voted out of office, to be replaced by Mrs Johns whose proposal, obviously reflecting the spirit prevailing in the women's game, was immediately embraced by the meeting. The formation of the English Women's Bowling Association was no doubt the most important action taken at the York Hotel on 7 October 1931, but the subsequent election of Mrs Johns to the office of President was to prove an extremely wise decision. Over the following three years she led the transformation of women's bowls with indomitable spirit, a frightening workload and supreme administrative skills. Equally effective on the green as she was off it, Mrs Johns, an England skip over 11 international series, won the EWBA singles championship in 1947 and skipped a rink from her own Cavendish Club to victory in the fours in 1933, '34 and '35.

The formation of the EWBA sparked off a rapid increase in the number of county bodies and, although originally conceived as an association of clubs, the EWBA was forced within two years to adopt the 'membership through county association' system as practised in the men's game, with the Kent County Women's BA being the first such body to affiliate to the National Association.

Of the major EWBA competitions, three, the singles (The Alpha Rose Bowl), pairs (Jacques Cup and Scolding Trophy) and fours (C. B. Collins Trophy) were all held for the first time in 1932. Mrs E. Tigg (Waddon Residents, Croydon), the singles winner of Mrs Johns' Eastbourne tournament, triumphed once again winning not only the Alpha Rose Bowl to become the first women's singles champion of England, but also led her Waddon Residents rink, completed by Mrs W. Privett, Mrs Holman and Mrs Gilchrist, to success in the fours. The early years of the EWBA were dominated on the green by bowlers from the Waddon Residents, who won 8 out of a possible 12 championship finals between 1932 and 1934, the Cavendish Club of Mrs Johns, and Strawberry Hill and Southgate, both situated in Middlesex. The EWBA triples competition, unlike that of the men's game, had a relatively early start, being introduced into the women's calendar in 1933 and, predictably, it was the Waddon Residents trio who registered another first. Inter-county matches in the women's game date from 1928 when bowlers of the South Wales and Monmouthshire BA played host to the ladies of Somerset at Newport, with the return at Weston-Super-Mare in 1929, thought to have been the first women's county match played in England.

The Johns Trophy

The value of these representative games, an important feature of the EBA calendar through the Middleton Cup since 1911, was quickly appreciated by Mrs Johns who presented a trophy expressly for the purpose of inter-county competition in 1934. The Johns Trophy competition is played on a knock-out basis by teams of six rinks (24 players) to 21 ends. Surrey, with Mrs Tigg inevitably in the forefront, emerged as the first winners of the trophy, defeating Kent in the 1934 final.

Wales

After only five months in splendid isolation as the sole national women's association in the British Isles, the EWBA found the ladies of Wales following their example with representatives of just six clubs forming the Welsh Women's Bowling Association in March 1932. Mrs Roland Pugh (Thomastown) was elected president with Mrs Mabel Brown the first hon. secretary.

Early records of the Welsh Women's BA Championships which date from 1933 are sketchy to say the least but we do know that Mrs Insell of Newport was the first singles champion and that Thomastown won the fours.

Scotland

The women of Scotland were the next to organize albeit by a tortuous route. In a country strong on independence of spirit, the first women's association of any note was the East Renfrewshire Ladies Bowling Association formed in 1933 with Mrs I. McLean (Busby) installed as first secretary-treasurer, a post she held for 21 years, and Mrs J. M. Guest (Kingswood) founder president. The Scottish Women's Bowling Association, Eastern Section was founded one year later by nine clubs moulded into one unit by Mrs H. Murphy (Blackhall, Edinburgh), secretary of the new body. At the founding meeting held on 2 February 1934, Mrs Murphy was empowered to undertake the formation of one national association and it was largely through her efforts that the Scottish Women's Bowling Association was formed in March 1936. (In 1947 the title of the Scottish Women's BA, Eastern Section was changed to The East of Scotland Women's BA to save confusion with the major national body.)

National championships got under way in Scotland in 1936 with The Isobel Trophy (also known as the Founders Trophy), presented by

Mrs Murphy for the winner of the singles championship, going to Mrs Patton (Wallace and Weir). Mrs Murphy's club, Blackhall, Edinburgh, carried off the first pairs title and the T. C. Hills Trophy, while the Robert Carswell Trophy presented for the fours went to the Lanarkshire-based Bearsdon WBC.

Ireland

Last of the Home Countries to form a National Women's Association was Ireland which, following a morale-boosting tour by members of the EWBA, finally organized with eight clubs in 1947. Mrs J. McMaster (Whitehead, County Antrim) was elected as first president with Mrs Liddle, hon. secretary. In 1948, Mrs I. M. Nesbitt (Chichester, Belfast) took over as secretary, with Mrs McMaster taking on the role of treasurer. Formed along the same lines as the men's IBA, the Irish Women's BA represents bowlers from both the North and South of Ireland and by 1972 the membership had risen to 56 clubs with some 1900 lady bowlers. The Irish Women's Bowling League was formed in 1952 with a Junior League added

in 1964. Also under IWBA control are the NI Women's Private Greens League, the NI Women's Bowling Association (Parks), the Ladies Bowling League of Ireland (Eire) and the Provincial Towns Women's BA, all formed in 1969.

At the outset, the IWBA's national championships were restricted to competition for pairs (Lady Baird Cup), won initially by the Alexandra Club of Belfast, the fours (Lady Nevill Cup) which also went to a Belfast club, Cavehill, and a knock-out four-rink tournament won by the Whitehead Club of Co. Antrim. Singles were added to the championships in 1964 with Mrs S. Heron of the Alexandra Club taking the Hall-Thompson Trophy and the title. Other major trophies in Irish Women's Bowls include the senior league (Nesbitt Shield) first won by the Alexandra Club in 1952; junior league (Aiken Shield) won by Wingrave (Belfast) in 1964; and since 1970 an inter-association tournament (Jean Hayes Cup) which saw the NI Women's Private Greens League stamp their authority on the game in Ireland by winning the tournament for the first three years.

'Cleaner than I would have ever thought possible'. The first committee of the EWBA select the Ladies' uniforms. (EWBA).

EWBA National Championships

Singles (Four-wood)

1932 Mrs Tigg *Wadden Residents, Surrey*
1933 Mrs King *Wadden Residents, Surrey*
1934 Mrs Holman *Wadden Residents, Surrey*
1935 Mrs McDanell *Devon*
1936 Mrs L. Parnell *Somerset*
1937 Mrs Batsford *Middlesex*
1938 Miss Culling *Essex*
1939 Miss Howard *Devon*
1940–5 War Years
1946 Mrs Chillman *Sussex*
1947 Mrs Johns *Sussex*
1948 Mrs Woodhead *Devon*
1949 Mrs Chillman *Sussex*
1950 Mrs Buckland *Surrey*
1951 Mrs Burden *Kent*
1952 Miss Colley *Devon*
1953 Mrs Lavender *Sussex*
1954 Mrs Franklin *Surrey*
1955 Mrs A. Beath *Yorkshire*
1956 Miss F. Whalley *Somerset*
1957 Miss E. Wilson *Sussex*
1958 Mrs H. Evans *Somerset*
1959 Mrs J. Lucking *Berkshire*
1960 Mrs L. Coxall *Kent*
1961 Miss M. Steele *Middlesex*
1962 Miss M. Steele *Middlesex*
1963 Mrs F. Carvell *Middlesex*
1964 Mrs D. Dowling *Surrey*

1965 Mrs J. Auld *Durham*
1966 Mrs D. Hills *Northumberland*
1967 Mrs D. Payne *Dorset*
1968 Mrs L. Bufton *Warwickshire*
1969 Miss M. Steele *Middlesex*
1970 Mrs N. Colling *Somerset*
1971 Mrs C. Frost *Devon*
1972 Mrs M. Ward *Suffolk*
1973 Miss E. King *Dorset*
1974 Mrs V. Peck *Suffolk*
1975 Mrs I. Lawson *Durham*
1976 Mrs J. Croot *Gloucestershire*
1977 Mrs B. Stubbings *Yorkshire*
1978 Mrs E. Logan *Middlesex*
1979 Mrs L. Hawes *Berkshire*
1980 Mrs P. Derrick *Surrey*
1981 Mrs N. Madden *Yorkshire*
1982 Mrs W. Clarke *Hampshire*
1983 Mrs J. Valls *Surrey*
1984 Mrs O. Henery *Wiltshire*
1985 Mrs E. Clarke *Leicestershire*

Singles (Two-wood)

1939 Mrs L. Parnell *Somerset*
1940–5 War Years
1946 Mrs Osey *Berks & Bucks*
1947 Mrs Coxall *Kent*
1948 Mrs Carvell *Middlesex*
1949 Mrs Chillman *Sussex*
1950 Mrs Dickinson *Devon*
1951 Mrs Wright *Durham*
1952 Mrs Courtenay *Somerset*
1953 Mrs Griffiths *Devon*
1954 Mrs Taylor *Essex*

1955 Mrs A. Thomas *Essex*
1956 Mrs M. Rubery *Essex*
1957 Mrs L. Clark *Nottinghamshire*
1958 Mrs A. Beath *Yorkshire*
1959 Mrs F. Careswell *Middlesex*
1960 Mrs G. Webber *Devon*
1961 Mrs M. Darlington *Warwickshire*
1962 Mrs M. Smith *Essex*
1963 Mrs L. Cudmore *Hampshire*
1964 Mrs E. Buckland *Surrey*
1965 Mrs N. Evans *Somerset*
1966 Mrs M. Harrison *Warwickshire*
1967 Mrs I. Burns *Warwickshire*
1968 Mrs E. Britton *Nottinghamshire*
1969 Mrs J. Hunt *Hampshire*
1970 Mrs P. Derrick *Surrey*
1971 Mrs N. Galloway *Durham*
1972 Miss B. Atherton *Nottinghamshire*
1973 Mrs W. Stevenson *Surrey*
1974 Mrs L. Maynard *Hertfordshire*
1975 Mrs J. Hunt *Hampshire*
1976 Miss E. King *Dorset*
1977 Mrs W. Hall *Middlesex*
1978 Mrs N. Shaw *Durham*
1979 Mrs I. Molyneux *Oxfordshire*
1980 Mrs B. Newborn *Leicestershire*
1981 Mrs E. Gascoigne *Nottinghamshire*
1982 Mrs K. Steer *Warwickshire*
1983 Mrs N. Shaw *Durham*
1984 Mrs V. Vintiner *Middlesex*
1985 Mrs J. Bryant *Hampshire*

EWBA National Championships

Pairs

1932 Mrs Roberts, Craxford *Southgate*
1933 Mrs Privett, Tigg *Surrey*
1934 Mrs Privett, Tigg *Surrey*
1935 Mrs Hopewell, Palmer *Kent*
1936 Mrs Merralls, Hallett *Kent*
1937 Mrs King, Privett *Surrey*
1938 Mrs Howard, Quick *Devon*
1939 Mrs Graham, Haynes *Surrey*
1940–5 War Years
1946 Mrs Franklin, Mew *Surrey*
1947 Mrs Monkcom, Stoat *Essex*
1948 Mrs Joyce, Coleman *Surrey*
1949 Mrs Winslow, Holmes *Wilts*
1950 Mrs Dickinson, Broughton *Devon*
1951 Mrs Gibson Coxall *Kent*
1952 Mrs Tomblin, Bannister *Northants*
1953 The Misses Colley *Devon*
1954 Mrs Winslow, Holmes *Wilts*
1955 Mrs McDowall, Hallatt *Glos*

1956 Mrs R. Evan, L. Johnson *Kent*
1957 Mrs M. D. Nunn, H. R. Gibson *Essex*
1958 Mrs M. Goodman, E. Youldon *Devon*
1959 Mrs D. T. Winterburn, F. E. Careswell *Middlesex*
1960 Mrs L. Bufton, M. Powell *Warks*
1961 Mrs J. R. Freeman, E. Wilson *Northants*
1962 Mrs F. A. Morgan, V. C. Doyle *Sussex*
1963 Mrs L. Stewart, K. Fairbairn *Hants*
1964 Mrs V. Stevens, Miss M. Steele *Middlesex*
1965 Mrs E. Routledge, L. Wise *Cumberland*
1966 Mrs H. O'Donnell, P. Derrick *Surrey*
1967 Mrs F. Lewis, M. Pickvance *Herts*
1968 Mrs D. Crutchley, I. Oliver *Kent*
1969 Mrs D. Barclay, F. E. Jarvis *Kent*
1970 Mrs B. Tregonning, D. Leese *Middlesex*

1971 Mrs Bartlett, M. Steele *Middlesex*
1972 Mrs M. Light, L. Parkhurst *Hants*
1973 Mrs B. Norbury, I. Burns *Warks*
1974 Mrs P. Mortimer, W. Hollow *Devon*
1975 Mrs I. Hunt, B. Taylor *Hants*
1976 Mrs M. Lockwood, I. Molyneux *Oxon*
1977 Mrs E. Scrorer, E. Rutherford *Northumberland*
1978 Mrs A. Pascoe, G. Thomas *Cornwall*
1979 Mrs A. Kaye, A. Steventon *Devon*
1980 Mrs M. Burnett, N. Shaw *Durham*
1981 Mrs S. Simmons, I. Smith *Herts*
1982 Mrs J. Valls, M. E. Wessier *Surrey*
1983 Mrs J. Valls, M. E. Wessier *Surrey*
1984 Mrs A. Pascoe, E. Pearett *Devon*
1985 Mrs D. Lewis, P. M. Green *Leics*

Triples
Players titles not recorded after 1981

1933 Mrs Morton, Rodgers, King *Waddon Residents*
1934 Mrs Soppitt, Damon, Brown *Strawberry Hill*
1935 Mrs Barnes, Privett, Tigg *Surrey*
1936 Mrs Barnes, Privett, Tigg *Surrey*
1937 Mrs Crawford, Excel, Dennis *Glos*
1938 Mrs Gale, Burge, Elliott *Sussex*
1939 Mrs Hole, Nelson, Thorne *Berks/Bucks*
1940–5 War Years
1946 Mrs Isaac, Blay, Osey *Berks/Bucks*
1947 Mrs Cadbury, Davis, Martin *Glos*
1948 Mrs Horn, Slade, Tolchard *Devon*

1949 Mrs Beck, Collins, Karn *Devon*
1950 Mrs Bettridge, Bowyer, Jarrett *Middx*
1951 Mrs Finch, Whitfield, Rivers *Berks/Bucks*
1952 Mrs Capstick, Carvell, Green *Middx*
1953 Mrs Murdock, Dawes, Garner *Hunts*
1954 Mrs Speight, Calvert, Walker *Northumberland*
1955 Mrs Linney, Purviss, Jackson *Surrey*
1956 Mrs R. Clarke, Dyos, Merry *Surrey*
1957 Mrs C. Tyler, Wrigelsworth, Hyland *Sussex*
1958 Mrs M. Scott, Howe, Marshall *Durham*
1959 Mrs W. Hall, E. McCree, W. Lambert *Middx*

1960 Mrs D. Hamer, M. A. Shoesmith, P. Sawyer *Hants*
1961 Mrs D. Penicud, G. Foreman, G. Wood *Berks*
1962 Mrs L. Bufton, L. Randall, M. Powell *Warks*
1963 Mrs K. Hedges, M. Tildesley, Miss V. Hedges *Worcs*
1964 Mrs I. Kelly, M. Newbury, W. Hollow *Devon*
1965 Mrs F. Sharp, H. McCarthy, M. Blick *Berks*
1966 Mrs W. Anderson, J. Mills, J. Sparkes *Essex*
1967 Mrs H. Garner, O. Marshall, E. Buckland *Surrey*
1968 Mrs L. Robertson, V. Stevens, M. Steele *Middx*
1969 Mrs M. Blanch, G. Taylor, J. V. Howes *Sussex*
1970 Mrs P. Briggs, B. Coombs, I. Mouland *Hants*
1971 Mrs I. Cassidy, E. Dean, C. Gosling *Essex*
1972 Mrs P. Carrott, W. Anderson, J. Sparkes *Essex*
1973 Mrs Parson, B. Taylor, M. Welling *Hants*
1974 Mrs R. Ley, M. Lockwood, I. Molyneux *Oxon*
1975 Mrs G. Davis, K. Saill, E. Howe *Glos*
1976 Mrs B. Colgate, P. White, M. E. Wessier *Surrey*
1977 Mrs P. Kauz, D. Williams, M. Momber *Glos*
1978 Mrs M. Martin, B. Ansell, G. Danvers *Leics*
1979 Mrs B. Trafford, M. Lockwood, I. Molyneux *Oxon*
1980 Mrs A. Tucker, S. Goodenough, D. Fletcher *Hants*
1981 J. Searle, J. Briggs, M. Poots *Dorset*
1982 J. Jones, M. Clark, N. Shaw *Durham*
1983 T. Tull, A. Stone, D. Cave *Kent*
1984 G. Rochester, M. Atkinson, R. Fuller *Middx*
1985 B. Jacob, W. Line, E. Fairhall *Hants*

Fours
1932 Mrs Gilchrist, Tigg, Privett, Holman *Surrey*
1933 Mrs Fry, White, Llewelyn, Johns *Cavendish*
1934 Mrs Fry, White, Llewelyn, Johns *Cavendish*
1935 Mrs Fry, White, Llewelyn, Johns *Cavendish*
1936 Mrs Nash, Foord, Tyler, Line *Sussex*
1937 Mrs Swann, Reed, West, Wardle *Somerset*
1938 Mrs L. Sharpe, Allen, E. Sharp, Woolridge *Middx*
1939 Mrs Holmes, Reader, Fulton, Bassett *Sussex*
1940–5 War Years
1946 Mrs Holmes, Barnes, Lambert, King *Surrey*
1947 Mrs Carvell, Banstead, Green, Culverhouse *Middx*
1948 Mrs Mill, Gomm, Ainsley, Cale *Sussex*
1949 Mrs Twigger, Hemming, Brooks, Barlow *Warks*
1950 Mrs Lucy, Kerslake, Dale, Woodhead *Devon*
1951 Mrs Buckland, Medland, Durban, George *Surrey*
1952 Mrs Grievson, Nesbit, Punton, Wright *Northumberland*
1953 Mrs Capstick, Warfield, Carvell, Green *Middx*
1954 Mrs Wake, White, Wilkinson, Spowart *Northumberland*
1955 Mrs Wrigley, Pitcher, Gilchrist, Wright *Lincs*
1956 Mrs I. Linney, Cuckney, Purkiss, Jackson *Surrey*
1957 Miss Vincent, Mrs Lucas, Miss Wilson, Mrs Webster *Sussex*
1958 Mrs Delnevo, Turner, Stew, Lynn *Oxon*

1959 Mrs Turner, Welsman, Slater, Robertson *Middx*
1960 Mrs Garrod, Marjoram, Sayer, Smith *Suffolk*
1961 Mrs Riddlestone, Panks, Williams, Rule *Suffolk*
1962 Mrs Hall, Churcher, McCraue, Lambert *Middx*
1963 Mrs Robertson, Smith, Stevens, Steele *Middx*
1964 Mrs Sharp, Needham, Watchorn, Wrigley *Leics*
1965 Mrs Sansom, Ashdown, Swain, Young *Beds*
1966 Mrs Rudkin, Jones, I. L. Jones, Hornsby *Essex*
1967 Mrs Mulhern, Barnston, Hills, Kinnersley *Northumberland*
1968 Mrs Wright, Easto, Young, Bryant *Hants*
1969 Mrs Mackferness, Bartlett, Stevens, Steele *Middx*
1970 Mrs Woodhouse, Marigold, Albery, Smith *Sussex*
1971 Mrs Robertson, Clifford, Turner, Gould *Surrey*
1972 Mrs Bates, Steeks, Johnson, Wright *Lincs*
1973 Mrs Chiltern, Hopkinson, Ward, Francis *Yorks*
1974 Mrs Neal, Redgrave, Annison, Youngs *Norfolk*
1975 Mrs Edginton, Lee, Greaves, Harris *Leics*
1976 Mrs Moore, Jones, Gibson, Marlow *Lancs*
1977 Mrs Johnson, Clark, Burnett, Shaw *Durham*

Mrs E. Tigg of Surrey, the first winner of the EWBA national singles championship in 1932. (BBC Hulton Picture Library).

1978   Mrs Kaye, Walsh, Allsop, Steventon *Devon*
1979   Mrs Davies, Rolf, Moffett, Bruntnell *Hereford* ˙
1980   Mrs Kennedy, Williams, Amos, Doubleday *Kent*
1981   Mrs Clarke, Hicks, Croad, Fairhall *Hants*
1982   Mrs Rochester, Lilly, Atkinson, Fuller *Middx*
1983   Mrs Gill, Chapman, Symonds, Doggett *Norfolk*
1984   Mrs Anderson, Gordon, Burdess, Wailes *Durham*
1985   Mrs C. Webb, P. Emery, J. Andrews, J. Roylance *Norfolk*

Most titles: World (Women) Outdoor Merle Richardson (Australia) won singles and pairs gold medals at 1985 Women's World Championships at Melbourne. Elsie Wilkie (New Zealand) won singles gold medals in Women's World Championships 1969 and 1974.

16–25 Singles
1983   Miss S. Smith *Norfolk*
1984   Miss S. Smith *Norfolk*
1985   Miss S. Franklin *Norfolk*

McCarthy & Stone Mixed Pairs
1985   Mr & Mrs J. Kilyon *Leicestershire*

Inter-County (Johns Trophy)
1934   Surrey
1935   Surrey
1936   Sussex
1937   Surrey
1938   Middlesex
1939   Devon
1940–5 War Years
1946   Surrey
1947   No results
1948   No results
1949   No results
1950   Hampshire
1951   Devon
1952   Kent
1953   Surrey
1954   Surrey
1955   Kent
1956   Warwickshire
1957   Surrey
1958   Devon
1959   Durham
1960   Nottinghamshire
1961   Nottinghamshire
1962   Sussex
1963   Surrey

1964   Sussex
1965   Suffolk
1966   Devon
1967   Warwickshire
1968   Durham
1969   Nottinghamshire
1970   Suffolk
1971   Middlesex
1972   Surrey
1973   Middlesex
1974   Durham
1975   Middlesex
1976   Durham
1977   Durham
1978   Surrey
1979   Durham
1980   Devon
1981   Middlesex
1982   Surrey
1983   Yorkshire
1984   Kent
1985   Norfolk

Double Rink
1958   Warwickshire
1959   Durham
1960   Devon
1961   Gloucestershire
1962   Surrey
1963   Yorkshire
1964   Nottinghamshire
1965   Suffolk
1966   Suffolk
1967   Middlesex
1968   Hertfordshire
1969   Devon
1970   Somerset
1971   Middlesex
1972   Devon
1973   Hampshire
1974   Surrey
1975   Warwickshire
1976   Lincolnshire
1977   Somerset
1978   Essex
1979   Warwickshire
1980   Middlesex
1981   Middlesex
1982   Devon
1983   Oxfordshire
1984   Middlesex
1985   Surrey

Wales

WWBA National Championships

Singles
Players titles not recorded after 1974
1933   Mrs Insell *Newport*
1934   Mrs M. Brown *Newport*
1935   Mrs M. Brown *Newport*
1936   Mrs Hopkins *Merthyr*
1937   Mrs W. Harris *Skewen*
1938   Mrs D. Porter *Beechwood*
1939   Mrs Thomas *Llandrindod*
1940–5   War Years
1946   Mrs E. Howells *Port Talbot*
1947   Mrs E. Howells *Port Talbot*
1948   Mrs E. Howells *Port Talbot*
1949   Mrs H. Webber *Porthcawl*
1950   Mrs L. Davies *Beechwood*
1951   No Record
1952   No Record
1953   Mrs L. Webster *Mackintosh*
1954   Mrs E. Thomas *Port Talbot*
1955   Mrs E. Thomas *Port Talbot*
1956   Mrs Lane *Pengelli*
1957   Mrs Evans *Abergavenny*
1958   Mrs E. Howells *Port Talbot*
1959   Mrs E. G. Howell *Mackintosh*
1960   Mrs Parkhouse *Swansea Victoria*

1961   Mrs C. Leek *Pontypool*
1962   Miss Mair Jones *Pengelli*
1963   Mrs L. Nicholas *Ebbw Vale*
1964   Mrs L. Nicholas *Ebbw Vale*
1965   Mrs Pomeroy *Howard Gardens*
1966   Mrs W. Gilmore *Grange*
1967   Mrs L. Nicholas *Ebbw Vale*
1968   Mrs E. Morgan *Porth*
1969   Mrs M. Pomeroy *Howard Gardens*
1970   Mrs L. Nicholas *Ebbw Vale*
1971   Mrs L. Nicholas *Ebbw Vale*
1972   Mrs L. Parker *Knighton*
1973   Mrs M. Pomeroy *Sophia Gardens*
1974   M. Laverty *Rhiwbina*
1975   E. Howells *Port Talbot*
1976   M. Pomeroy *Sophia Gardens*
1977   D. Hemming *Barry Plastics*
1978   L. Nicholas *Nevill*
1979   E. Thomas *Port Talbot*
1980   J. Ackland *Penarth Belle Vue*
1981   M. Pomeroy *Sophia Gardens*
1982   L. Nicholas *Nevill*
1983   J. Davies *Port Talbot*
1984   B. Morgan *Llandrindod*

1985   J. Davies *Port Talbot*

Pairs
Players names were not recorded until 1966.
1933–48   No record
1949   Pontypridd
1950–2   No record
1953   Pontypridd
1954   Port Talbot
1955   Port Talbot
1956   Pontypridd
1957   Thomastown
1958   Penarth Windsor
1959   Port Talbot
1960   Port Talbot
1961   Penarth Windsor
1962   Port Talbot
1963   Rumney Gardens
1964   Rumney Gardens
1965   Ebbw Vale
1966   Mrs Evans, Thomas *Romilly Park*
1967   Mrs Bowen, Jones *Ebbw Vale*
1968   Mrs Wright, Baylis *Beechwood*

1969 Mrs Osborne, Pomeroy *Howard Gardens*
1970 Mrs Hemmings, Breed *Dinas Powis*
1971 Mrs Atkins, Miss Hutchings *Penarth Windsor*
1972 Mrs Chapman, Thatcher *Rumney Gardens*
1973 Mrs Williams, Lake *Port Talbot*
1974 Mrs Williams, Lake *Port Talbot*
1975 Miss Proctor, Mrs Pomeroy *Sophia Gardens*
1976 Mrs Price, Owen *Knighton*
1977 Mrs Davies, Thorne *Llandovery*
1978 Mrs Watts, Pipe *Pontypool*
1979 Mrs Dainton, Stanton *Barry Plastics*
1980 Mrs Mills, Morgan *Llandrindod*
1981 Mrs Dainton, Stanton *Barry Plastics*
1982 Miss Proctor, Mrs Pomeroy *Sophia Gardens*
1983 Mrs Nicholas, Howells *Nevill*
1984 Mrs Ricketts, Jenkins *Bailey Park*
1985 Miss Proctor, Mrs Pomeroy *Sophia Gardens*

Triples
No records before 1952. Players names not recorded until 1971.
1952 Pontypridd
1953 No record
1954 Mackintosh
1955 Mackintosh
1956 Newport
1957 Port Talbot
1958 Not played
1959 Port Talbot
1960 Porth
1961 Penarth Windsor
1962 Ebbw Vale
1963 Ebbw Vale
1964 Not played
1965 Rumney Gardens
1966 No record
1967 Porth
1968 Ebbw Vale
1969 Swansea Victoria
1970 Pengelli
1971 D. Evans, I. Bishop, B. Stanton *Barry Plastics*
1972 A. Thomas, J. Osborne, M. Lewis *Howard Gardens*
1973 J. Watts, E. Hill, J. Pipe *Pontypool*
1974 E. Chapman, J. Pryor, W. Thatcher *Rumney Gardens*

The English and Welsh teams line up prior to the first Women's Home International match at Brooklands Park, Blackheath in 1932. (EWBA).

1975 N. Hooper, M. Buchanan, J. Mills *Porth*
1976 D. Evans, A. Dainton, D. Hemming *Barry Plastics*
1977 J. Griffiths, J. Howells, L. Nicholas *Nevill, Abergavenny*
1978 N. Williams, C. Williams, J. Ackland *Penarth, Belle Vue*
1979 S. Proctor, D. Kingaby, M. Pomeroy *Sophia Gardens*
1980 J. Davies, L. Evans, E. Thomas *Port Talbot*
1981 J. Davies, L. Evans, E. Thomas *Port Talbot*
1982 M. Evans, C. Gwilt, L. Parker *Knighton*
1983 J. Evans, M. Jenkins, J. Ricketts *Bailey Park*
1984 N. Hopkins, P. Price, J. Mills *Porth*
1985 S. Proctor, M. Jones, M. Pomeroy *Sophia Gardens*

Fours
Players names were not recorded.
1933 Thomastown
1934 Thomastown
1935 Skewen
1936 Abercynon
1937 Skewen
1938 Llandrindod Wells
1939 Newport
1946 Pontypridd
1947 Llandrindod Wells
1948 Penarth

1949 Llandaff
1950 Port Talbot
1951 Cwmbran
1952 Mountain Ash
1953 Cwmbran
1954 Mackintosh
1955 Cwmbran
1956 Port Talbot
1957 Mackintosh
1958 Penarth Windsor
1959 Abergavenny, Nevill
1960 Abergavenny, Nevill
1961 Porth

1962 Pengelli
1963 Penarth, Belle Vue
1964 Pengelli
1965 Bridgend
1966 Grange
1967 Pengelli
1968 Beechwood
1969 Port Talbot
1970 Rumney Gardens
1971 Porth
1972 Port Talbot
1973 Penarth, Belle Vue
1974 No record

1975 Sophia Gardens
1976 Penarth, Belle Vue
1977 Llandrindod Wells
1978 Pontypool
1979 Port Talbot
1980 Sophia Gardens
1981 Penarth, Belle Vue
1982 Penhill
1983 Llandrindod Wells
1984 Whitchurch
1985 Sophia Gardens

Scotland

SWBA National Championships

Singles

Players titles dropped after 1974.
1936 Mrs Paton *Wallace and Weir*
1937 Mrs Kent *Clarkston*
1938 Mrs Murphy *Blackhall*
1939 Mrs A. Reid *Foxley*
1946 Mrs G. McMurtie *Hawkhill*
1947 Mrs T. McGill *Mauchline*
1948 Mrs W. Copland *Linthouse*
1949 Mrs C. Westwood *Nethertown*
1950 Mrs J. Barr *Overtown and Waterloo*
1951 Mrs H. McGeachen *Halfway and District*
1952 Mrs W. Miller *Ayr*
1953 Mrs T. McGill *Mauchline*
1954 Mrs G. Cameron *Maitland*
1955 Mrs H. McGeachen *Cambuslang*
1956 Mrs N. Carmichael *Springburn*
1957 Mrs E. Allardice *Dalmuir*
1958 Mrs E. Skeldon *Port William*
1959 Mrs J. Leck *Glasgow Transport*
1960 Mrs M. Chambers *Drumoyne*
1961 Mrs J. Allardyce *Callendar MW*
1962 Mrs N. Young *Inverkeithing*
1963 Mrs A. Knowles *Kilbarchan*
1964 Mrs J. Baguley *Weatermains*
1965 Mrs Rodgers *Valleyfield*
1966 Mrs J. Hendry *Hamilton Caledonian*
1967 Mrs J. Sharp *Wardie*
1968 Mrs D. Sinclair *Mosspark*
1969 Mrs R. Bell *Westerton*
1970 Mrs N. Carroll *Newport-on-Tay*
1971 Mrs J. Frame *Newmains*
1972 Mrs B. Todd *Riddrie*
1973 Mrs E. Clark *Croftfoot*
1974 Mrs E. Ireland *Dalbeattie*
1975 S. Valentine *Lugar*
1976 E. Neil *Kirkhill*
1977 E. Clark *Croftfoot*
1978 C. McParland *Whitburn*
1979 N. Hyslop *Kingarth*
1980 M. Carroll *Irvine Park*
1981 J. Lawson *Ardeer*
1982 H. Wright *Cumbernauld*
1983 M. Smith *Belvidere*
1984 J. Barnes *Templeton*
1985 C. McLean *Cardonald*

Pairs

Players names not recorded until 1966.
1936 Blackhall
1937 Shettleston
1938 Radnor Park
1939 Hyndland
1946 Fauldhouse
1947 Hawkhill
1948 Halfway and District
1949 Bonnyrigg
1950 Hawkhill
1951 Shawlands
1952 Lockerbie
1953 Ardrossan
1954 St Clair
1955 Milngavie
1956 Bonnyrigg
1957 Chryston and District
1958 Dudley
1959 Crosshill
1960 Hillington Estate
1961 Kelvindale
1962 Carnoustie
1963 Fauldhouse
1964 Rankin Park
1965 Crosshill
1966 Mrs Innes, Summers *Blantyre*
1967 Mrs Dow, Denovan *Alloa East End*
1968 Mrs Gourlay, Leslie *Annabank*
1969 Mrs Brown, McLeod *Queens Park*
1970 Mrs Smith, Wilson *Whitehouse and Grange*
1971 Mrs McCulloch, Kennedy *Drongan*
1972 Mrs Woods, McSorland *Lugar Works*
1973 Mrs Young, Chalmers *St Vincent*
1974 Mrs Frame, Rice *Marchmount*
1975 Mrs Clark, Russell *Bonnybridge*
1976 Mrs Wilson, Williamson *Thornhill*
1977 Mrs Cooper, Allison *Craigentinny*
1978 Mrs McGregor, McDonald *Mount Vernon*
1979 Mrs Mathew, Reid *Ayr*
1980 Mrs McMillan, Picken *Gissnock*
1981 Mrs I. Johnstone, M. Archibald *Eddlewood*
1982 Mrs M. Gray, A. Knowles *Kilbarchan*
1983 Mrs A. Carson, S. Morrison *Newbattle*
1984 Mrs M. Scott, A. Leslie *Annabank*
1985 Mrs J. Thomson, R. Price *Overtown and Waterloo*

Triples

1981 N. Cross, J. Duncan, M. Bryson *Dalserf*
1982 Mrs Alder, Spiers, Hughes *Riverside, Sterling*
1983 R. Quate, M. Anderson, I. Hay *Orbiston*
1984 P. Galloway, M. Graham, M. Brockett *Bishopbriggs*
1985 E. McGarvie, A. Graham, F. Whyte *Priorscroft*

Fours

Players names not recorded until 1966.
1936 Bearsdon
1937 Moffat
1938 Kirkhill
1939 Linthouse
1946 Clydebank
1947 Cambuslang
1948 Blackhill
1949 Irvin Winton
1950 Hamilton Caledonian
1951 Busby
1952 Milngavie
1953 Bridge of Allen
1954 Auchengeich
1955 Halfway and District
1956 Caldercraig
1957 Tollcross
1958 Ardrossan
1959 Hurlford
1960 Killermont
1961 Wattfield
1962 West Kilbride
1963 Ayr
1964 Woodend
1965 Bishopbriggs
1966 Mrs Anderson, Goldie, Barbour, Clements *Troon*
1967 Mrs Watson, Liddle, Manzie, Bain *Carrick Knowe*
1968 Mrs Fairweather, Liddle, Watson, Manzie *Carrick Knowe*
1969 Mrs McClellan, Spiers, McFarlane, White *Inkerman*
1970 Mrs Cooper, Mrs Good, Miss Tinning, Mrs Stewart *Maxwelltown*
1971 Mrs Logan, Smith, Barbour, Bunten *Mauchline*
1972 Mrs Barclay, Nicoll, Thomson, Walker *Crossgate Fife*
1973 Mrs Quigley, Coupe, Cleland, Parker *Darvel*
1974 Mrs Simpson, Ross, Aitkin, McFarlane *Kelvindale*
1975 Mrs Brown, Douglas, Bennett, Stewart *Rutherglen*
1976 Mrs Jackson, Dunlop, Waterson, Jackson *Coatbridge*
1977 Mrs Young, Lovell, Rennison, Halliday *Fairfield*
1978 Mrs Thomson, Mrs McKenzie, Miss Stark, Mrs Halliday *Whitburn*
1979 Mrs Williams, Wilson, Cameron, Black *Kingston*
1980 Mrs Cumming, Jackson, Wilson, Anderson *Castlehill*
1981 M. Bain, M. Gardiner, N. Hamilton, J. Menzies *Douglas*
1982 D. Pettigrew, S. Young, T. Powell, M. Logan *Mauchline*
1983 J. Wilson, J. Coulston, H. Hamilton, S. Kelly *Stranraer*
1984 S. Auld, M. Kelly, I. Temple, G. Crawford *Drumoyne*
1985 Mrs Boyd, Auld, Mitchell, Graham *Tarbolton*

Youngest EBA club champion Duncan Hayne, Lostwithiel, Cornwall. Won Bodmin BC singles 1983 aged 13.

Most titles: World (Men) David John Bryant (England) won singles gold medal in 1966 and 1980.

Ireland

IWBA National Championships

Singles
1964 S. Heron *Alexandra*
1965 A. Sterrett *Ward Park*
1966 E. Cameron *Belfast*
1967 E. Furlonger *Holywood*
1968 M. Ross *Ward Park*
1969 B. McKeag *Wingrave*
1970 M. Brown *Leinster*
1971 M. Brown *Leinster*
1972 B. Sharpe *Herbert Park*
1973 E. Bell *Saintfield*
1974 N. Burnett *Herbert Park*
1975 N. Burnett *Herbert Park*
1976 N. Burnett *Herbert Park*
1977 M. Brown *Leinster*
1978 E. Cameron *Belfast*
1979 N. Burnett *Herbert Park*
1980 M. Montgomery *Cavehill*
1981 N. Gibson *Blackrock*
1982 E. Bell *Belfast*
1983 H. Hamilton *Belfast*
1984 M. Johnston *Ballymoney*
1985 E. Bell *Belfast*

Pairs
Players names were not recorded until 1966. Players titles dropped after 1974.
1947 Alexandra
1948 Londonderry
1949 Kenilworth
1950 Kenilworth
1951 Ward Park
1952 Ward Park
1953 Ward Park
1954 Castleton
1955 Chichester (later Salisbury)
1956 Ward Park
1957 Pickie
1958 York Road Civil Defence
1959 Castleton
1960 Salisbury
1961 Knock
1962 Salisbury
1963 Ward Park
1964 Whitehead
1965 Ward Park
1966 Mrs Houston, Lockhart *Whitehead*
1967 Mrs Cameron, Morrow *Wingrave*
1968 Mrs Barnes, Beattie *Brookvale*
1969 Mrs Lewis, Bailey *Lisnagarvey*
1970 Mrs Collins, Wilson *Deramore*
1971 Mrs McGrath, Stevenson *Belfast*
1972 Misses Morrison and Thompson *Saintfield*
1973 Mrs McDowell, Cameron *Belfast*
1974 M. Middleton, F. Byrne *Leinster*
1975 I. Reddock, F. Andrews *Ballymena*
1976 P. Marchant, A. Prodohl *Blackrock*
1977 N. Allely, D. Fraser *Donaghdee*
1978 M. Wilson, A. Brown *Holywood*
1979 N. Allely, D. Fraser *Donaghdee*
1980 T. Costley, L. Simpson *Knock*
1981 K. McGrath, E. Cameron *Belfast*

The poise and concentration of Ireland's new star Margaret Johnston. (Duncan Cubitt, *Bowls International*).

1982 S. Adair, A. Hewitt *Belfast*
1983 P. Nolan, M. Barber *Blackrock*
1984 M. Johnston, M. McCullough *Ballymoney*
1985 M. Paul, M. McCullough *Ballymoney*

Triples
1979 J. Murphy, E. O'Hara, N. Burnett *Herbert Park*
1980 J. Hollinger, P. Dillon, N. Allely *Donaghdee*
1981 R. O'Neill, M. Henry, M. Paul *Ballymoney*
1982 F. Elliott, D. Turner, M. Ross *Belfast*
1983 M. Montgomery, A. Elliott, J. Mulholland *Dunluce*
1984 E. Clements, E. Morrison, M. Mallon *Lisnagarvey*
1985 K. Megrath, H. Hamilton, E. Bell *Belfast*

Fours
Players names not recorded until 1973.
1947 Cavehill
1948 Kenilworth
1949 Londonderry
1950 Alexandra
1951 Leinster
1952 Ward Park
1953 Chichester
1954 Ward Park
1955 Chichester
1956 Castleton
1957 York Road Civil Defence
1958 Whitehead
1959 Belmont
1960 Pickie
1961 Castleton
1962 Knock
1963 Wingrave
1964 Forth River
1965 Brookvale
1966 York Road Civil Defence
1967 Salisbury
1968 Lisnagarvey
1969 Herbert Park
1970 Ballyholme
1971 Lisnagarvey
1972 Knock
1973 A. Allan, G. Beattie, M. Gennett, N. Gibson *Lady Neill*
1974 M. Kennedy, I. Reddock, F. Andrews, E. Nichol *Ballymena*
1975 A. Allen, M. Jennett, M. Beattie, N. Gibson *Lisnagarvey*
1976 R. Porter, S. Herron, R. Wilson, A. Patton *Deramore*
1977 M. Kelly, E. McMillan, I. Smyth, D. Blackstock *Deramore*
1978 J. Mulligan, M. McMurray, M. Wilson, A. Brown *Deramore*
1979 P. Marchant, P. Nolan, M. Barber, A. Prodohl *Blackrock*
1980 A. McNulty, J. Spencer, L. Watts, A. Tunney *Kenilworth*
1981 W. Boylan, M. Webb, B. McKelvey, K. Toner *Falls*
1982 F. Elliott, E. Wilkinson, E. Bell, M. Ross *Belfast*
1983 M. Dunlop, A. McAlary, M. McCullough, M. Johnston *Ballymoney*
1984 K. Megrath, H. Hamilton, E. Bell, E. Cameron *Belfast*
1985 K. Megrath, H. Hamilton, D. McGill, E. Bell *Belfast*

The Eve Trophy

Home International matches between the ladies of England and Wales got under way in 1932, with the newly formed WWBA tasting victory in its inaugural year, defeating the English on their own Blackheath greens by one shot. Without the benefit of any national championships to aid selection, the Welsh had achieved a remarkable result, but one they were unable to repeat until 1958.

The entry of the Scottish Women's Bowling Association into the international series in 1936 coincided with the presentation by Mrs Eve Craxford (Middlesex), then president of the EWBA, of the Eve Trophy for the championships. The England team, pride restored and in the process of notching up its fourth success in a row, became the first holders of the trophy, but were to find the ladies of Scotland just as eager to win as their male counterparts. Scotland took the trophy north of the border for the first time in 1937, keeping it there each year until the Second World War intervened in 1940. England won the first post-war encounter in 1946 but the Scots triumphed again in 1947–8 and 1949 before the English established their supremacy with a run of nine wins. Wales managed its third success in 1978 but, those Welsh victories apart, the Eve Trophy has been shared by the women of England and Scotland.

The Eve Trophy, presented by Mrs Eve Craxford of Middlesex in 1936 for the winner of the international series.

The Irish Women's Bowls Association have been represented in the series since 1948 but, with so few bowlers available, their role has, over the years, essentially been one of taking part. Ireland's finest performance to date came in the 1985 series held at Balgreen, Edinburgh in July where victories over Wales and England took them into second place behind Scotland. Margaret Johnston (Ballymoney) was to prove an inspiration to the Irish team with an unbeaten run as skip throughout the tournament including a laudable 23–14 victory over the Scottish four skipped by Marion Halliday.

For England, defending the Eve Trophy, the 1985 Championships began with a ten-shot defeat at the hands of the Scots on opening day and went downhill from there on. Further defeats by Wales (124–107) and Ireland (115–112) left a demoralized England party with the wooden spoon and a record which read, played 3, won 0, lost 3, points 0 and a shot difference of minus 30.

Women's Outdoor International Series
Eve Trophy

1936 England	1964 England
1937 Scotland	1965 England
1938 Scotland	1966 England
1939 Scotland	1967 England
1940–5 War Years	1968 England
1946 England	1969 Scotland
1947 Scotland	1970 England
1948 Scotland	1971 England
1949 Scotland	1972 England
1950 England	1973 England
1951 England	1974 England
1952 England	1975 England
1953 England	1976 England
1954 England	1977 England
1955 England	1978 Wales
1956 England	1979 England
1957 England	1980 England
1958 England	1981 Scotland
1959 Wales	1982 England
1960 England	1983 Scotland
1961 Scotland	1984 England
1962 Scotland	1985 Scotland
1963 England	

The British Isles Championships

The British Isles championships entered the Women's game on 22 June 1972 following the home international series held at Plymouth. England, having just won the Eve Trophy for the 21st time, might have been expected to carry off at least one of the individual prizes but these were destined for other hands with the host country managing to reach just one final. Mrs Lillian Nicholas (Sophia Gardens, Cardiff), winner of 19 WWBA titles in her career, just edged out England's Mrs H. Chris

Frost (Phear Park, Devon) 21–20 to win the singles while the Scottish duo of Mrs I. McCulloch and Mrs M. Kennedy proved too strong for Ireland's Mrs M. McGrath and Mrs R. Stephenson to win the pairs final 23–13. Ireland, however, gained a fine victory in the fours, E. Patterson, S. McCrone, G. Burnett and Q. Bailey defeating N. Hooper, J. Mills, C. Jones and E. Morgan of Wales 20–15.

The second British Isles championships in 1973 were also to prove fruitless for England, the major honours going to Wales who won the fours and pairs with Betty Todd of Scotland defeating Mrs Sharpe of Ireland to take the singles title. Betty Norbury and Ivy Burns were the first English bowlers to experience success in the championships winning the pairs title in 1974 with a crushing 28–7 victory over the Welsh combination of E. Williams and K. Lake.

Triples were introduced into the championships in 1982 with England the first winners through the efforts of J. Searle, I. Briggs and M. Poots.

England created a record by winning all four titles in 1984 with Surrey's Jean Valls successful in both singles and pairs. One year later the Irish contingent, with their best result in the international series behind them completed a memorable week emulating England's 1984 performance with a British Isles grand slam. Margaret Johnston from Ballymoney retained her outstanding form shown in the internationals to win overwhelmingly against Betty Morgan of Wales by 21 shots to 10 in the singles, adding the pairs crown when joining Murial McCulloch to edge past Myra Jenkins and Joan Ricketts of Wales 20–19.

British Isles Championships

Singles
1981 P. Derrick *England*
1982 P. Madden *England*
1983 E. Bell *Ireland*
1984 J. Valls *England*
1985 M. Johnston *Ireland*

Pairs
1981 T. Costly, L. Simpson *Ireland*
1982 S. Simmons, I. Smith *England*
1983 M. Gray, A. Knowles *Scotland*
1984 J. Valls, C. Wessier *England*
1985 M. Johnston, M. McCullough *Ireland*

Triples
1981 Not held
1982 J. Searle, I. Briggs, M. Poots *England*
1983 J. Jones, M. Clarke, N. Shaw *England*
1984 T. Tull, A. Stone, D. Cave *England*
1985 E. Clements, E. Morrison, M. Mallon *Ireland*

Fours
1981 G. Miles, S. Proctor, J. Osborn, M. Pomeroy *Wales*
1982 A. Barberini, J. Downs, M. James, R. Radford *Wales*
1983 B. Pettigrew, S. Young, T. Powell, M. Logan *Scotland*
1984 P. Gill, V. Chapman, S. Symonds, M. Doggett *England*
1985 K. Megrath, H. Hamilton, E. Bell, E. Cameron *Ireland*

The Women's British Isles Records are incomplete at time of writing. In the interests of accuracy I have therefore given only those results dating from 1981.

Women's Indoor Bowls

With drawing skills and 'touch' being the prime requisites of indoor play, it is hardly surprising that this version of the game has found such favour with women bowlers, especially in the British Isles where outdoor vagaries of weather and green often call for the addition of physical strength to the more obvious attributes.

England

The Welsh Ladies Indoor BA had operated as a section of the WIBA since 1947 with a membership of five clubs, but it was the English women, led once again by the indefatigable Mrs Clara E. Johns, who formed the first separate body, The English Women's Indoor Bowling Association, at a meeting held on 24 April 1951. Such was the enthusiasm among England's women bowlers that the new association soon boasted a healthy growth rate. The initial tally of eight clubs rose to 90 by the early seventies and the latest figures show no less than 174 clubs representing a membership of over 21 000 players.

The earliest EWIBA competition was the inter-club four-rink championship, the Yetton Trophy, which dates from 1954. The Aird Trophy, a two-wood triples competition, ran from 1968–76 when it was superseded by the present three-wood triples event thus enabling entry into the British Isles Championships as a national competition alongside the singles, pairs and fours established in the season 1972/3.

Lowest-scoring match Indoors Spring League triples match played at Worthing Indoor BC 11 February 1983. Gordon Sparks, Stan Kirkham and G. H. (John) Scadgell (skip) beat Don Davis, Gordon Jones and Richard Twine (skip) 9–8. The total of 17 shots being one less than the number of ends played. The first end was tied and only one shot per end scored thereafter.

EWIBA National Championships

Singles
1973 Mrs E. Fairhall *Atherley*
1974 Mrs O. Freeman *Diss*
1975 Mrs E. Smith *Worthing*
1976 Mrs B. Norbury *Rugby Thornfield*
1977 Mrs E. Collins *Cyphers*
1978 Mrs N. Shaw *Teesside*
1979 Mrs T. Barton *Croydon*
1980 Mrs N. Shaw *Teesside*
1981 Mrs N. Shaw *Teesside*
1982 Mrs I. Molyneux *Cherwell*
1983 Mrs N. Shaw *Teesside*
1984 Mrs R. Campbell *Teesside*
1985 Mrs M. Price *Desborough*

Pairs
1973 Mrs Hendry, Cater *Barking*
1974 Mrs Bates, Wright *Boston*
1975 Mrs Crees, Grove *Exonia*
1976 Mrs Green, Mist *King George*
1977 Mrs Spence, Shaw *Teesside*
1978 Mrs O'Donoghue, Logan *Mansfield*
1979 Mrs Marlow, Valls *Richmond*
1980 Mrs Spence, Shaw *Teesside*
1981 Mrs McPherson, Furness *Rugby Thornfield*
1982 Mrs Spence, Shaw *Teesside*
1983 Mrs Spence, Shaw *Teesside*
1984 Mrs Hargrave, Tozer *Folkestone*
1985 Mrs J. Pacey, V. Grooby *Lincs*

Triples
3-wood
1977 Mrs McLeod, Mordaunt, Smith *Folkestone*
1978 Mrs Tucker, Bunce, Woodward *Desborough*
1979 Mrs Weal, Annison, Youngs *County Arts*

1980 Mrs Shepherd, Thomas, Barnes *Barking*
1981 Mrs Clemmy, Talbot, Lawrence *Folkestone*
1982 Mrs Batchelor, Mills, Thornback *Falcon*
1983 Mrs Parker, Burns, Buckby *Wellingborough*
1984 Mrs Hall, Pratt, Lamb *Picketts Lock*
1985 Mrs E. Townsend, S. Perkins, E. West *Crystal Palace*

Fours
1973 Desborough (No names recorded)
1974 Mrs Johnson & co. (No other names recorded) *Boston*
1975 Mrs Johnson & co. (No other names recorded) *Boston*
1976 Mrs R. Campbell, B. Johnson, P. Spence, N. Shaw *Teesside*
1977 Mrs B. Norbury, K. Orton, I. Burns, I. Dunford *Coventry*
1978 Mrs K. Bullen, B. Chambers, M. Wessier, W. Stevenson *King George*
1979 Mrs M. Rawlinson, B. McGillivray, M. Marlow, J. Valls *Richmond*
1980 Mrs G. Davis, D. Powell, N. Clarke, M. Baker *Moonrakers-Christie Miller*
1981 Mrs B. Alvey, J. Adamson, P. Davis, T. Barton *Croydon*
1982 Mrs B. Trafford, B. Hudson, G. Harding, I. Molyneux *Cherwell*
1983 Mrs L. Braun, D. Pike, T. Drayton, K. Green *King George*
1984 Mrs F. Dawkes, J. Thompson, L. Hawkins, M. Tims *Avon Valley*
1985 Mrs A. Talbot, E. Crooks, L. Miller, P. Mather *Gateshead*

Yetton Trophy Winners
1954 Richmond
1955 Bramley
1956 Richmond
1957 Alexandra Palace
1958 Boston
1959 Richmond
1960 Hounslow
1961 Alexandra Palace
1962 Alexandra Palace
1963 Bexhill
1964 Hounslow
1965 Birmingham
1966 Wandsworth
1967 Ascot
1968 Century
1969 Boston
1970 West Mersea
1971 Falcon
1972 West Mersea
1973 Folkestone
1974 Cotswold
1975 Folkestone
1976 Worthing
1977 Cherwell
1978 Cherwell
1979 Richmond
1980 Teesside
1981 Cherwell
1982 Essex County
1983 St Neots
1984 Sunderland
1985 Folkestone

Wales

In 1952 the Welsh Ladies Indoor BA severed its ties with the main Welsh indoor body, becoming an association in its own right and that same year saw the inauguration of the international matches between England and Wales. Welsh women's national indoor championships began with the fours in 1948 with singles and pairs added in 1949.

WLIBA National Championships

Singles
No records for 1974–9. Players titles omitted after 1981.
1949 Mrs E. Morgan *Porth*
1950 Mrs E. Morgan *Porth*
1951 Mrs H. Difford *Caerphilly*
1952 Mrs G. Best *Penarth*
1953 Mrs C. Williams *Penarth*
1954 Mrs D. Powell *Roath*
1955 Miss Q. Hutchings *Penarth*
1956 Mrs B. Heathfield *Roath*
1957 Miss M. Hutchings *Penarth*
1958 Mrs E. Morgan *Trealaw*
1959 Mrs B. Heathfield *Roath*
1960 Mrs C. Williams *Penarth*
1961 Mrs N. Williams *Penarth*
1962 Mrs E. Morgan *Trealaw*
1963 Mrs P. Williams *Penarth*
1964 Mrs M. Lane *Trealaw*

1965 Mrs D. Hemmings *Dinas Powis*
1966 Mrs A. Williams *Sully*
1967 Miss M. Hutchings *Penarth*
1968 Mrs J. Mills *Trealaw*
1969 Mrs N. Williams *Penarth*
1970 Mrs C. Williams *Penarth*
1971 Mrs J. Pryor *Roath*
1972 Mrs J. Pryor *Roath*
1973 Mrs M. Arkin *Penarth*
1974 No Record
1975 No Record
1976 No Record
1977 No Record
1978 No Record
1979 No Record
1980 E. Thomas *Swansea*
1981 P. Griffiths *Merthyr*
1982 A. Dainton *Vale of Glamorgan*
1983 A. Dainton *Vale of Glamorgan*
1984 A. Dainton *Vale of Glamorgan*
1985 R. Jones *Merthyr*
1986 A. Dainton *Vale of Glamorgan*

Pairs
No records for 1962, 1974–9.
Players names not recorded until 1980.

1949	Porth	1956	Trealaw
1950	Porth	1957	Trealaw
1951	Penarth	1958	Trealaw
1952	Roath	1959	Roath
1953	Penarth	1960	Trealaw
1954	Caerphilly	1961	Penarth
1955	Trealaw	1962	No Record

1963	Field's Park	1972	Dinas Powis
1964	Trealaw	1973	Penarth
1965	Field's Park	1974	No Record
1966	Trealaw	1975	No Record
1967	Trealaw	1976	No Record
1968	Penarth	1977	No Record
1969	Sully	1978	No Record
1970	Dinas Powis	1979	No Record
1971	Sully		

1980 M. Pomeroy, S. Proctor *Cardiff*
1981 P. Skinner, J. Watts *Cardiff*
1982 S. Proctor, M. Pomeroy *Cardiff*
1983 P. Skinner, J. Watts *Cardiff*
1984 P. Skinner, J. Watts *Cardiff*
1985 A. Toms, J. Ward *Cardiff*
1986 J. Davies, S. Oliver *Swansea*

Triples
Triples were introduced into the Welsh Ladies National Championships in 1976. No full records were kept however until the season 1979–80.
1980 M. Pomeroy, S. Proctor, J. Osborne *Cardiff*
1981 C. Davies, B. Stanton, A. Dainton *Vale of Glamorgan*
1982 A. Barbarini, J. Downes, I. Radford *Vale of Glamorgan*
1983 E. Thomas, L. Evans, J. Davies *Swansea*
1984 E. Thomas, L. Evans, J. Davies *Swansea*
1985 J. Scoular, E. Brown, A. Dainton *Vale of Glamorgan*
1986 F. Lewis, V. Howell, P. Griffiths *Merthyr*

Fours
No records 1962 and 1974–9.
Players names not recorded until 1980.

1948	Trealaw	1964	Penarth
1949	Trealaw	1965	Dinas Powis
1950	Trealaw	1966	Barry
1951	Penarth	1967	Sully
1952	Penarth	1968	Sully
1953	Penarth	1969	Dinas Powis
1954	Caerphilly	1970	Dinas Powis
1955	Sully	1971	Dinas Powis
1956	Sully	1972	Barry
1957	Penarth	1973	Rhiwbina
1958	Trealaw	1974	No Record
1959	Roath	1975	No Record
1960	Sully	1976	No Record
1961	Penarth	1977	No Record
1962	No Record	1978	No Record
1963	Field's Park	1979	No Record

1980 A. Dainton, G. Bellamy, J. Whalley, J. Osborne *Vale of Glamorgan*
1981 J. Ward, D. Hemming, W. Williams, J. Howells *Cardiff*
1982 B. Green, E. Mantle, J. Mills, M. Jones *Cardiff*
1983 G. Wallis, C. Williams, A. John, J. Ackland *Penarth*
1984 D. Wallace, C. Williams, A. John, J. Ackland *Penarth*
1985 B. Green, E. Mantle, J. Mills, M. Jones *Cardiff*
1986 A. Toms, N. Hopkins, B. Stanton, J. Ward *Cardiff*

Scotland

Since the formation of the Scottish Women's Indoor BA on 26 May 1961, its bowlers have carved out a useful record in the home international series which they won for the first time in 1963. National championships however were not held until the season of 1971–2.

SWIBA National Championships

Singles
1972 M. Young *West of Scotland*
1973 F. Whyte *Paisley*
1974 A. Blair *Glasgow*
1975 J. Bain *Bainfield*
1976 M. Ross *Ardrossan*
1977 C. McParland *Lanarkshire*
1978 M. Ross *Ardrossan*
1979 C. Mathews *Lanarkshire*
1980 F. Whyte *Paisley*
1981 M. Black *Arbroath*
1982 J. Docherty *Aberdeen*
1983 M. Gray *Dundee*
1984 S. Gourlay *West of Scotland*
1985 J. Conlan *Midlothian*

Pairs
1972 W. Massey, R. Henderson *Ayr*
1973 C. Allison, A. McAlpine *Bainfield*

Sally Smith of Norfolk, winner of the EWBA 16–25 singles championship in 1983 and 1984. (Duncan Cubitt, *Bowls International*).

1974 A. Drummond, A. Walker *East Fife*
1975 I. Wilkie, S. Michie *Dundee*
1976 E. Stewart, J. Morrison *Aberdeen*
1977 M. Campbell, M. Reid *Ayr*
1978 J. Logan, M. Reid *Ardrossan*
1979 M. Gray, F. Whyte *Paisley*
1980 M. Martin, I. Dockrell *Ardrossan*
1981 M. Scott, A. Leslie *Prestwick*
1982 A. Scott, E. Gemmell *Ayr*
1983 J. Christie, T. Powell *Prestwick*
1984 S. Cox, J. Mitchell *Headwell*
1985 W. McRae, M. Hargreaves *Irvine*

Triples

1972 N. Watson, A. Carson, E. Neil *West of Scotland*
1973 D. Fair, M. Brockett, I. Dockrell *Glasgow*
1974 H. Jardine, O. Sharp, B. Russell *Lanarkshire*
1975 N. Dickenson, M. Thomson, M. Jamieson *Prestwick*
1976 J. Campbell, B. Webster, M. Franchi *Dundee*
1977 E. Clark, B. Murray, S. Bradley *West of Scotland*
1978 M. McMillan, N. French, R. Pettigrew *Blantyre*
1979 J. Christie, J. McColl, M. Jamieson *Prestwick*
1980 N. Wylie, J. Millar, C. Webster *Paisley*
1981 J. McGregor, M. Crawford, N. MacDougal *West of Scotland*
1982 J. McGregor, M. Crawford, N. MacDougal *West of Scotland*
1983 N. Thomson, N. Skenridge, J. Frame *Lanarkshire*
1984 D. Malone, J. Stenhouse, N. Bell *Midlothian*
1985 H. Young, A. Watson, M. McRae *Midlothian*

Fours

1972 A. Foster, P. Roseweir, I. Douglas, S. Dallas *West of Scotland*
1973 M. Young, P. Roseweir, I. Douglas, S. Dallas *West of Scotland*
1974 M. Dunn, L. Drummond, M. McDougall, N. McCallum *Glasgow*
1975 N. Johnstone, J. Cain, N. French, E. Summers *Blantyre*
1976 M. McDonald, R. Horne, N. MacDougall, M. Carmichael *West of Scotland*
1977 N. Watson, I. Walker, A. O'Hara, I. Black *West of Scotland*
1978 M. Ramsay, J. Baxter, R. Hill, N. Flood *Ardrossan*
1979 L. Hobson, M. Galbraith, J. Bell, A. McAlpine *Bainfield*
1980 A. Sangster, J. Armour, J. Allan, J. Henderson *Aberdeen*
1981 E. Serafin, I. Maiden, H. Torie, M. Maiden *Arbroath*
1982 E. Hood, N. Watson, C. Lyle, E. Paul *Edinburgh*
1983 N. Mulholland, I. Gracie, J. Barclay, M. Ross *Ardrossan*
1984 A. McCusker, L. Paulley, E. Christie, M. Munroe *Coatbridge*
1985 L. Paulley, S. Dewar, M. Mungall, J. Adamson *Coatbridge*

Most Titles International (Outdoor) With 34 victories (including 11 consecutive wins 1965 to 1975) Scotland head the winners table in the outdoor international series (inst. 1903). England with 22 have won the last three series (1983 to 1985), Wales have 13 and Ireland 3.

Ireland

Ireland, although for many years restricted to one full-size indoor venue, the Percy Watson Stadium in Belfast, organized a ladies section of the Belfast IBC on 17 September 1966. Knock-out competitions were organized in 1972 for singles, pairs and fours, with the winners gaining entry into the British Isles Indoor Championships.

By far the greater number of Irish women bowlers play the short mat game as members of some 600 clubs affiliated to the Irish Indoor BA. While new facilities such as the Jim Baker Stadium will certainly benefit Ireland's bowlers in international competition, the short mat game, which has produced the country's finest woman prospect for years in Margaret Johnston, will continue to play an important role in Irish bowls for many years to come.

IWIBA National Championships

Singles
1973 Mrs E. Cameron *Belfast*
1974 Mrs E. Cameron *Belfast*
1975 Mrs S. Adair *Belfast*
1976 Mrs E. Bell *Belfast*
1977 Mrs M. Ross *Belfast*
1978 Mrs D. Roy *Belfast*
1979 Mrs H. Hart *Belfast*
1980 Mrs M. Wilson *Belfast*
1981 Mrs E. Bell *Belfast*
1982 Mrs E. Bell *Belfast*
1983 Mrs E. Bell *Belfast*
1984 Mrs E. Bell *Belfast*
1985 Mrs F. Elliott *Belfast*

Pairs
1973 Mrs E. Bell, M. Ross *Belfast*
1974 Mrs E. Bell, L. Simpson *Belfast*
1975 Mrs E. Smith, D. Fraser *Belfast*
1976 Mrs B. McKeag, E. Cameron *Belfast*
1977 Mrs L. Simpson, A. Patton *Belfast*
1978 Mrs B. McKeag, E. Cameron *Belfast*
1979 Mrs L. Beck, E. Edgar *Belfast*
1980 Mrs B. Lamont, D. Roy *Belfast*
1981 Mrs H. Hart, N. Gibson *Belfast*
1982 Mrs S. Adair, A. Hewitt *Belfast*
1983 Mrs E. Wilkinson, E. Bell *Belfast*
1984 Mrs F. Elliott, M. Ross *Belfast*
1985 Mrs H. Hart, N. Gibson *Belfast*

Triples
1976 Mrs E. Smith, L. Simpson, D. Fraser *Belfast*
1977 Mrs M. McGrath, D. Milligan, P. Jackson *Belfast*
1978 Mrs E. Smith, L. Simpson, D. Fraser *Belfast*
1979 Mrs M. McGrath, H. Hart, M. Ross *Belfast*
1980 Mrs S. Adair, E. Wilkinson, E. Bell *Belfast*
1981 Mrs M. Colvin, M. Johnston, R. Stevenson *Belfast*
1982 Mrs F. Elliott, D. Turner, M. Ross *Belfast*
1983 Mrs B. McKeag, M. Martin, E. Cameron *Belfast*
1984 Mrs S. Adair, E. Wilkinson, E. Bell *Belfast*
1985 Mrs B. McKeag, M. Martin, E. Cameron *Belfast*

Fours
1973 Mrs M. McGrath, B. Lamont, D. Roy, R. Stevenson *Belfast*
1974 Mrs H. Harrison, M. Patterson, R. McBriar, B. Stirling *Belfast*

1975 Mrs G. Beattie, A. Allen, M. Jennet, N. Gibson *Belfast*
1976 Mrs M. McGrath, H. Hart, P. Jackson, M. Ross *Belfast*
1977 Mrs M. McGrath, H. Hart, P. Jackson, M. Ross *Belfast*
1978 Mrs S. Adair, B. Lamont, E. Bell, D. Roy *Belfast*
1979 Mrs E. Bell, M. McGrath, H. Hart, M. Ross *Belfast*
1980 Mrs M. McGrath, E. McKibben, H. Hart, N. Gibson *Belfast*

1981 Mrs F. Elliott, E. Wilkinson, E. Bell, M. Ross *Belfast*
1982 Mrs F. Elliott, E. Wilkinson, E. Bell, M. Ross *Belfast*
1983 Mrs M. McGrath, E. McKibben, H. Hart, N. Gibson *Belfast*
1984 Mrs K. Megrath, B. McKeag, M. Martin, E. Cameron *Belfast*
1985 Mrs M. McGrath, S. Little, H. Hart, N. Gibson *Belfast*

Women's British Isles Indoor Championships*

Singles
1981 N. Shaw *England*
1982 I. Molyneux *England*
1983 A. Dainton *Wales*
1984 S. Gourlay *Scotland*
1985 J. Conlan *Scotland*

Pairs
1981 H. Hart, N. Gibson *Ireland*
1982 S. Proctor, M. Pomeroy *Wales*
1983 P. Spence, N. Shaw *England*
1984 A. Toms, J. Ward *Wales*
1985 J. Davies, S. Oliver *Wales*

* The Women's British Isles Records are incomplete at time of writing. In the interests of accuracy I have therefore given only those results dating from 1981.

Triples
1981 J. McGregor, M. Crawford, N. MacDougall *Scotland*
1982 J. McGregor, M. Crawford, N. MacDougall *Scotland*
1983 N. Thomson, N. Skenridge, J. Frame *Scotland*
1984 J. Scoular, E. Brown, A. Dainton *Wales*
1985 H. Young, A. Watson, M. Macrae *Scotland*

Fours
1981 E. Serafin, I. Maiden, H. Torrie, M. Maiden *Scotland*
1982 E. Hood, N. Watson, C. Lyle, E. Paul *Scotland*
1983 M. McGrath, E. McKibben, H. Hart, N. Gibson *Ireland*
1984 B. Green, E. Mantle, J. Mills, M. Jones *Wales*
1985 N. Allely, S. Little, E. Archibald, N. Gibson *Ireland*

Women's Indoor International Series

1952	England	1969	Scotland
1953	England	1970	Scotland
1954	England	1971	Scotland
1955	England	1972	Scotland
1956	England	1973	Scotland
1957	England	1974	England
1958	England	1975	Scotland
1959	England	1976	Scotland
1960	England	1977	Wales
1961	England	1978	England
1962	England	1979	England
1963	Scotland	1980	Wales
1964	England	1981	Wales
1965	England	1982	Scotland
1966	Scotland	1983	England
1967	Scotland	1984	Wales
1968	Scotland	1985	England

Lewes Castle Bowling Green Society. The bowls – the jack – the trig and the clock (no longer in use). (BBC Hulton Picture Library).

The Lewes Bowling Green Society An ancient form of bowls harking back to the seventeenth century is still enjoyed in Sussex where the Lewes Bowling Green Society has its green on the site of a tilting ground within the precincts of Lewes Castle. Heavily biased woods, some over 200 years old, are trundled over a distinctly uneven surface which dates from 1753 when the club was originally formed. The jack, black and biased, is delivered by a bowler standing with one foot (at least) behind the 'trig', a small copper disc placed where the jack of the previous end finished. As in the crown green game, the jack can be cast anywhere on the green, an area of about three-quarters of an acre, but any bowl lying more than two yards from the jack is disregarded in the count.

Only two bowls per player are used and these weigh on average 1 lb 12 oz and have a diameter of $4\frac{1}{2}$ in (11.5 cm).

4 World Tournaments

AN EARLY World Tournament of sorts was staged in Los Angeles during the Olympic Games of 1932, but it was perhaps with the competition for the Vitalite World Singles Trophy, organized by the magazine *World Bowls* in 1957, that we find the first truly world-wide tournament. This bowling oddity was however far removed from the normal bowls tournament in that it was concerned solely with only one aspect of the game, drawing to the jack. Two trial ends were permitted before competitors, playing on their home greens, bowled five ends of four bowls each end. The distances of bowls from the jack were measured after every end, figures totalled and sent to the sponsors in London who duly passed on the information to the other competitors. The player with the lowest grand total measurement was then adjudged the winner.

Players nominated by the various countries participating in that inaugural year were Percy Baker (England), David Cambell (USA), Felix Cobbson (Ghana), David Dall (Scotland), A. T. 'Bert' Evans (Wales), A. P. 'Pinky' Danilowitz (South Africa) and 'Ham' Pirret (New Zealand). Baker, at that time the outstanding bowler in England and the only man to have won the EBA singles four times, began his challenge well with a total of 43 ft 6 in (13.26 m) despite having to contend with

Vitalite Trophy Winners

1957 David Dall *Scotland* 42 ft 0¾ in (12.8 m) 5 ends
1958 Walter Woodhard *Guernsey* 57 ft 2¾ in (17.54 m) 8 ends
1959 Bert Evans *Wales* 64 ft 8¼ in (19.57 m) 8 ends
1960 Tom Flemming *England* 54 ft 7$\frac{1}{16}$ in (16.6 m) 8 ends
1961 Tom Flemming *England* 66 ft 10¼ in (20.4 m) 8 ends
1962 Tom Flemming *England* 54 ft 9⅞ in (16.7 m) 8 ends
1963 Tom Flemming *England* 56 ft 7⅜ in (17.3 m) 8 ends
1964 Tom Flemming *England* 58 ft 1$\frac{9}{16}$ in (17.7 m) 8 ends
1965 N. S. 'Snowy' Walker *S. Africa* 53 ft 6$\frac{5}{16}$ in (16.3 m) 8 ends
1966 Tom Flemming *England* 54 ft 0¾ in (16.5 m) 8 ends
1967 Bob Veitch *USA* 53 ft 6$\frac{13}{16}$ in (16.3 m) 8 ends
1968 Tom Flemming *England* 64 ft 4$\frac{11}{16}$ in (19.6 m) 8 ends

strong winds at his home club of Poole Park, Dorset. Not so happy with the Dorset 'mistral' was the Ghanaian representative, Felix Cobbson. Acting as a last-minute substitute for Patrick Patnelle of Sierra Leone, Cobbson, a relative newcomer to the game and in England on a scholarship, registered a disheartening 122 ft 6½ in (37.4 m). Pirret, who was the 1950 Commonwealth Games singles gold medallist, had the misfortune of having to play on a green that had been under water the night before. Despite that and the cruel luck which saw him trailing the jack away from his first three bowls with his final delivery of the last end, Pirret managed a creditable total of 45 ft 3½ in (13.8 m). The eventual winner however proved to be the unfancied Scottish international, David Dall from Blantyre with 42 ft 0¾ in (12.8 m), with Bert Evans of Wales second and Percy Baker third. Walter Woodhard of Guernsey caused an even greater surprise by his victory in the competition, now over eight ends, in 1958 with England's Norman King in third place and the inaugural winner Dall in fourth.

Bert Evans of Wales took the title in 1959 but over the following nine years it was England international Tom Flemming from the Albert Park BC, Middlesbrough who was to put a firm stranglehold on the Vitalite Trophy with seven victories, including an unbeaten five-year run from 1960 to 1964. The South African singles champion, Snowy Walker, interrupted Flemming's remarkable sequence by winning in 1965 and Bob Veitch of the Berkley Lawn Bowling Club, California took the trophy to the United States in 1967. Flemming, however, followed each of these fleeting successes by promptly taking it back. After his last winning effort in 1968 the organizers, perhaps wisely, called 'enough', replacing this unique world event with a domestic club competition.

World Championships

First World Championships

With bowls excluded from the 1966 Commonwealth Games in Jamaica due to a lack of facilities, a suggestion by Dr Neil Benjamin of the Australian Bowls Council that the sport should have its own world championship, was greeted with enthusiasm by the bowling nations and officially approved by the International Bowling Board in May 1965. Sixteen countries were represented at the inaugural World Bowls Championships, held under IBB laws and staged at the Kyeemagh Bowling Club near Sydney from 10–23 October 1966. The formula was the normal singles, pairs, triples and fours matches with a special honour, the W. M. Leonard Trophy, earmarked for the country producing the best all-round performance.

Poor weather conditions led to fewer spectators than expected, despite heavy advertizing, and the financial assistance from AMPOL Petroleum and Quantas became of vital importance to the organizers. The ultra fast Australian greens combined with a blustery wind, were to cause many overseas bowlers to perform well below expectations, but one man, David Bryant, the English champion, had prepared himself both mentally and physically for any eventuality. By switching to a smaller, but maximum weighted bowl, Bryant successfully negotiated the greens and tamed the conditions with an opening sequence of ten wins before losing a close 21–18 contest to Mal Evans of Wales. Australian champion, Geoff Kelly was then unfortunate enough to catch the sharp edge of the Clevedon man's game and was promptly despatched 21–9, his worst defeat of the Championships. Three more victories, including a 21–18 beating of the 1965 Vitalite Trophy winner, Norman 'Snowy' Walker of South Africa, earned Bryant the title of first World Singles Champion with 14 wins from 15 matches and a total of 312 shots to his credit and just 196 against.

Geoff Kelly, a New South Wales bank manager, showed typical Aussie resilience by bouncing back from his mauling by Bryant in the singles, to skip teammate Bert Palm to a victory in the pairs which included a 22–15 defeat of Bryant and his partner, Cedric Smith, in the final stages. Don Collins, Athol Johnson and John Dobbie added the triples title to the Australian tally before joining up with Bert Palm to clinch second place in the fours behind the New Zealand quartet of N. Lash, R. Buchan, G. Jolly and W. O'Neill, putting the host country in an unassailable position at the head of the Leonard Trophy table with 11 points.

Although viewed as a successful innovation, the World Championships were clouded somewhat by a complicated and, at times, alarmingly unfair system of scoring in pairs, triples and fours. The participating countries were split into two sections but sectional points scored, once the preliminary rounds were over, were completedly disregarded. Having reached the final stage, countries played only those from the opposite first stage group. Thus, good early performances meant nothing in terms of points while, in the case of a points tied situation, only shots for were taken into account. The injustice of this system is well illustrated in the case of the England pair who lost just two of their total 11 matches, yet only managed third place behind Australia who lost four!

Second World Championships

The 1972 Championships held at Beach House Park, Worthing proved a notable success. The mistakes of Sydney were rectified and the English Bowling Association rejected the idea of direct sponsorship in favour of an insurance scheme provided by bowlers. The wisdom of this became apparent when an operating loss of some £13 000 was paid off leaving a credit balance of £14 500 for future development. The anomalies of the 1966 scoring system were eradicated by simply scrapping sectional play and instituting a shots for and against method of resolving a points-tied situation.

As might have been expected, the Australian bowlers could make little progress on the slower English greens but more surprising was the lacklustre performance of the English contingent. Despite the home advantage England's team ended the fortnight with a welcome victory in the fours for Norman King, Cliff Stroud, Ted Hayward and their skip, Peter Line, but precious little else. David Bryant, the defending singles champion, opened with a victory over Bob McDonald of New Zealand but then stumbled, losing 21–16 to Hong Kong's Eric Liddell and 21–14 to Bob Henderson of Papua New Guinea on the opening day of the singles. Two further losses, a 20–21 nip and tuck affair to Harry Lakin of Malawi and a 21–6 thrashing at the hands of the eventual winner, Mal Evans of Wales, put paid to any hopes Bryant may have cherished of retaining his title. In the 1966 Championships it was Evans who had inflicted the sole defeat on Bryant and this victory made a satisfying double for the schoolmaster from Tonypandy and was certainly a most important result in his run to the world title.

Eric Liddell and Cecilio Clemente took the pairs title back to Hong Kong, certainly an outstanding achievement for such a small bowling country. It was, however, the performance of Bill Miller, Clive Forrester and skip Dick Folkins in capturing the triples title for the USA, a minnow in bowling terms, that really caught the imagination in 1972. Scotland, who finished in fourth place in this event, three points adrift of the winners, found themselves on the short end of a highly contentious umpiring decision in their match with Fiji. With the scores tied at 11–11, the Scots held three shots on the final end with only the last bowl of Jock McAtee, their skip, still to be played. Not surprisingly the prudent Scot, quite in keeping with the laws of the game, elected not to deliver it, content to take the match at 14–11. Scorecards were duly signed by both skips and the head broken up when, to the surprise of all six bowlers, the umpire, Walter Phillips, ordered the end to be replayed as all of the bowls had not been delivered. Obviously shaken by this eccentric decision, the deflated Scots dropped two shots on the replayed end, losing the match 13–11. Despite strong protests by the Scottish team manager, Tom Moffat, to the Umpires Committee and questions on the legality of the umpire's ruling from IBB representatives, the decision was upheld and the result stood. Although hardly adequate compensation, the one point McAttee and his men earned from the triples debacle ensured Scotland of first place in the Leonard Trophy table, one point ahead of South Africa and the USA with seven apiece.

Third World Championships

Johannesburg was the scene of the third World Bowls Championships which got under way on 18 February 1976 amid the most lavish of settings. Huge grandstands seating a total of 10 500 paying customers were erected around the three greens at Zoo Lake at a cost of £49 000. A scoreboard, designed to show the state of play in 18 games simultaneously was complimented by closed circuit television punching out pictures and information to nine bars scattered about the complex. Budget for the championships was £260 000 of which the South African government forked out a useful £40 000. It was not, however, just the South African administrators who had prepared themselves well for the championships: their bowlers made a clean sweep of all four events and completed their nap hand by taking the Leonard Trophy with a maximum 16 points.

With only one defeat, a 21–10 'nothing to lose' affair against David Bryant in the final round, Doug Watson seized the singles crown from Welshman, Mal Evans, signalling his intentions early with an emphatic 21–9 second round victory over the 1972 champion. For Bryant a bright start clouded when Bob Middleton of Australia beat him 21–18 in the

fourth round and a 21–5 hammering from New Zealander Kerry Clarke hardly helped his cause. The Englishman picked up his game over the second half of the championships but those defeats pushed him down into third place with only a bronze medal to show for his efforts. Dick Folkins, a superb draw bowler, began his singles challenge with four victories, but then found Watson just too strong, the South African outlasting him to win an important tie 21–19. Folkins however then teamed up with Neil McInnes in the pairs and, with only two defeats, 25–15 to Rhodesia and 22–14 to England, did well enough to win a silver medal for the USA. David Bryant, with Tom Armstrong and Bill Irish took a silver in the triples beating the eventual winners, South Africa 25–13 in the 13th round. Any hopes of gold however were snuffed out by defeats against New Zealand (35–11), Ireland (20–14) and the USA (20–7).

Like Rhodesia and Western Samoa, Japan, a true fledgling bowling country, was making its World Championship debut and the experience was to prove a painful one with a series of massive defeats. The pairs found them going under 47–2 to Israel, 51–8 to England, 66–3 to Australia and 60–6 to Hong Kong and the sorry tale continued into the triples, with losses to Rhodesia by 69–4, New Zealand 52–4 and Ireland 49–3.

Fourth World Championships

Undeterred by the misfortunes of their South African adventures, a Japanese squad turned up at the fourth World Championships held at Frankston, Australia from 16 January–2 February, 1980. Unfortunately their play had hardly reached world championship standards during the intervening period and the triples promptly found them on the receiving end of a world record 63–1 thrashing at the hands of Swaziland. Absent from the championships however were the South Africans, political victims of their government's apartheid policy and effectively barred from defending their five titles.

At Frankston, the triples and pairs events featured a number of close matches with the Australian pairing of Alf Sandercock and Peter Rheuben scraping home 21–20 against John Bell and Mal Hughes of England, and using that victory as a springboard to success in the pairs. In the triples Australia drew 19–19 with Fiji but then went down 18–17 to the English trio of Jim Hobday, Tony Allcock and David Bryant after a four-hour battle. With only one defeat in 19 games, a 22–14 loss to Bert McWilliams, Clive Forrester and Dick Folkins of the USA, England powered their way to the triples title beating Scotland, their closest challengers, 28–11 in their final match, with 24-year-old Allcock becoming the youngest ever gold medal winner in bowling history. The third historic event of the 1980 championships, one which earned the loudest cheer, came when Japan registered their first ever World Championship victory, beating Papua New Guinea 21–19 in the 16th round of the triples.

David Bryant entered the singles fray with something to prove and did so in emphatic style with 11 consecutive wins to put himself at the head of the singles table. Only Arthur McKernan of Jersey was able to better the determined Englishman with a 21–19 victory in the 12th round and although Russell Evans of Wales had him on the rack in their match with a 7–1 lead, Bryant steadied to win 21–16 and from that point on, closed his hands on the gold medal and a second World Singles title. After coming so close in the triples, Scotland were denied once again in the fours. Level on points with Hong Kong as the two teams met in the final round the Scots led 17–16 going to the last end, but dropped two heartbreaking shots to lose the match and the gold medal 18–17.

Fifth World Championships

Despite scoring their first success at Frankston, the Japanese opted out of the Fifth World Championships held at Aberdeen's Westburn Park 6–28 July 1984, their place being taken by Argentina. To the disgust of many bowlers, notably the defending champion, David Bryant, the idea of sectional play was re-introduced despte much protest. This one area of contention apart, the championships were handsomely staged with a budget of some £500 000, part of which was raised by a levy of £2 from each male bowler in Scotland, to be paid over a four-year period. Ten major sponsors, British Airways, Clydesdale Bank Ltd, Dewars Scotch Whisky, General Accident, Homestead Eggs/Day Lay Eggs, Scottish Brewers Ltd, Thomas Cook Ltd and Thomas Taylor (Bowls) Ltd, committed £10 000 apiece and there were many minor sponsors also helping to get the 1984 championships under way.

The singles, not unnaturally, found David Bryant installed as firm favourite and, with a recent victory in the Gateway Masters tournament at Worthing, the great man had fully justified that position. Bryant's first task, however, lay in the pairs, in which he formed a potent partnership with Tony Allcock and, with seven wins in a row, things looked distinctly promising for the English duo. A surprise 26–23 defeat by Canada combined with a series of victories by a Scot and a Hong

Kong-born American, however, spelt trouble for the Englishmen and every other fancied pair in the event. Following a 23–14 victory over Papua New Guinea and a 21–11 loss to Kenya, the US lost their pairs lead, 66-year-old Jim Candelet, who retired with a back injury and was replaced from the pool of reserves by Scottish reject, George Adrain. Adrain and US skip 'Skippy' Arculli quickly formed a well-nigh unbeatable rapport and, by a quirk of fate, met and defeated the Scots pairing of Willie Wood and David Gourlay by the score of 22–15 in their first match together. With a 19–18 loss to Australia already on their card this defeat put paid to the hopes of Wood and Gourlay but, in contrast, Arculli and Adrain were now riding high, beating the Aussie pair of Kenny Williams and Bob Middleton 22–15. Almost inevitably the final encounter found England and America locked in combat, battling out a match of fluctuating fortunes which ended in a completely unforeseen 21–20 victory for the United States.

The triples featured a number of strong combinations from the world's top bowling nations including George Turley, Julian Haines, John Bell (England), Philip Chok, Majid Hassan, George Souza (Hong Kong), Brian Rattray, Doug Lambert, David Gourlay (Scotland), Stan Espie, Sammy Allen, Jim Baker (Ireland), Peter Rheuben, Doug Sherman, Keith Poole (Australia) and Rowan Brassey, Jim Scott, Morgan Moffatt (New Zealand). Of these all but Hong Kong, surprisingly beaten 21–9 by Jersey, won their first matches. The England men lost their way, however, after defeats by Israel and Zimbabwe

The Duchess of Roxburgh delivers the silver jack to get the 1984 World Championships under way at Westburn Park, Aberdeen. (E. Hyslop).

while the New Zealanders went down 27–9 to Western Samoa. At the end of the sectional play Ireland and Scotland remained unbeaten but the promise of a closely contested final was unfulfilled. Espie, Allen and Baker were collectively on song and while the Scots infuriated their home crowd with their most inept display of the tournament, it was Ireland collecting the gold medal with a 29–11 victory in a disappointingly one-sided final.

There were no unbeaten teams at the end of the fours sections. New Zealand's Rowan Brassey, Jim Scott, Morgan Moffatt and Phil Skoglund were involved in a three-way tie at the head of Section A, losing to Wales and Ireland and drawing with Israel, but entered the final on shot count. In Section B England's George Turley, Julian Haines, John Bell and Tony Allcock, with just one defeat against Jersey, finished ahead of Scotland who lost their first and last matches to England and Australia respectively. Superb skipping by Allcock and an inspired spell by his number three, John Bell, saw the England foursome safely home in a tight final played in pouring rain from start to finish.

A seven-shot advantage in Section A of the singles put Scotland's Willie Wood into the final at the expense of David Bryant, the defending champion, after each man had scored nine victories out of a possible ten. With the burly little Scot succumbing to Canada's pint-sized bowler, Ronnie Jones, in the fifth round, the progress of the Section A leaders rested, fittingly, on their final match – against each other. After what has been described by one knowledgeable observer as 'the greatest match ever', it was Wood who emerged triumphant with a 21–18 victory and a place in the final against the ex-rugger player from New Zealand, Peter Belliss. Belliss, runner-up to Bryant in the Gateway Masters in June, had wisely remained in the UK to prepare for the most important tournament of his life. With just one defeat, a surprising loss to John Jones from Jersey, Belliss handed out a 21–7 thrashing to the highly fancied Australian challenger, Kenny Williams on his way to a place in the final and was in superb form.

In the final it was Belliss first into his stride, taking a 10 shots to 3 lead by the seventh end and playing all the delicate shots that New Zealanders are not supposed to know about. In contrast, Wood was forced to play a typical 'down under' forcing game in an effort to stay in touch. Seven winning ends and 11 shots, however, put the Scot into the lead for the first time at 14–11 but threes on the 21st and 23rd ends saw the big New Zealander level at 19 all. By the 25th it was 20 all and tension caused each man to bowl probably their worst opening deliveries of the match and follow those with even more forgettable attempts. Both were closer with their third bowls, Belliss just behind, Wood jack-high. The Scot then put his last bowl just in front of the jack to lie definite shot and the pressure swung on to Belliss. The young man from Wanganui, however, was equal to the challenge and choosing the drive as his final weapon, played the shot bowl out of the head to leave umpire Jim Muir with the unenviable task of measuring for the winner. A much vaunted 'sonic' measuring device chose that moment to develop a fault and so it was down to the time-honoured tape which showed Belliss as the winner and the new world champion.

Although without a win to their name the Scots took the Leonard Trophy with a total of 80 points.

First World Championships
Sydney, Australia 1966

Singles
Gold D. Bryant *England*
Silver J. Henshaw *Scotland*
Bronze R. Fulton *Ireland*

Pairs
Gold A. Palm and G. Kelly *Australia*
Silver J. Harvey and N. S. Walker *South Africa*
Bronze C. Smith and D. J. Bryant *England*

Triples
Gold D. Collins, A. Johnston, J. M. Dobbie *Australia*
Silver A. Houston, K. D. Beacom, J. Henderson *Canada*
Bronze K. Lightfoot, J. Prest, L. Kessel *South Africa*

Fours
Gold N. Lash, R. Buchan, G. Jolly, W. P. O'Brien *New Zealand*
Silver W. Collins, A. Palm, A. Johnston, J. M. Dobbie *Australia*
Bronze W. Adrain, W. Dyett, R. Thompson, H. Reston *Scotland*

W. M. Leonard Trophy
Gold G. Kelly, D. Collins, A. Palm, A. Johnston, J. M. Dobbie. Manager, W. J. Spear *Australia*

Second World Championships
Worthing, England 1972

Singles
Gold M. Evans *Wales*
Silver R. Bernard *Scotland*
Bronze J. Harvey *South Africa*

Pairs
Gold C. C. Delgado and E. J. Liddell
Hong Kong
Silver J. F. Candelet and R. W. Folkins
USA
Bronze J. A. Harvey and B. G. Ellwood
South Africa

Triples
Gold W. M. Miller, C. Forrester, R.
Folkins *USA*
Silver E. L. Davey, J. A. Marsh, D. G.
Watson *South Africa*
Bronze J. R. Evans, H. Andrews, G.
Humphreys *Wales*

Fours
Gold N. King, C. Stroud, E. H.
Hayward, P. Line *England*
Silver A. R. Logan, A. McIntosh, J.
McAttee, H. Reston *Scotland*
Bronze C. C. Delgado, A. R. Kitchell, R.
E. da Silva, G. A. Souza *Hong Kong*

W. M. Leonard Trophy
Gold R. Bernard, A. R. Logan, A.
McIntosh, J. McAtee, H. Reston.
Manager, T. Moffatt *Scotland*

Third World Championships
Johannesburg, S. Africa 1976

Singles
Gold D. Watson *South Africa*
Silver R. J. Middleton *Australia*
Bronze D. J. Bryant *England*

Pairs
Gold W. Moseley and D. Watson
South Africa
Silver N. McInnes and R. W. Folkins
United States
Bronze D. A. Woolnough and R. J.
Middleton *Australia*

Triples
Gold K. Campbell, N. Gatti, K.
Lightfoot *South Africa*
Silver D. J. Bryant, W. C. Irish, T. W.
Armstrong *England*
Bronze W. Murray, D. Hull, J. Higgins
Ireland

Fours
Gold K. Campbell, W. Moseley, N.
Gatti, K. Lightfoot *South Africa*
Silver D. A. Woolnough, L. Bishop, B.
Salter, K. Poole *Australia*
Bronze J. C. Evans, W. C. Irish, T.
Armstrong, P. Line *England*

W. M. Leonard Trophy
Gold D. Watson, K. Campbell, W.
Moseley, N. Gatti, K. Lightfoot.
Manager, Leon Kessel *South Africa*

Fourth World Championships
Frankston, Australia 1980

Singles
Gold D. Bryant *England*
Silver J. Snell *Australia*
Bronze D. McGill *Scotland*

Pairs
Gold A. Sandercock, P. Rheuben
Australia
Silver B. Gill, G. Jarvis *Canada*
Bronze P. Skogland, K. Darling *New
Zealand*

Triples
Gold J. Hobday, A. Allcock, D. Bryant
England
Silver J. Summers, D. McGill, W.
McQueen *Scotland*
Bronze J. Malcolm, N. Unkovitch, M.
Moffatt *New Zealand*

Fours
Gold P. Chok, G. Souza Jnr., E.
Liddell, O. K. Dallah *Hong Kong*
Silver J. Summers, W. Wood, W.
McQueen, A. McIntosh *Scotland*
Bronze J. Malcolm, K. Darling, M.
Moffatt, P. Skogland *New Zealand*

W. M. Leonard Trophy
Gold D. Bryant, J. Bell, M. Hughes, A.
Allcock, J. Hobday *England*

Fifth World Championships
Aberdeen, Scotland 1984

Singles
Gold Peter Bellis *New Zealand*
Silver Willie Wood *Scotland*
Bronze David Bryant *England*

Pairs
Gold Skippy Arculli, Jim Candelet
(George Adrain sub) *USA*
Silver David Bryant, Tony Allcock
England
Bronze Kenny Williams, Bob
Middleton *Australia*

New Zealand's Peter
Belliss (left) and Willie
Wood of Scotland
practise their close
order drill during their
1984 World
Championship singles
duel at Aberdeen.
(E. Hyslop).

Guess who won. Belliss (left) and Wood face the press after the 1984 final. (E. Hyslop).

Triples
Gold Stan Espie, Sammy Allen, Jim Baker *Ireland*
Silver Brian Rattray, Doug Lambert, Jim Boyle *Scotland*
Bronze Rowan Brassey, Jim Scott, Morgan Moffat *New Zealand*

Fours
Gold George Turley, Julian Haines, John Bell, Tony Allcock *England*
Silver Rowan Brassey, Jim Scott, Morgan Moffat, Phil Skoglund *New Zealand*
Bronze Brian Rattray, Doug Lambert, Jim Boyle, David Gourlay *Scotland*

W. M. Leonard Trophy
Gold Joe Bogle, Brian Rattray, Doug Lambert, Jim Boyle, David Gourlay, Willie Wood *Scotland*

The International Women's Bowling Board

Bearing in mind the high degree of organization established among women bowlers within the British Isles, it is perhaps surprising to find that they were not represented at a meeting held in Sydney, Australia on 4–5 December 1969 at which the International Women's Bowling Board was formed. Delegates from Australia, Canada, Fiji, New Zealand, Papua New Guinea, South Africa and the United States were present and these, with the exception of Fiji, at that time without a National Women's Association, were to be the founder members. Provisional membership was however granted to England, Ireland, Scotland and Wales in 1972 and confirmed on 3 December 1973 at the IWBB meeting in New Zealand.

First Women's World Championships Sydney, Australia 1969

The first Women's World Bowls Championships, held under the auspices of the IWBB, were staged in December 1969 at the Elizabethan Women's BC, Sydney, Australia with six countries taking part. The South African team, by far the strongest contingent, featured in every final on offer, being denied only once, when Mrs Gladys Doyle of Papua New Guinea defeated Mrs E. McDonald to win the singles. In the pairs however Mrs McDonald teamed up with M. Cridlan to defeat P. Hart and J. Turnbull of Australia in the final. The triples went to S. Sundelowitz, Y. Emanuel and C. Bidwell and this trio, with the addition of Mrs Cridlan, also won the fours.

Countries taking part
Australia, Fiji, New Zealand, Papua New Guinea, South Africa, USA.

Second Women's World Championships Wellington, New Zealand 1973

Political pressure led to the exclusion of the powerful South African team from the Second World Championships held at the Victoria BC, Wellington, New Zealand in 1973. Although three British Isles associations were due to take part, the Welsh unfortunately were forced to withdraw through lack of finance leaving England and Ireland as the sole UK representatives. Mavis Steele (Middlesex) represented England in the singles event, bowling with skill and tenacity to master the unfamiliar conditions and a tricky wind. She lost to New Zealand's Elsie Wilkie 21–13 in the opening singles match and the New Zealander went through the tournament undefeated earning 14 points while the Middlesex player, comfortably winning her remaining matches, ended in second place with 12. In the pairs it was to be the same end result for Miss Steele and her partner, Phyl Derrick of Surrey, despite the encouragement of a superb last end, last bowl victory over New Zealand in the first round. Behind 17–20, Miss Steele delivered her final effort with sufficient force and accuracy to remove most of the New Zealand bowls from the head, scoring the five precious shots which earned a thrilling 22–20 victory for England. Defeat by the same score against Sadie Little and Jean Hayes of Ireland however put paid to English hopes of outright success in the pairs leaving them with the same points total as Australians Lorna Lucas and

Dot Jenkinson and reduced to second place on shots difference, despite a 21–14 victory over the Aussies in the final match.

With three victories – singles, triples and fours – the New Zealand team collected 13 points to win the *Sydney Daily Mirror* award for the best overall performance.

Countries taking part

Australia, Canada, England, Fiji, Ireland, New Zealand, Papua New Guinea, USA.

Third Women's World Championships Worthing, England 1977

Jock Munro's famous greens at Beach House Park, Worthing in England provided the setting for the Third Women's World Bowls Championships in 1977 and, with 14 countries competing, the event was gaining real credibility. Elsie Wilkie (New Zealand), the defending singles champion, took some while to adjust to the slower English greens, suffering an uncomfortable 21–16 first round defeat against Helen Gordon of Israel. Further losses to Eva Neil of Scotland (21–12), Australia's Norma Massey (21–10) and Helen Wong of Hong Kong (21–12), opened the door to any singles player able to master the conditions and seize Miss Wilkie's crown, but the offer was spurned and the New Zealander made up lost ground to retain her singles title despite a 21–12 last round defeat by Lillian Nicholas of Wales.

Home advantage brought scant reward to the English team who failed to win a single event, although only a 21–17 defeat at the hands of the Scots in their final match pushed Margaret Lockwood, Joan Hunt, Mabel Darlington and Joan Sparkes into second place in the fours behind Australia's Lorna Lucas, Connie Hicks, Merl Richardson and Dot Jenkinson. Helen Wong and Elvie Chok underlined the emerging power of Hong Kong by winning the pairs with a last match victory over Norma Le Motte and Marion Bramwell of Papua New Guinea by 21–12 despite losing a six on the final end! To their everlasting credit it was the bowlers of Wales who saved the blushes of the UK teams with an outstanding performance in winning the triples with Joan Osborne, Margaret Pomeroy and Enid Morgan, and collecting bronze medals in both pairs and fours.

Countries taking part

Australia, Canada, England, Guernsey, Hong Kong, Ireland, Israel, Jersey, Malawi, New Zealand, Papua New Guinea, USA, Wales.

Fourth Women's World Championships Toronto, Canada 1981

If Elsie Wilkie had been the star of the previous two world championships, England's Norma Shaw made those of 1981, held at Willowdale, Toronto, Canada, all her own. Better known in England for her indoor prowess, Mrs Shaw, National Indoor Champion in 1977/8, 1979/80 and 1980/81, added her second British Isles indoor title to an impressive tally just prior to the championships, but her outdoor record at the time featured just the national two-wood title won in 1978. At Toronto, however, she was to prove herself the dominant woman singles player in the world, playing impeccable drawing bowls throughout the championships to win the premier honour with just two lapses, a 21–11 defeat by Scotland's Esther Clark and a close run 21–20 loss to Eileen Bell of Ireland. For defending champion Elsie Wilkie, 1981 proved little short of disastrous as, unable to come to terms with the dreadful greens, she finished 18th out of 18!

The silver medal position was filled by Anna Bates of Zimbabwe whose 13 victories included a 21–5 thrashing of the luckless Miss Wilkie and an almost as severe 21–9 defeat of Scotland's Esther Clark. Third-placed Helen Wong of Hong Kong was forced to withdraw from the pairs event completely exhausted from her efforts in the singles, and was soon joined 'on the bench' by England pairs and fours player Gloria Thomas of Devon who had fallen ill with sunstroke and a throat infection after completing nine matches out of a scheduled 17 in the fours. Mrs Thomas was replaced by England manageress, Irene Molyneux who, with ample international experience, proved the ideal substitute as the English quartet produced 13 wins to collect the gold medal with 26 points.

UK bowlers struck again in the pairs, the gold medal going to Eileen Bell and Nan Allely of Ireland at the cost of just two matches out of 16. The scratch English pairing of Norma Shaw and Irene Molyneux (the latter once again substituting for Gloria Thomas) did well enough to add a bronze to England's two gold medals although Mrs Molyneux was forced to switch from skip's position after nine games, but the silver went to the Fiji pairing of Maraia Lum On and Willow Fong.

The final day's play of the Championships were rained off and, but for this 'unnatural break', England may well have picked up a third gold medal in the triples. Positions in the event were finely balanced, with Linda King, Rae O'Donnell and Lena Sadick of Hong

Kong just two points clear of England's Eileen Fletcher, Betty Stubbings and Mavis Steele who held the better shot average. The final day's encounter between the two countries would decide the championship and, while the outcome was by no means a foregone conclusion for the English, it was a cruel fate which denied them the opportunity of proving their superiority. However, with two gold, one silver and one bronze medals, England carried off the overall team prize with 91 points, 11 clear of second placed Hong Kong.

Eighteen nations took part in the 1981 Championships with Swaziland included as a last minute replacement for Samoa. Unable to field a team due to the aftermath of a General Strike, Samoa were forced to withdraw from the championships just two weeks prior to the opening ceremony.

Countries taking part

Australia, Canada, England, Fiji, Guernsey, Hong Kong, Ireland, Israel, Jersey, Malawi, New Zealand, Papua New Guinea, Scotland, Swaziland, USA, Wales, Zambia, Zimbabwe.

Fifth Women's World Championships Melbourne, Australia 1985

While the greens at Toronto, scene of the championships in 1981, came in for heavy criticism, those at the venue for the 1985 Championships in Australia, the Reservoir Bowling Club at Preston, eight miles from Melbourne, left little to be desired. Defending singles champion, England's Norma Shaw, was well fancied to retain her title but experienced unsettled form, having to battle back from a seven-shot deficit to beat Julie Davies of Wales 21–19 in her opening match before slumping to a disastrous 21–18 defeat by Maria Laura Dufour de Gismondi of Argentina. Worse was to come for the 1981 champion. Kathy Sigimet of Papua New Guinea handed her a 21–3 beating and New Zealand's Rhoda Ryan beat her 21–6 in the ninth round. While this desperate buffeting of Mrs Shaw's hopes was taking place a new champion was emerging in the person of Australia's Merle Richardson who had powered her way through 13 rounds without defeat. Such was the impressive form of this 55-year-old grandmother from New South Wales that it soon became apparent that the main competition would be for second place.

Norma Shaw restored at least some of her confidence by inflicting a record 21–0 defeat on Alice Mayers from Kenya in the seventh round and must have raised an eyebrow when, seven

rounds later, Mrs Mayers became the sole victor over Mrs Richardson, beating her by 21 shots to 18.

That lapse, however, was to prove no more than a hiccup in the progress of the Australian who duly won her remaining games to win the singles gold medal for the host country.

The pairs found Mrs Richardson still in a dominating mood as she and her partner, Fay Craig, put together an impresssive string of 11 victories before succumbing 22–16 to England's Norma Shaw and Jean Valls in a match which saw the English at last strike form. The Australians, however, went off the boil, losing three matches in succession and only a last gasp 21–13 victory over Israel's Helen Gordon and Rina Lebel ensured them of a gold medal, thanks to shot average, over Maraia Lum On and Willow Fong who took the silver medal for the second time in succession.

Australia struck gold again in the triples with Dorothy Roche, Norma Massey and Mavis Meadowcroft proving almost unbeatable – until a surprising 21–11 defeat by Barbara le Moignan, Kath Hickman and Doreen Gay of Jersey brought a momentary pause to their run in the 18th round. A 16–12 victory in their final match against Israel's Rina Lebel, Miriam Jankelowitz and Bernice Katz, however, restored their faith, as challengers Hong Kong and England fell away. Hong Kong, represented by Sandi Zakozke, Rae O'Donnell and Helen Wong came back with a last round win over Kenya to grab second place silver from the Welsh trio of Rita Jones, Mair Jones and WWBA Secretary, Linda Parker, who finished one point behind.

With wildly contrasting weather conditions making results something of a lottery for the less experienced bowlers, it was the established nations which adjusted their games the quicker in the fours. Dot Roche, Norma Massey, Fay Graig and Mavis Meadowcroft were determined to make it a clean sweep of all the gold medals for Australia while England's quartet of Jean Valls, Brenda Atherton, Betty Stubbings and Mavis Steel seemed a potent blend of experience and enthusiasm. The key match between the two ended in a 24–14 victory for the host country and good victories for the English against Argentina (40–2), Canada (27–12) and Fiji (27–9) were offset by disappointing performances in important games against Hong Kong, Wales and Zimbabwe.

With attention focused on the Australians, the talented Scottish four, Sarah Gourlay, Elizabeth Christie, Annette Evans and Francis Whyte were quietly stringing together an impressive run of victories, beating Fiji (34–7), who had earlier defeated the Australians in a close match, and Jersey 36–8. Another crucial victory came in their final match against the USA, out of contention but still dangerous after defeating Wales 30–13. Against the determined Scots, however, Jo Gilbert, Edith Denton, Isabella Forbes and Corinna Folkins could muster only six shots in reply to their opponents 31 and Scotland had won a gold medal for the first time in the history of the championships, with Australia one point behind in second place and England in third.

This fine result by the English four brought Miss Steele her fourth World Championship medal in the 12 years, one gold, two silver and one bronze, making her the top medal winner since the Championships began.

Countries taking part

Argentina, Australia, Botswana, Canada, England, Fiji, Hong Kong, Ireland, Israel, Jersey, Kenya, New Zealand, Papua New Guinea, Scotland, Swaziland, USA, Wales, Western Samoa, Zimbabwe.

Women's World Championships

First World Championships
Sydney, Australia 1969

Singles
G. Doyle *Papua New Guinea*

Pairs
E. McDonald, M. Cridlan *South Africa*

Triples
S. Sundelowitz, Y. Emanuel, C. Bidwell *South Africa*

Fours
S. Sundelowitz, Y. Emanuel, C. Bidwell, M. Cridlan *South Africa*

Second World Championships
Wellington, New Zealand 1973

Singles
E. Wilkie *New Zealand*

Pairs
L. Lucas, D. Jenkinson *Australia*

Triples
New Zealand

Fours
New Zealand

Third World Championships
Worthing, England 1977

Singles
E. Wilkie *New Zealand*

Pairs
H. Wong, E. Chok *Hong Kong*

Triples
J. Osborne, M. Pomeroy, E. Morgan *Wales*

Fours
L. Lucas, C. Hicks, M. Richardson, D. Jenkinson *Australia*

Fourth World Championships
Toronto, Canada 1981

Singles
N. Shaw *England*

Pairs
E. Bell, N. Allely *Ireland*

Triples
L. King, R. O'Donnell, L. Sadick *Hong Kong*

Fours
E. Fletcher, B. Stubbings, G. Thomas, M. Steele *England*

Fifth World Championships
Melbourne, Australia 1985

Singles
Gold Merle Richardson *Australia*
Silver Maraia Lum On *Fiji*
Bronze Rhoda Ryan *New Zealand*

Pairs
Gold Fay Craig, Merle Richardson *Australia*
Silver Maraia Lum On, Willow Fong *Fiji*
Bronze Norma Shaw, Jean Valls *England*

Triples
Gold Dorothy Roche, Norma Massey, Mavis Meadowcroft *Australia*
Silver Sandi Zakoske, Rae O'Donnell, Helen Wong *Hong Kong*
Bronze Rita Jones, Mair Jones, Linda Barker *Wales*

Fours
Gold Sarah Gourlay, Elizabeth Christie,, onnette Evans, Francis White *Scotland*
Silver Dorothy Roche, Fay Craig, Norma Massey, Mavis Meadowcroft *Australia*
Bronze Jean Valls, Brenda Atherton, Betty Stubbings, Mavis Steele *England*

Team Prize
Jean McKinnon, Fay Craig, Norma Massey, Mavis Meadowcroft, Merle Richardson, Dorothy Roche *Australia*

British Commonwealth Games

Singles

1930 1 Robert G. Colquhoun *England*
2 J. C. Thoms *South Africa*
3 W. Fielding *New Zealand*
1934 1 Robert Sprot *Scotland*
2 W. S. Macdonald *Canada*
3 A. Harvey *South Africa*
1938 1 Horace Harvey *South Africa*
2 Frank Livingstone *New Zealand*
3 Jack I. Low *Australia*
1950 1 James R. Pirret *New Zealand*
2 Albert E. Newton *Australia*
3 Lionel F. Garnett *Fiji*
1954 1 Ralph F. Hodges *S. Rhodesia*
2 James Pirret *New Zealand*
3 Arthur W. Saunders *South Africa*

1958 1 Phineas (Pinkie) Danilowitz *South Africa*
2 E. Percy Baker *England*
3 William J. R. Jackson *Rhodesia*
1962 1 David J. Bryant *England*
2 J. Watson Black *Scotland*
3 Alan D. Bradley *Rhodesia*
1970 1 David J. Bryant *England*
2 Neail Bryce *Zambia*
3 Roy Fulton *N. Ireland*
1974 1 David J. Bryant *England*
2 Clive White *Australia*
3 William Wood *Scotland*
1978 1 David J. Bryant *England*
2 Sydney John Snell *Australia*
3 John Russell Evans *Wales*
1982 1 William Wood *Scotland*
2 Robert Parrella *Australia*
3 Peter Belliss *New Zealand*

Pairs

1930 1 T. C. Hills and G. W. A. Wright *England*
2 W. Fielding and Peter McWhannell *New Zealand*
3 A. S. Reid and W. W. Moore *Canada*
1934 1 T. C. Hills and G. W. A. Wright *England*
2 W. G. Hutchinson and A. A. Langford *Canada*
3 T. R. Davies and S. Weaver *Wales*
1938 1 L. L. Macey and William Denison *New Zealand*
2 Phillip L. Hutton and Harold Mildren *Australia*
3 D. A. Adamson and J. R. Appleford *South Africa*
1950 1 Robert Henry and Evan P. Exelby *New Zealand*
2 W. Gibb and H. J. van Zyl *South Africa*
3 James E. Poulton and Leslie G. Brown *Fiji*
1954 1 William J. Rosbotham and Percy T. Watson *N. Ireland*
2 Samuel C. Gardiner and Richard L. Williams *Canada*
3 George B. Budge and John W. J. Carswell *Scotland*
1958 1 John M. Morris and Richard E. Pilkington *New Zealand*
2 John A. Myrdal and Rudolph J. J. van Vuuren *South Africa*
3 William G. Yuill and Hector Philp *Rhodesia*
1962 1 Robert L. McDonald and Hugh H. J. (Robbie) Robson *New Zealand*
2 Michael W. Purdon and Thomas F. Hamill *Scotland*
3 Charles S. Bradley and William J. R. Jackson *Rhodesia*
1970 1 Norman King and Peter A. Line *England*
2 Robert L. M. McDonald and Hugh H. J. (Robbie) Robson *New Zealand*
3 Jimmy Donnelly and Syd Thompson *N. Ireland*
1974 1 John Christie and Alex McIntosh *Scotland*
2 John C. Evans and Peter A. Line *England*
3 Phil Skoglund and Robert L. N. McDonald *New Zealand*
1978 1 Clementi Cecil Delgado and Eric John Liddell *Hong Kong*
2 William Walker Wood and Alexander McIntosh *Scotland*
3 James Arthur Morgan and Raymond Williams *Wales*
1982 1 John Watson, David Gourlay *Scotland*
2 Lyn Perkins, Spencer Wilshire *Wales*
3 Denis Dalton, Peter Rheuben *Australia*

Ladies Triples

1982 1 Florence Kennedy, Anna Bates, Margaret Mills *Zimbabwe*
2 Pearl Dymond, Joyce Osborne, Jennifer Simpson *New Zealand*
3 Mavis Steele, Betty Stubbings, Norma Shaw *England*

Fours

Year	1	2	3
1930	**1 ENGLAND**	**2 CANADA**	**3 SCOTLAND**
	E. F. Gudgeon	Jimmy Campbell	David Fraser
	J. Edney	Mitch Thomas	Thomas M. Chambers
	P. Hough	W. (Billy) Rae	William Campbell
	J. Frich	Harry J. Allen	John Orr
1934	**1 ENGLAND**	**2 N. IRELAND**	**3 SCOTLAND**
	R. Slater	Cecil Curran	James Brown
	P. D. Thomlinson	George Watson	James P. Morrison
	E. F. Gudgeon	Charlie Clawson	Charles W. Tait
	F. Biggin	Percy T. Watson	William S. Lowe
1938	**1 NEW ZEALAND**	**2 SOUTH AFRICA**	**3 AUSTRALIA**
	W. Bremner	J. G. Donaldson	Thomas Kinder
	William Whittaker	H. S. Walker	Aub Murray
	H. Alec Robertson	Samson	H. F. Murray
	E. Jury	Stevenson	Charlie H. McNeill
1950	**1 SOUTH AFRICA**	**2 AUSTRALIA**	**3 NEW ZEALAND**
	Harry Atkinson	John Cobley	Noel E. Jolly
	H. Currer	Len Knight	Fred T. Russell
	A. Blumberg	Charles Cordary	John A. Engebretsen
	N. S. Walker	James Cobley	Thomas T. Skoglund
1954	**1 SOUTH AFRICA**	**2 HONG KONG**	**3 S. RHODESIA**
	George L. Wilson	Jose A. da Luz	Alan D. Bradley
	John W. H. Anderson	Alfred E. Coates	Fred D. Hockin
	Frank N. Mitchell	Robert S. Gourley	Alex Pascoe
	Wilfred A. Randall	Raoul F. E. da Luz	Ronald H. Turner
1958	**1 ENGLAND**	**2 SOUTH AFRICA**	**3 RHODESIA**
	John H. Bettles	Wilfred A. Randall	Charles S. Bradley
	Norman King	E. S. G. Stuart	Alex Pascoe
	Walter F. Phillips	N. S. Walker	Ronald H. Turner
	George H. Scadgell	E. A. Williams	Basil Wells
1962	**1 ENGLAND**	**2 SCOTLAND**	**3 RHODESIA**
	George T. Fleming	Michael W. Purdon	Malcolm M. J. Bibb
	David J. Bryant	Thomas F. Hamill	Victor Blyth
	John L. Watson	J. Watson Black	John M. D. Milligan
	Sidney Drysdale	William Moore	Ronald H. Turner
1970	**1 HONG KONG**	**2 SCOTLAND**	**3 N. IRELAND**
	Clement C. Delgado	John Slight	John Higgins
	Abdul R. Kitchell	Norman Pryde	Edward Gordon
	Roberto E. da Silva	David G. Pearson	Harold Stevenson
	George A. Souza	Alex McIntosh	William Tate
1974	**1 NEW ZEALAND**	**2 AUSTRALIA**	**3 SCOTLAND**
	Kerry Clark	Robert King	Morgan Moffat
	Dave Baldwin	Errol Bungey	John Y. Marshall
	John Somerville	Errol G. Stewart	William G. Scott
	Gordon Jolly	Keith F. Poole	John McRae
1978	**1 HONG KONG**	**2 NEW ZEALAND**	**3 WALES**
	Kin Fun P. Chok	David C. Baldwin	Ellis G. Stanbury
	Majid Hassan Jr.	John E. Malcolm	Ian C. Sutherland
	Robert O. E. Desilva	D. Morgan Moffat	John D. H. Thomson
	Omar Kachong Dallah	Philip C. Skoglund	Gwyn F. Evans
1982	**1 AUSTRALIA**	**2 NEW ZEALAND**	**3 N. IRELAND**
	Robert Dobbins	Rowan Brassey	Samuel Allen
	Bert Sharp	Danny O'Connor	John McCloydhlin
	Don Sherman	Jim Scott	Frank Campbell
	Keith Poole	Morgan Moffat	Willie Watson

5 Crown Green Bowls

CROWN GREEN BOWLS is an intriguing, highly competitive version of the game, quite unlike any other and played, as the name suggests, on a surface which slopes down from a raised centre or 'crown', to the edges. The major ruling body is the British Crown Green Bowling Association which recommends that the height of the crown on a 40 yd × 40 yd (36.6 m × 36.6 m) green should be 12 in (306 mm) and pro rata on greens of other dimensions. Singles, 21 up and played with two bowls is the predominant mode of play and a high degree of skill is required successfully to negotiate the sloping surface. The jack, unlike that used in either IBB or EBF flat green codes is biased (full no. 2) and subject to stringent weight and size restrictions. Delivery point is fixed by a small round mat called a footer with a diameter of not less than 5 in (128 mm) and not more than 6 in (153 mm). At the commencement of the game, law no. 2 of the Association stipulates that the footer should be placed, by the leader, within 117 in (3 m) to either the right or left of the entrance of the green and 39 in (1 m) from the edge. The position of the entrance is determined as being 'as near the centre of any one side' and must be clearly marked. The idea of separate and distinct rinks as favoured by the flat green code is an alien concept to the free-spirited crown green player. With direction of play unhindered by such restrictions, however, it is not unusual, on greens where more than one match is in progress, to find bowls and jacks criss-crossing each other in a most hazardous manner and, at times, colliding, so necessitating a replayed delivery of either bowl or jack.

While the flat green bowler must concentrate on line and length, his crown green counterpart must also contend with the sloping surface. The crown green will always pull the bowl away from the raised centre and, with few greens conforming to the recently suggested standard, top bowlers will normally own several sets of woods, each of different bias and weight, which help them cope with a variety of conditions. Fortunately there are no restrictions on weight, bias or size of woods in the crown green game, the most popular being around 2 lb 12 oz in weight with a no. 2 full bias. However, the ability to match the pull of the green with the bias of bowl and jack requires a degree of skill not easily attained. Unlike the flat green bowler who must always keep the weightier side of the bowl toward the jack, the crown green player has a choice, depending on the position of the jack on the crowned surface. While the bias of the bowl remains constant, the slope of the green, unless a bowl is delivered over precisely the same route each time, will vary with each delivery. The mastery of this particular feature of the game is of vital importance and the bowler will switch bias in his attempts to utilize the inherent characteristics of the green. In the 'straight peg' shot the slope of the green is used in direct opposition to the bias of the bowl, resulting, if correctly judged, in an almost straight bowl. The 'round peg' shot finds the bowler using the slope of the green together with the bias of the bowl to increase its curving run to the jack.

The crown green code flourishes mainly in the North and North Midlands of England, in North Wales and the Isle of Man. Fifteen county associations are affiliated to the British Crown Green Bowling Association: Cheshire, Cumbria, Derbyshire, Greater Manchester, Lancashire, Merseyside, North Lancs and Fylde, North Midlands, Potteries, Shropshire, Staffordshire, South Yorkshire, Warwick and Worcestershire, Wales and Yorkshire. Many of these embrace both flat and crown green bowls and in one at least, Derbyshire, all three codes, IBB, Federation and Crown Green, are played. Unaffiliated clubs exist in Westmorland and an association formed in 1911 to cater for the thousands of bowlers active in public parks, the British Parks and Recreation Amateur Bowling Association, although playing to similar laws, remains to this day outside of the BCGBA.

Lancashire's amateur bowlers formed an association, the first of its kind, in 1888 with Cheshire as co-partner. This example was followed by Huddersfield and District in 1891, Yorkshire County in 1892, Manchester and District in 1896, Salford Parks in 1898 and Manchester and District Parks in 1904. In 1907 the formation of the British Crown Green Amateur Bowling Association (originally known as the British Crown Green Amateur County Association) gave the non-professional bowlers their first major unifying body. The professional crown green bowlers meanwhile had organized to protect their interests in 1905, with the owners of the greens on which they played already boasting their own association. In 1908, the amalgamation of these two bodies at a meeting in Manchester led to the formation of the Lancashire Professional Bowlers Association, its laws similar to those of the BCGABA but with games getting under way from the centre of the green and the leader having two chances at casting the jack to the required position or, in crown green parlance, casting a mark. In the professional game, bowlers formed what became known as 'The Panel' with only the most skilled and successful of the breed invited to join. The influence of this small but elite band was considerable as they drew large and enthusiastic audiences to their power base of Blackpool and greens at Wigan, Chorley and Bolton. Play took place on most days of the week and throughout the year. Betting was an accepted feature at these professional events and the bowlers, usually taking a percentage of the gate as their wage, were never short of vocal support.

Best known of today's crown green tournaments is the Waterloo Handicap, founded in 1907 and played annually on the famous green at the Waterloo Hotel in Blackpool. For many years, however, it was the Talbot Handicap, first staged at the same town's Talbot Hotel in 1873, that held pride of place in the crown green calendar. Such was the popularity of this Blue Riband event that entries rose from 84 in 1882 to 1000 in 1910, forcing the organizers to place a limit of 1024 on entrants. The Talbot green, now the site of a car park, became over the years something of a hallowed place. E. A. Lundy in his book *Crown Bowls* (Phoenix House, 1961) called it the 'Centre Court of Bowls' and recalled 'As at all historic places, and the "Talbot green" is one, an indefinable atmosphere prevails. It is as though the spirits of the past great ones are ever present, reviewing the scene of their personal triumphs, reluctant to leave it ever. The feeling, call it what you will, may be fostered in my own case by my great love of anything to do with bowls and bowlers, but except for visiting the Tower of London, nothing has impressed me quite as

much as my first visit to the "Talbot".' Joseph Fielding was the initial Talbot champion and the man to first register a double in the tournament was Dan Greenhalgh, a bowler of great repute, who won in 1888 and 1890. During the Second World War the Talbot green was out of commission and the tournament was transferred to Blackpool's strangely named No. 3 Hotel, and from there to the Raikes Hall Hotel where it remained until 1952 before returning to its original home, but by 1967 the site was already earmarked on somebody's plans and the old tournament began its final journey, back to the Raikes. Needless to say the 'Talbot' as a permanent fixture anywhere but at the Talbot green was bound to lose some of its charisma and in 1976 the essential backing from sponsors dried up and a piece of bowling action passed into history.

Although getting under way some 14 years after the 'Talbot', the Waterloo Handicap was soon to rival the older tournament in prestige and eventually outlived it. From 1907 on, the achievement most cherished among the top crown green bowlers was to win both tournaments in the same year, an honour which fell to an ex-Liverpool and England footballer, Jack Cox of Blackpool who pulled off the Talbot-Waterloo double in 1925. The Waterloo was played to the rules of the Lancashire Professional BA until 1981 when the organizer, Jack Lee, brought the tournament firmly under the laws of the British Crown Green Bowling Association. The way for such a move was cleared in 1973, when, under the clear-sighted guidance of its new Secretary, Eddie Elson, the code's major body dropped the word Amateur from its title.

The British Crown Green Individual Merit Competition is, virtually, the national championship of the crown green game. Entry to the final stages of this competition, which was instituted in 1910, is by performance in county merit competitions with selection 'strictly in order of merit'. No competitor is allowed to play on a green of which he is a playing member or compete for more than one county. E. Peers of Staffordshire was the first winner of the individual merit but it was Lancashire's Joe Gleave who pulled off the first trio of merit successes with victories in 1923, 1928 and 1934. The Parks Association run its own merit competition dating from 1911 and in which Yorkshire's Donald Haigh clocked up an impressive record over a ten-year span, with victories in 1948, 1951, 1954 and 1958. The majority of today's top performers however owe allegiance to the British Crown Green Bowling Association and in 1983 Stan Frith of Cheshire completed a notable trio of victories by winning

Eddie Elson, a major influence for progress in the crown green code. (Courtesy Eddie Elson).

the BCGBA Merit, the Waterloo Handicap and the Embassy Champions Trophy.

In recent years a number of crown green bowlers have taken to the flat green indoor game during the winter months. Big-money invitation tournaments held in crown green country have found the likes of Noel Burrows, Brian Duncan and Stan Frith giving a reasonable account of themselves before succumbing to the greater tactical awareness of the flat green stars. Before dismissing the future prospects of the crown green bowlers in this alien world, it would be as well to remember that Burrows, a past winner of the Waterloo, the Embassy Champions Trophy and the BCGBA Merit, reached the final stages of the British Indoor Bowling Association National Singles Competition in 1985, losing 19–21 in the quarter-finals to the eventual winner, Tony Allcock of Gloucestershire.

An inter-county competition for the Crosfield Cup is played between teams of 24 bowlers, 12 playing at home and 12 away in matches taking place on the same day. No player is permitted to take part in a match played on the green of any club of which he is a member; 'home' teams however are allowed to practise on the selected green up to the day of the match, and from 2.00 p.m. until 2.15 p.m. on the match day itself 'visitors' get one half-hour period to play themselves in, but all practice

Talbot Handicap

1887	T. Salisbury	1932	Jas. Heyes
1888	D. Greenhalgh	1933	T. Turner
1889	J. Bowden	1934	H. Hardman
1890	D. Greenhalgh	1935	H. Bury
1891	H. Rutter	1936	W. Grace
1892	Wm. Balmer	1937	G. Lomax
1893	John Peace	1938	W. Molyneux
1894	Thos. Berry	1939	(Abandoned)
1895	Gerard Hart	1940	W. J. Wilcock
1896	R. Mather	1941	J. Edmondson
1897	Thos. Meadows	1942	Geo. Croker
1898	Thos. Hayes	1943	F. Gillett
1899	John Peace	1944	W. Ashton
1900	Ed. Barton	1945	J. Jolly
1901	James Platt	1946	A. Raby
1902	James Ward	1947	R. Thomas
1903	W. Fairhurst	1948	J. H. Hill
1904	C. Farrington	1949	J. Molyneux
1905	M. Sharples	1950	J. Wolstenccroft
1906	W. Taylor	1951	W. Parr
1907	J. Bagot	1952	J. Timmins
1908	S. Massey	1953	J. Molyneux
1909	W. H. Law	1954	H. Wallwork
1910	R. Hart	1955	W. Simm
1911	F. Threlfall	1956	J. Rothwell
1912	Rd. Birchall	1957	J. E. Ball
1913	H. Southern	1958	R. Mercer
1914	J. Bromilow	1959	W. H. Frost
1915	T. Richardson	1960	W. Dalton
1916	R. Johnson	1961	W. Turner
1917	G. F. Hampson	1962	W. Dalton
1918	Eli Yates	1963	R. Kellett
1919	Ed. Whiteside	1964	J. Kirby
1920	L. Banks	1965	A. Milnes
1921	F. Threlfall	1966	S. Priestley
1922	W. Finch	1967	W. Dawber
1923	J. Farnworth	1968	F. Whitehead
1924	Tom Rose	1969	R. Peat
1925	Jack Cox	1970	K. Illingworth
1926	G. Beswick	1971	G. Rigby
1927	T. Monks	1972	W. Dalton
1928	G. Beswick	1973	C. E. Jackson
1929	W. R. Hardy	1974	B. Duncan
1930	H. Walkden	1975	S. Buckley
1931	R. Pendlebury		

must cease ten minutes prior to commencement of play. The early years of this competition were dominated by the might of Lancashire and Cheshire. As a combination they won the first inter-county competition in 1908 and repeated that success in 1909, on each occasion defeating Yorkshire in the final. The following 11 years saw the two, now playing as separate counties, share the title of county champions between them, Cheshire notching up a further six victories to Lancashire's five. Yorkshire, over the same period, were finalists on no less than six occasions eventually breaking the Cheshire–Lancs monopoly with a well deserved victory in 1922. The Embassy Champions Trophy and the Yorkshire Bank/*Daily Express* Crown King Championship are hotly contested, if relatively recent additions to the crown green calendar, both played on the Waterloo green. Perhaps more important to the future of the game however is the Junior Merit Competition, first contested in 1974 when J. Garbutt of Yorkshire defeated S. Leah 21–20 in the final. The Junior Merit is open to bowlers between the ages of 12 and 18 years and its value was underlined in 1982 when N. Cranston, Junior Merit winner in 1977, won the Embassy Champions Trophy beating the experienced Bernard Marrow 21–16.

Despite the code's determinedly 'macho' image, the ladies are taking to the crown green game with increasing enthusiasm. While, at present at least, there is no organizing body in women's crown green, various tournaments are in existence with, no doubt, the £3000 Waterloo Ladies Handicap for one to go for. The popularity of this event is already such that the 1984 entries numbered 1200, and finals day at the hotel attracted almost 2500 spectators who saw Liz Chapman from Preston, a former All England Ladies Champion, take the title.

Individual Merit Competition

1910 E. Peers *Staffordshire* beat J. Valentine *Lancashire* 21–11
1911 J. Stead *Yorkshire* beat G. Ashcroft *Lancashire* 21–18
1912 T. Dale *Cheshire* beat I. Rosa *Staffordshire* 21–12
1913 J. Chesters *Cheshire* beat J. Hart *Lancashire* 21–19
1914 A. Robinson *Staffordshire* beat P. Kilner *Yorkshire* 21–17
1915 J. Charnock *Lancashire* beat A. Robinson *Staffordshire* 21–19
1916 S. Sackville *Lancashire* beat J. Garthwaite *Yorkshire* 21–14
1917 J. Gough *Staffordshire* beat H. Parkin *Yorkshire* 21–14
1918 T. B. Burgess *Cheshire* beat P. Berry *Lancashire* 21–16
1919 J. Charnock *Lancashire* beat J. Bratt *Cheshire* 21–18
1920 W. Twist *Lancashire* beat J. Fort *Yorkshire* 21–19
1921 F. Dickinson *Yorkshire* beat J. Bradburn *Staffordshire* 21–11
1922 John Gleave *Lancashire* beat S. Davies *Staffordshire* 21–20
1923 Joe Gleave *Lancashire* beat E. Blackledge *Lancashire* 21–16
1924 E. Blackledge *Lancashire* beat J. A. Appleyard *Yorkshire* 21–13
1925 F. Bentley *Staffordshire* beat J. Walker *Lancashire* 21–13
1926 A. Booth *Yorkshire* beat W. J. Wilcock *Lancashire* 21–16
1927 P. Ainscough *Cheshire* beat E. Percival *Cheshire* 21–7
1928 Joe Gleave *Lancashire* beat W. J. Wilcock *Lancashire* 21–15
1929 J. Gough *Staffordshire* beat A. Bintcliffe *Yorkshire* 21–20
1930 G. A. Fielding *Yorkshire* beat S. Moss *Staffordshire* 21–11
1931 J. Fort *Yorkshire* beat L. Pickles *Yorkshire* 21–16
1932 C. Garside *Derbyshire* beat S. Hulse *Cheshire* 21–14
1933 J. Eyes *Cheshire* beat L. Holmes *Staffordshire* 21–18
1934 Joe Gleave *Lancashire* beat F. Clark *Lancashire* 21–18
1935 J. W. Pickering *Shropshire* beat W. Rhodes *Cheshire* 21–19
1936 G. Howells *Staffordshire* beat A. Skeath *Lancashire* 21–18
1937 W. Garrard *Cheshire* beat J. Metcalfe *Yorkshire* 21–9
1938 J. Davies *Cheshire* beat H. Hill *Lancashire* 21–10
1939 W. H. Garside *Cheshire* beat R. G. Meyrick *Shropshire* 21–16
1946 B. Longbottom *Yorkshire* beat A. Wells *Lancashire* 21–9
1947 H. King *Lancashire* beat H. Smith *Staffordshire* 21–14
1948 R. G. Meyrick *Shropshire* beat H. Pennington *Lancashire* 21–15
1949 A. Bebbington *Cheshire* beat J. J. A. Price *Shropshire* 21–14
1950 J. Barnsley *Warwick & Worcester* beat H. Heppenstall *Lancashire* 21–10
1951 J. Pilling *Lancashire* beat W. Worthington *Lancashire* 21–16
1952 A. A. Shore *Warwick & Worcester* beat E. Forrester *North Wales* 21–16
1953 W. Slater *Staffordshire* beat F. Clark *Lancashire* 21–12
1954 N. Norris *Cheshire* beat H. Fairhurst *Lancashire* 21–19
1955 H. Burgess *Cheshire* beat S. L. Ball *Yorkshire* 21–9
1956 E. Fish *Shropshire* beat W. Baldwin *N. Midlands* 21–14
1957 N. Hardman *Lancashire* beat R. Cross *Cheshire* 21–16
1958 C. Littlehales *North Wales* beat J. Wakefield *Staffordshire* 21–12

1959 E. Ashton *North Wales* beat T. J. Tickle *Lancashire* 21–8
1960 R. W. Hodson *Staffordshire* beat J. Howells *Staffordshire* 21–12
1961 R. G. Meyrick *Shropshire* beat E. Ashton *North Wales* 21–16
1962 R. G. Meyrick *Shropshire* beat T. Knott *Lancashire* 21–20
1963 F. Goulden *Lancashire* beat C. A. West *Cheshire* 21–13
1964 R. Green *Yorkshire* beat H. Gibson *Yorkshire* 21–15
1965 W. Baldwin *N. Midlands* beat G. Matthews *Yorkshire* 21–19
1966 R. G. Meyrick *Shropshire* beat D. I. Lawrence *Shropshire* 21–12
1967 A. A. Shore *Warwick & Worcester* beat J. Openshaw *Cheshire* 21–20
1968 R. Oakes *Cheshire* beat P. Spencer *Staffordshire* 21–13
1969 A. Johnson *Derbyshire* beat K. C. Birtwhistle *Cheshire* 21–18
1970 A. C. Dowley *Shropshire* beat M. Hinton *Shropshire* 21–19
1971 A. F. Poole *Shropshire* beat J. Openshaw *Cheshire* 21–6
1972 D. Mercer *Cheshire* beat D. J. Ripley *Yorkshire* 21–9
1973 W. Line *Cheshire* beat G. Wainwright *Shropshire* 21–15
1974 F. Whitehead *Yorkshire* beat A. F. Poole *Shropshire* 21–15
1975 R. Wilby *Yorkshire* beat C. Bordley *N. Midlands* 21–12
1976 E. N. Burrows *Lancashire* beat D. Blackburn *Yorkshire* 21–16
1977 R. Edkins *Warwick & Worcester* beat C. Bordley *N. Midlands* 21–20
1978 K. Widdowson *Derbyshire* beat B. Yardley *Cheshire* 21–16
1979 J. Hunt *Wales* beat W. Wilson *Wales* 21–5
1980 J. Hadfield *Lancashire* beat P. Atkin *Derbyshire* 21–10
1981 I. Ross *South Yorkshire* beat A. Thompson *Yorkshire* 21–15
1982 I. Bottomley *Yorkshire* beat M. Evans *Staffordshire* 21–8
1983 S. F. Frith *Cheshire* beat D. Monks *South Yorkshire* 21–7
1984 M. Leach *North Lancashire & Fylde* beat V. Seddon *Lancashire* 21–11
1985 T. Moss *Birmingham* beat B. Duncan *Lancashire* 21–18

Junior Merit

1974 J. Garbutt *Yorkshire* beat S. Leah *Lancashire* 21–20
1975 A. J. Matthews *Staffordshire* beat K. Robinson *Potteries* 21–20
1976 G. Jones *Wales* beat E. Burdett *North Midlands* 21–6
1977 N. Cranston *Yorkshire* beat M. Roach *Lancashire* 21–15
1978 R. Towle *Derbyshire* beat P. Varney *North Midlands* 21–10
1979 R. Crawshaw *Cheshire* beat P. Richardson *Lancashire* 21–15
1980 M. Burdon *North Midlands* beat T. Yardley *Warwick & Worcester* 21–10
1981 M. Halliwell *Wales* beat G. Wallis *South Yorkshire* 21–12
1982 D. Hales *Yorkshire* beat M. Shaw *Merseyside* 21–11
1983 C. Parker *Lancashire* beat J. Gommersall *Merseyside* 21–16
1984 A. Spragg *Derbyshire* beat K. Graham *Cheshire* 21–9
1985 A. Buckley *Gr. Manchester* beat D. Hales *Yorkshire* 21–10

Inter-County Championship Competition

1908 Lancs. and Cheshire	1928 Lancashire	1952 Lancashire	1970 Cheshire
1909 Lancs. and Cheshire	1929 Staffordshire	1953 Cheshire	1971 Cheshire
1910 Cheshire	1930 Yorkshire	1954 Lancashire	1972 Lancashire
1911 Cheshire	1931 Yorkshire	1955 Cheshire	1973 Cheshire
1912 Lancashire	1932 Staffordshire	1956 Lancashire	1974 Shropshire
1913 Cheshire	1933 Lancashire	1957 Yorkshire	1975 Lancashire
1914 Lancashire	1934 Lancashire	1958 Lancashire	1976 Warwick & Worcester
1915 Cheshire	1935 Lancashire	1959 Lancashire	1977 Lancashire
1916 Lancashire	1936 Yorkshire	1960 Lancashire	1978 Lancashire
1919 Lancashire	1937 Yorkshire	1961 Lancashire	1979 Lancashire
1920 Cheshire	1938 Staffordshire	1962 Lancashire	1980 Yorkshire
1921 Cheshire	1939 Cheshire	1963 Lancashire	1981 Greater Manchester
1922 Lancashire	1946 Cheshire	1964 Warwick & Worcester	1982 Potteries
1923 Yorkshire	1947 Lancashire	1965 Lancashire	1983 South Yorkshire
1924 Cheshire	1948 Lancashire	1966 Lancashire	1984 Lancashire
1925 Yorkshire	1949 Yorkshire	1967 Cheshire	1985 Yorkshire
1926 Lancashire	1950 Cheshire	1968 Yorkshire	
1927 Yorkshire	1951 Lancashire	1969 Cheshire	

The Waterloo Handicap

1907 Jas. Rothwell *West Leigh*	1951 J. Waterhouse *Middleton*
1908 Geo. Beatty *Burnley*	1952 L. Thompson *St Helens*
1909 Tom Meadows *West Leigh*	1953 B. Kelly *Hyde*
1910 No Handicap	1954 B. Kelly *Hyde*
1911 John Peace *Huddersfield*	1955 J. Heyes *Aspull*
1912 Thos. Lowe *Weshoughton*	1956 J. Sumner *Blackpool*
1913 Gerard Hart *Blackrod*	1957 W. Lacy *Wigan*
1914 John Rothwell *Atherton*	1958 F. Salisbury *Preston*
1915 W. Fairhurst *Standish*	1959 W. Dawber *Wrightington*
1916 J. Parkinson *Oldham*	1960 H. Bury *Blackpool*
1917 Geo. Barnes *Westhoughton*	1961 J. Featherstone *Leigh*
1918 W. Simms *Aspull*	1962 J. Collier *Pendleton*
1919 Len Moss *Denton*	1963 T. Mayor *Bolton*
1920 E. Whiteside *Lytham*	1964 W. B. Heinkey *Birmingham*
1921 J. Bagot *South Shore*	1965 J. Pepper *Salford*
1922 W. A. Smith *Old Trafford*	1966 R. Collier *Little Hulton*
1923 J. Martin *Westhoughton*	1967 Eric Ashton *Towyn*
1924 Rowland Hill *Brynn*	1968 Billy Bennett *Warrington*
1925 Jack Cox *Blackpool*	1969 G. T. Underwood *Blackpool*
1926 T. Roscoe *Blackpool*	1970 Jack Everitt *Willenhall*
1927 H. Waddecar *Midge Hall*	1971 J. Bradbury *Romiley*
1928 T. Whittle *Ashton-in-M*	1972 N. Burrows *Withington*
1929 Chas. Halpin *Blackpool*	1973 A. Murray *Partington*
1930 J. Chadwick *Westhoughton*	1974 W. Houghton *Freckleton*
1931 A. Gleave *Warrington*	1975 J. Collen *Bury*
1932 T. E. Booth *West Didsbury*	1976 K. Illingworth *Blackpool*
1933 A. Ogden *Failsworth*	1977 L. Barrett *Whitefield*
1934 W. Derbyshire *Burnley*	1978 A. Murray *Partington*
1935 C. Roberts *Fearnhead*	1979 B. Duncan *Leigh*
1936 H. Yates *Preston*	1980 V. Lee *Blackpool*
1937 A. King *Windermere*	1981 R. Nicholson *Brighouse*
1938 J. W. Whitter *Standish*	1982 D. Mercer *Stockport*
1939 Abandoned	1983 S. Frith *Weaverham*
1940 H. Holden *Blackpool*	1984 S. Ellis *Blackpool*
1941 W. J. Wilcock *St Helens*	1985 T. Johnstone *Manchester*
1942 T. Bimson *Hardhorn*	
1943 S. Ivell *Little Hulton*	
1944 T. Tinker *Huddersfield*	
1945 W. Grace *Blackpool*	
1946 C. Parkinson *Pemberton*	
1947 W. Dalton *Fleetwood*	
1948 A. E. Ringrose *Bradford*	
1949 J. Egan *Birkdale*	
1950 H. Finch *Blackpool*	

Stan Frith completed a unique hat trick of crown green victories in 1983 winning the Waterloo Handicap, the All-England competition and the Champion of Champions. (*Bowlers World*).

Yorkshire Bank/Daily Express

1975 H. Pennington *Lancashire* beat A Murray *Cheshire* 21–7

1976 A. F. Poole *Shropshire* beat E. Davies *Wales* 21–12

1977 M. Leach *Lancashire* beat J. Hunt *Wales* 21–16

1978 K. Burrows *Cheshire* beat S. V. Ellis *Lancashire* 21–6

1979 J. Hunt *Wales* beat A. F. Poole *Shropshire* 21–18

1980 J. Hunt *Wales* beat A. R. Green *Wales* 21–17

1981 M. Gilpin *Cumbria* beat L. Higginbottom *Lancashire* 21–20

1982 M. Walker *Potteries* beat D. Rawlins *North Midlands* 21–16

1983 R. B. Conway *Wales* beat K. Strutt *Greater Manchester* 21–16

1984 N. Burrows *Greater Manchester* beat P. Atkin *Derbyshire* 21–8

1985 V. Lee *Blackpool* beat R. Coombes *Potteries* 21–18

Embassy Championship

1974 J. Hadfield *Lancashire* beat B. Warr *British Parks* 21–10
1975 J. Collen *Waterloo* beat A. F. Poole *Shropshire* 21–20
1976 A. F. Poole *Shropshire* beat K. Beaman *Staffordshire* 21–19
1977 C. Bordley *North Midlands* beat J. Andrews *Cheshire* 21–11
1978 N. Burrows *St Bruno* beat K. Burrows *Hepworth/D. Express* 21–14
1979 T. Turner *Midlands Masters* beat A. Murray *Cheshire* 21–20
1980 N. Burrows *Man. Evening News* beat V. Lee *Waterloo* 21–16

1981 D. Ellis *Cheshire* beat R. Nicholson *Waterloo* 21–18
1982 N. Cranston *Yorkshire* beat B. Marrow *Thwaites Classic* 21–16
1983 S. F. Frith *B.C.G.B.A.* beat N. Burrows *Greater Manchester* 21–20
1984 A. Poole *Shropshire* beat K. Fletcher *Isle of Man* 21–13

In 1985 Greenall Whitley replaced Embassy as tournament sponsors.

1985 R. Hitchen *Yorkshire* beat N. Burrows *Greater Manchester* 21–17

Noel Burrows (left) has only just delivered his bowl but Stan Frith has seen enough to know that he has won the 1983 Embassy Champions trophy at Blackpool's Waterloo Hotel. (*Bowlers World*).

Glossary of Crown Bowls Terms

Barracking remarks or criticisms made by spectators.

BCGABA British Crown Green Amateur Bowling Association.

Bias the heavy side of a wood or jack.

Block another word for the jack.

Blue-eye a wood which finishes touching the jack.

BPRABA British Parks and Recreation Amateur Bowling Association.

Bobby a wood effectively blocking the way to the jack.

Button the centre of the green and/or the marker used to show this.

Cut the ditch or gully round the edge of the green.

Dead end an end which is void.

Dead wood a wood from which no points can be scored as the result of rule infringement by the bowler.

Dry rub an expression to describe a game in which one player fails to score.

End the process and completion of play over a mark.

Falling land the sloping parts of any green which cause the jack and woods to fall against the bias.

Feet the cry to warn players of approaching woods.

Fire another word for strike.

Flags the 4-yard markers on the green edges.

Grandmother another word for luck.

Heavy or slow a slow running green.

In-off a wood which is diverted to the jack by striking another.

Jack header a wood in front of and touching the jack.

Length correct judgement of distance from mat to jack.

Mark a jack bowled 21 yards or over constitutes a mark.

Mat the rubber on which players must stand whilst delivering.

Narrow wood a wood bowled inside the line of the jack.

Nothing for short an expression meaning short woods are useless and that the bowler should make sure his woods reach the 'end'.

Pan all four woods of partners to count in a foursome.

Pull the working of the bias.

Quick wood a wood which is thrown at a speed greater than that required to reach the jack in order to displace jack or woods.

Rabbit the weakest member of a team.

Round peg when the jack and woods are bowled with the bias facing away from the crown.

Scratching time the time by which players must present themselves at the green or be disqualified.

Short a wood failing to reach the jack.

Stopper another word for a bobby.

Straight peg a jack or wood thrown out with the bias facing the crown.

Tapes measures.

Thin another word for a narrow wood.

Trickle the running on of a wood after seeming about to stop, usually on a fast green.

Through a wood which runs beyond the jack.

Wide a wood delivered outside the line of the jack.

Wobbler a wood not delivered true.

Brian Duncan (centre) in action during a BBC *Top Crown* tournament. His partner Keith Fletcher is on the extreme right. (*Bowlers World*).

Lyons find a use for the old crocks Part of a sports complex built as a war memorial in 1920, the Lyon's BC green at Sudbury Hill, Middlesex has a drainage base of broken crockery garnered from the Lyons tea shops and Corner Houses. Frank Fullijames, the club's honorary treasurer, reported that following a cloudburst which had interrupted a 70th anniversary match against the Middlesex County BC, the green was perfectly playable within ten minutes.

Tony Allcock

The rich talents and tactical nous which have made Tony Allcock one of the most respected bowlers of modern times surfaced at Mortlake in 1972. Allcock and Paul Clark, at 17 Leicestershire county pairs champions, reached the third round of the EBA national finals before losing 21–17 to the eventual champions, Charlie Price and Ray Dawes.

Two years later Allcock lost to David Cutler in the final of the National Junior Singles but was back, collecting the title in 1975, making it a double in 1978 and completing his hat-trick in 1981.

Indoor international honours came in 1976, outdoor two years later, but it was in the 1980 World Championships at Frankston, Australia that Allcock made his first notable impact. Selected for the triples with Jim Hobday and David Bryant he played his part in a famous English success which made him, at 24, the youngest ever gold medal winner in the history of the championships.

There have been many Allcock success stories since then. Undefeated as an England skip, he entered 1984 in tremendous singles form winning the Prudential Under-31's title, the Daihatsu Welsh Classic and the Lombard Champion of Champions. It was to be as a skip, however, that he experienced glory that year. With David Bryant he won silver in the pairs at the World Championships in Aberdeen, a fine performance but merely a prelude to the superb tactical battle he was to wage in the final of the fours, skipping George Turley, Julian

Haines and John Bell. Allcock's uncanny ability and concentration enabled him to conjure up any shot required at precisely the right pace in appalling conditions, giving his men an edge over the strong New Zealand rink skipped by Phil Skoglund, and bringing England its lone gold medal of the Championships. The year ended with Allcock embroiled in another epic struggle in the final of the CIS UK Indoor Singles. This he lost to Terry Sullivan of Wales, but nine thrilling sets, played out before a television audience of 7.2 million, did wonders for the game's image.

In 1985 Allcock represented England in the Australian Mazda Masters, beating world champion, Peter Belliss and Willie Wood before succumbing to Kenny Williams in the final by the odd shot. Returning home he repaired the one omission in his record by winning a major national title, the Prudential EIBA singles, and followed that by taking the Croft Original Open with revenge over Terry Sullivan.

Tony Allcock, born at Thurmaston, Leicestershire on 11 June 1955, began playing bowls at the age of ten under the watchful eye of his parents Ernie, a Leicestershire Middleton Cup player and Joan, an England International. At 30, with the game entering a crucial stage in its development, he may soon find himself at a crossroads in his career. There is no limit to what he can achieve given his skills and temperament but, as head of a Social Education Centre for Mentally Handicapped Adults in Gloucestershire, he has other commitments which will weigh heavily in any decision concerning his future.

Concentration and determination have helped Tony Allcock rise to the very top level of bowls. (S. J. Line).

E. Percy Baker

Edwin Percy Baker was, by any standards, one of the great men of bowls. By winning the English National Singles title in 1932, 1946, 1952 and 1955 he created a remarkable record only surpassed by David Bryant in 1973.

Percy Baker, four times the English national singles champion, in action on Watney's green at Mortlake. (C. M. Jones).

Born at Weston-Super-Mare, Somerset on 18 July 1895, Baker, a photographer by trade, was persuaded onto the green in 1921 after playing billiards with members of the Poole Park BC, a club he subsequently joined and remained faithful to throughout his career. Two years after taking up the game he won the club handicap and in 1931 recorded his first victory in the club singles, a tournament he was to win no less than 22 times. The Dorset singles also fell to him in 1931, the first of 11 county singles

titles over a 37-year period. He played as skip in Dorset's Middleton Cup side from 1927 to 1969 taking part in the only Dorset victory in the competition in 1938. International honours came in 1933 but it was not until 1949 that he was able firmly to establish his place, captaining England in 1950 and stringing together a run of 11 years under the English badge.

Although professing little time for tournament play away from home, Baker played in the Test Matches against South Africa in 1948 and Australia in 1950 and won a silver medal in the Commonwealth Games held at Cardiff in 1958. Competing in the Games soon after a serious illness, Baker recovered from a disappointing 21–14 defeat by Pinky Danilowitz of South Africa to register

a number of important wins including a 21–10 thrashing of the much vaunted Australian, Glyn Bosisto. But an unexpected 21–18 defeat by Bill Jackson of Rhodesia ruined any chances of a gold medal and, by a strange quirk of fate, Baker and Jackson played off for the silver the very next day, but this time the scores were reversed, Baker winning 21–18.

In 1971, at the grand age of 76, Percy Baker, his elegant style and gentlemanly demeanour intact, registered his final tournament success by winning the Bournemouth Open Pairs, one of the toughest open competitions around. Sadly in poor health and totally blind, he celebrated his 90th birthday in 1985 at his home in Poole, safe in the knowledge that his reputation in a game he grew to love was as high as ever.

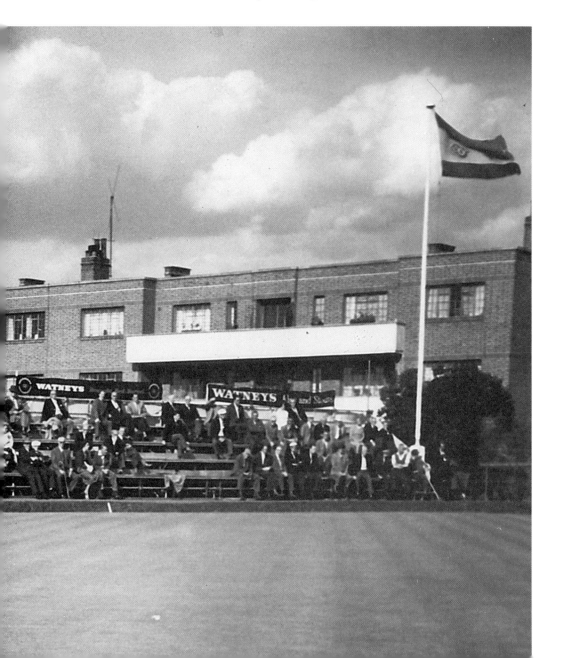

Jim Baker

On the green Jim Baker, born into a bowling family in Belfast on 18 February 1958, speaks quietly and carries a very big stick indeed. His performances as an Irish skip reveal that ruthless streak so essential for sporting success and once he gets his nose in front he is the very devil to catch.

Runner-up in the World Indoor Singles Championship in 1982, he won the title two years later defeating the youthful giant-killer, Nigel Smith with a dazzling display of the bowling arts. Later that year Baker skipped Stan Espie and Sammy Allen to a triples gold medal at the World Championships, revealing a knowledge of the game well beyond his 26 years.

'Tough to Beat' – Jim Baker. (Duncan Cubitt, *Bowls International*).

James Green Baker began his bowling career in the short-mat game at the age of 12, joining the Carrs Glen BC one year later. His first achievement of note came in the 1978 Bangor Open Pairs, won in the company of a cousin, Cecil Worthington. Seeking to raise the standard of his game, Baker joined the Private Greens League club Cliftonville and won representative honours for the league after only two matches. In 1979 he took the next step by making his international debut in both the indoor and outdoor Irish teams and met the two men he credits as being his main inspirations, Irish internationals Jimmy Donnelly and 'Big' Syd Thompson. In 1981 he became Irish indoor singles champion and confirmed a growing reputation by adding the British Isles title to an already impressive crop of honours.

Jim Baker is the most successful Irish bowler of modern times, a man whose natural modesty and quiet manner completely belie the attacking ferocity of his play. He is, for many observers, the complete bowler, with all the right shots and the ideal temperament. At 28 years of age Baker is already an experienced sportsman and there is no reason to believe he has reached anything like his peak. He is now beginning to reap some of the rewards of fame and in 1984 had the honour of seeing Ireland's second indoor stadium bear his name.

One of the quiet Irishman's finest performances came in the final of the 1985 UK Singles championship at Preston. After losing the first two sets to Scotsman John Watson, Baker, employing a heady mixture of power and finesse, completely dominated his opponent to win the next five, thus gaining revenge over the man who beat him in the 1982 World Indoor Singles final.

Jim Baker acknowledges a standing ovation after his success in the 1984 Embassy World indoor singles at Coatbridge, Scotland. (Duncan Cubitt, *Bowls International*).

John Bell

England's 1984 World Championship fours gold medal was undeniably the result of a supreme team effort. As skip, Tony Allcock, at his most brilliant and audacious best, was able to wrest the initiative from the grasp of tough New Zealander, Phil Skoglund, in the crucial middle period of the match, a task made possible by the dominant play of John Bell at number three.

Opposite John Bell unleashes one of his size seven Henselites. (S. J. Line).

Below 'Big John' celebrates after his 1984 British Isles singles victory. (Alan North, Gateway Building Society).

Undeterred by appalling conditions, Bell responded to Allcock's instructions with pinpoint accuracy and complete mastery of a rain-soaked green producing superb trail shots on the fourth and tenth ends to convert losing situations into winning positions. But it was on the 16th that he ensured the gold medal by running the jack away from the New Zealand shot bowl and into the ditch to give England two shots. Allcock then drew two more with stunning accuracy to score his rink's only four of the match, and although only able to muster two further singles, England's quartet had done enough, winning by 18 shots to 17.

John Nicholson Bell – 'Big John' – born on 14 December 1947 in Wigton, Cumbria is a natural ball player, winning county schoolboy honours at cricket and later playing full-back in Cumbria's rugby union side. Introduced to bowls at the age of 12 by his father, a county bowler, Bell's first taste of the game's big time came in 1966 when, still a schoolboy, he qualified for the final stages of the National Singles Championships. One year later he won his county fours and was launched on a career in which he has become not only highly successful but a man regarded by bowlers at all levels with something much deeper than just respect.

On the green this friendly, affable man dominates by his very presence; he is after all a 'big fella', but his prowess with those huge number 7 Henselites is equally impressive and an acute tactical awareness makes him always difficult to beat. It was this combination which enabled him to win the premier prize of the English game, the EBA national singles in 1983, and the manner in which he manoeuvred his opponent, Kevin Bone, into playing his weaker backhand in the final was an education in itself. John Bell's game however encompasses much more than just singles play. He is, to date, the most successful current English skip indoor and out and in that position won the EBA Triples in 1976, the EBA Top Fours in 1983, the Newcastle (NSW) International Pairs in 1978 and a host of other county and open tournaments.

There is more to bowls than winning, though, and John credits his late father, Jack, with teaching him how to lose with dignity and sportsmanship. Those lessons were never more important than in 1984 when success in the EIBA singles at Hartlepool would have earned Bell the distinction of holding both indoor and outdoor national titles at the same time. It was not to be after demolishing David Bryant 21–12 in the semis he lost 21–19 to Andy Ross in the final, and his immediate remark – 'I didn't deserve to win that one, Andy played well and I didn't' – effectively cloaked what must have been bitter disappointment. Salve came later that year at Aberdeen, revealing another Bell quality – the ability to bounce back with a vengeance. The 1985 Gateway Masters found him embroiled in one of the finest matches of his career, a classic encounter with Tony Allcock played in good humour throughout but with no quarter offered or given by either man. After taking an early lead, Bell was eventually forced to call upon his drive to save the game on two occasions but, at 20-all, the big Cumbrian ended matters with a precise draw to the jack. John never quite reached those heights again in the tournament but his match with Allcock is one which will be remembered for a long time for the variety and precision of shots employed, and for the spirit in which it was played.

Above The Mighty Mite
– Ronnie Jones
(Canada) during the
1985 Gateway Masters.
(*World Bowls*).
Above right David
Cutler (left) and Steve
Halmai. (*World Bowls*).
Scotland's David
Gourlay urges a bowl
into the head during the
1985 Home
International series at
Worthing's Beach
House Park. (*World
Bowls*).

Above Billy McKelvey (Ireland). (*World Bowls*).
Left Checking out the opposition – Sammy Allen (left) and Jim Baker (Ireland) survey the scene at the 1985 Gateway Home International series. (*World Bowls*).
Below Andy Thomson (Kent and England). (*World Bowls*).

Above Bill Hobart indicates the way in. (*Author*).
Above left EBA national singles champion 1985 –
Ron Keating of Devon. (*World Bowls*).

The Bowling Green,
Adelaide, 1906. From
an early postcard.
Right The David Bryant
Bowls Centre, Cabrera,
Spain. (*World Bowls*).

Several Commonwealth nations have issued stamps
depicting bowls but, so far, not the British Isles.

98

Peter Belliss

After introducing their son and heir Peter to bowls as a toddler of eight Mr and Mrs Belliss of Wanganui, New Zealand, waited 11 years before he joined the local Aramaho Club. The wait was worth it! In 1984, at the age of 33, Peter Belliss won the game's premier honour, the World Championship singles gold medal on the greens of Aberdeen in the most dramatic fashion.

Peter Belliss – the world champion from Wanganui. (Alan North, Gateway Building Society).

Belliss in action during the 1984 Gateway Masters. His opponent in the background is Frank Souza of the USA. (*World Bowls*).

During his first year at Aramaho, Belliss won the Junior Club Championship and in 1973 reached the semi-finals of the New Zealand fours. Two years later he was semi-finalist in the National Singles and won the Invitation Pairs at Matamata. His first big singles victory came in a top 'Masters' event at Manawatu in 1977 and the 6 ft 3 in (1.9 m) Belliss was launched towards the front rank of New Zealand bowls.

The year 1981 saw him involved in the final stages of eight major tournaments, including victories in the Air New Zealand World Open Singles, the McLean-Duff Invitation Pairs, the Pacific Permanent 2000 Singles and, most important of all, the New Zealand National Singles. That year however the young kiwi also received a few lessons competing in the Kodak Masters at Worthing, at the hands of South Africa's Doug Watson, David Bryant and Kenny Williams of Australia. A rocket-like drive rescued him on occasion and was popular with the crowd but, with one victory, the New Zealander came in sixth out of eight. To his credit, once realizing that there was more to bowls than the New Zealand game of 'drive or draw', Belliss set about correcting his deficiencies and has shown improvement on each subsequent UK visit.

Undeterred by his Worthing experience Belliss kept his form and the titles continued to accumulate. In 1982 he won the Mazda Masters at Melbourne, collected a singles bronze in the Commonwealth Games at Brisbane and, returning to Worthing, reached the semi-finals of the Kodak. He did it again in 1983 and added the Champion of Champion International Singles title to his growing list with victory in Belfast. It was in 1984 that Belliss, now a full-time bowler, showed true professionalism. After losing to David Bryant in the final of the Gateway Masters (Kodak withdrew support after 1983), Belliss remained in Britain, quietly acquainting himself with the conditions he would meet at Aberdeen. By the time the World Championships arrived he was in devastating form. The renowned drive was supplemented by the 'wrest', the 'yard on' and the 'push and lay' and his drawing skills remained as accurate as ever.

In section play, an unlikely 21–17 defeat at the hands of John Jones of Jersey was balanced by a 21–7 drubbing of old adversary Kenny Williams, and he entered the final against Scotland's Willie Wood, his conqueror in the 1982 Commonwealth Games, in a determined mood. Playing an English-style game, Belliss took an early lead at 11–3 with the Scot reduced to the drive as a lifesaver. Wood clawed back to level at 11-all, led at 18–12 and

Belliss, his back to the wall, then scored 8 shots over 5 ends to reclaim the lead at 20–19. By the 25th end it was 20-all and tension caused the worst head of the match. Wood lay jack high, but wide, Belliss was just through. Wood drew one close with his final delivery and at that point the New Zealander turned to his favourite shot, driving the Scot's shot bowl from the head and bringing in umpire Jim Muir, for the most crucial task of his career. An electronic measure failed and eventually it was the tape that showed that the back bowl lay shot and New Zealand had a world champion.

In 1988 Belliss will defend his title on his own turf and it will then be up to the world's bowlers to adapt their games to New Zealand's greens as he did to Britain's.

An overjoyed Belliss celebrates his 1984 World Championship singles victory over Scotland's Willie Wood. (*Bowls International*).

David Bryant CBE

On the green he is unmistakable. The steel-framed spectacles, the poised crouch, the ferocious drive and, above all, the pipe have helped to make David John Bryant synonymous with bowls throughout the world. Almost single-handedly this one-time schoolmaster, born 27 October 1931, has transformed the game from a gentle pursuit for the elderly into a sport which is fast proving irresistible to the media and sponsors selling everything from insurance to whisky.

The great man – David Bryant CBE, twice world outdoor singles champion, three times world indoor champion, four times Commonwealth Games champion and the winner of 16 national titles. (S. J. Line).

Coming from a bowling family – grandfather Bill played Middleton Cup for Somerset, great uncle Sam founded an indoor club and father Reg won indoor international honours – no doubt pointed the young Bryant in the right direction, but the style, the temperament, the concentration and the success are all of his own making. He is largely self-taught, but values the unstinting advice and encouragement he received from his father.

Bryant's style, honed before his teens through hours of practice on the family lawn, brought him his first title, the handicap singles at his beloved Clevedon BC, when he was 17 and has rarely let him down since. In 1949 he reached the semi-finals of the Somerset singles, winning his County Badge in 1953 with victory in the pairs at the age of 21. National honours came in 1957 when, with his father Reg, and another father and son pairing of L.G. and Roger Harris, he won the EBA fours at Paddington.

International recognition followed in 1958 and on that foundation Bryant has built a record that will probably never be equalled. Twice World Championship singles gold medallist, four times Commonwealth Games singles champion, three times world indoor champion, world triples champion in 1980, Commonwealth Games fours champions skip in 1962, British Isles outdoor champion four times and indoor champion four times, five times Masters champion, English outdoor champion six times and English indoor champion nine times. These and countless other tournament successes have made this amiable, unassuming man, awarded the MBE in 1969, one of the most respected figures in sporting history.

In 1970 Bryant took the first steps towards a full-time career in the sport, abandoning his teaching post for a partnership in a Bristol sports shop. Bowls was on the threshold of breaking out of its 'old man's' mould and the Clevedon ace found himself in the forefront of a revolution.

The long-standing record of four English National Singles victories, set by the great Percy Baker in 1955, fell to Bryant in 1973 when he completed a hat-trick of wins in the competition, and by this stage even the dyed-in-the-wool traditionalists were happy to acknowledge that the ancient game of bowls

The most feared sight in bowls – Bryant cocks the hammer as Ireland's Paul McVeigh offers up a prayer. (Duncan Cubitt, *Bowls International*).

had never seen anything quite like him. Wider recognition came in 1979 when the hard-boiled but knowledgeable sports writers of Fleet Street presented him with an award for 'Outstanding Achievement in Sport'.

Apart from his uncanny ability to find the exact line and weight of shot more quickly than most, Bryant's drive, while not as fast as the top Australian and New Zealand bowlers, is usually just as effective. For this shot he eschews the familiar crouch, the speculative quest for the 'right line'; he stands, right shoulder hunched up to his chin, bowl held threateningly high and pipe clenched firmly in his teeth as he takes a bead on his target. It's showmanship, unconscious maybe, but guaranteed to send a buzz of anticipation through any bowls audience. In the inaugural Kodak Masters tournament held in 1978 at Beach House Park, Worthing, Bryant employed the drive to maximum effectiveness in his match with Dick Folkins of the USA. Folkins, a superb draw bowler, could only look on in dismay as the Clevedon man coolly fired his way out of trouble end after end before reverting to his own drawing game to deliver the *coup de grâce* against a dispirited American. This victory was part of a sequence which has seen Bryant acquire the habit of winning new tournaments. The World Championship, the World Indoor Championship, the UK Indoor Singles and the Granada Superbowl are just some of the titles he has collected, along with the Masters, first time round. His performance in the final of the inaugural UK Indoor Singles had seasoned observers casting around for superlatives and his opponent, Scotsman Bob Sutherland believing 'it's as though he's got a large pipe running to the jack and just pops his bowls down it'. Many, including his pairs partner, England international David Rhys Jones, rate Bryant's game that day as the finest of his career; indeed, it may have been his peak.

Temperament and concentration are, in Bryant's view, two of the most vital qualities required for success in bowls and he is well endowed with both. 'Temperament,' he insists, 'is a self-discipline, not something you're born with, and when you're at the top you have to be even more disciplined to stay there.' This philosophy is always evident in Bryant's game: he usually chooses the right shot in any given situation, playing the percentages to a nicety. Like any other top bowler, however, he can be upset by a poorly prepared green but his opponent will probably never be aware of the fact. Bryant never gives the impression of being in trouble even when behind, and his grace when losing is a credit to the game, although, even at 54 years of age, that doesn't happen too often.

As a full-time professional bowler, the first in the game, David Bryant has carved an unassailable niche for himself. He has a number of business interests including indoor bowling surfaces and, of course, the Thomas Taylor-manufactured Bryant's Drakelite Bowl, which the company developed to his specifications. Most recent is the David Bryant Bowling Centre at Almeria in Spain, an ambitious project comprising property and holidays centred around four grass greens. He has recently produced his second book, *Bowl with Bryant*, described as the best instructional volume on the game ever published. In 1980 he received the OBE from the Queen but one suspects that the greatest honour in his eyes is the Honorary Life Membership of the English Bowling Association bestowed on him in 1984.

Master again! Bryant has won the International Masters title on no less than five occasions. (Alan North, Gateway Building Society).

Jimmy Carruthers

James Gillespie Carruthers created bowling history in 1905 by winning the inaugural singles championships of the English Bowling Association, defeating a fellow expatriate Scot, James Telford, 21—11 in a final marked by W. G. Grace, later to become a firm and admiring friend.

Carruthers, born in the small Dumfriesshire town of Lockerbie in 1874, was drawn to the game at the age of 16, joining his local club three years later and winning its Open Singles Championship for the first time in 1902. In 1904 he moved to England and, after a short spell in Liverpool, travelled south to London, joining the Muswell Hill BC and remaining an honoured member of that club until his death in 1958.

In 1905, the year of his historic victory over Telford, Jimmy Carruthers began a remarkable record of 19 international appearances for his adopted country which stood for 29 years until passed by Roy Kivell in 1968. The singles championship of Muswell Hill fell to him 19 times, his first success coming in 1911 and his last in 1953, just five years before his death at the age of 84. His singles record includes victories in both indoor and outdoor competitions. He won the coveted London and Southern Counties Gold Badge in 1916 and 1923, the EBA Invitation Singles in 1924, Middlesex Singles in 1926, the Paddington Indoor Singles in 1939 and 1944 and countless other top level competitions throughout the country. Although happily domiciled in London, Carruthers never forgot he was a Scot and kept his links with his birthplace. He returned to win the Lockerbie Open Singles for the second time in 1910 and skipped the Dumfriesshire rink to victory in the London Scottish Championships of 1919.

In 1938, his indoor international debut at Bournemouth was marked by yet another record-making performance. Skipping F. C. Gooding, W. Jasper and George Crane, Carruthers inflicted a crushing 62–3 defeat on his luckless Welsh opponents and followed that with a 32–11 win over a Scottish rink – a total of 94 shots to 14. Although unable to prevent the Scots winning the Championship, Carruthers and his men contributed the lion's share of England's 99-shot advantage with an astounding performance.

Jimmy Carruthers was a man with all the shots and all the graces, a superb sportsman, an inspiration to his players and a lasting influence on the game he loved.

Jimmy Carruthers – the first EBA national singles champion. (BBC Hulton Picture Library).

JAMES GILLESPIE CARRUTHERS 1874–1958
Lockerbie Bowling Club (Scotland), 1893–1903.
Muswell Hill Bowling Club, 1904–1958.

Record of Chief Events

Winner of numerous Club prizes in Lockerbie B.C.
Winner Lockerbie Confined Tournament, 1897.
Winner Lockerbie Open Single-handed Tournament, 1902, 1910.
Winner Powfoot Open Single-handed Tournament, 1903; Runner-up, 1902.
Finalist for Dumfriesshire in Scottish Single-handed Championship, 1903.
Winner Middlesex District of E.B.A. Single-handed Championship, 1905 and 1913.
Winner Single-handed Championship of England, 1905; 2nd, 1913.
English International Player (19 times), 1905, 1909, 1910, 1911, 1912, 1921, 1925, 1927, 1928, 1929, 1930, 1931, 1932, 1933, 1934, 1935, 1937, 1938 and 1939.
Divided First Prize Crystal Palace Open Single-handed Tournament, 1905; Runner-up, 1909.
Member Muswell Hill Team, Winners L. & S.C.B.A. Silver Shield, 1908 and 1909; Runners-up, 1921.
Section Finalist Welsh Open Single-handed Championship, 1910.
Runner-up Alexandra Palace Indoor Single-handed Championship, 1910.
Winner Single-Rink Championship, L. & S.C.B.A., 1910.
Skipped most successful Rink for L. & S.C.B.A. v. Midland Counties B.A., 1910, 1913 and 1919.
Member of the E.B.A. Council, 1911, 1912 and 1913.
Member of L. & S.C.B.A. Executive, 1922.
Winner Muswell Hill B.C. Single-handed Championship, 1911, 1912, 1914, 1915, 1916, 1917, 1922, 1923, 1925, 1928, 1931, 1932, 1937, 1938, 1939, 1942, 1949, 1950 and 1953.
Winner London & Southern Counties B.A. Single-handed Championship (Gold Badge), 1916 and 1923.
Winner John Weir Gold Cup, 1923.
Skipped Dumfriesshire Rink, winners London Scottish Championship, 1919.
Winner Lord Lonsdale's Gold Trophy, 1925 and 1936; 2nd, 1932.
Winner St. Dunstan's Open Single-handed Tournament, 1924.
Winner Hastings Open Pairs Tournament, 1924, 1927, 1934, 1946.
Winner E.B.A. Invitation Single-handed Tournament, 1924.
Skipped for Middlesex County B.A., winners English County Championship, 1925.
Skipped Muswell Hill B.C. Single-Rink, winners *Star* Newspaper Gold Cup, 1925.
Winner Single-handed Championship, Middlesex, 1926; 2nd, 1931.
Winner Pairs Championship, Middlesex, 1928.
Winner Hastings Open Rink Tournament, 1929; Runner-up, 1931.
Runner-up London & Southern Counties B.A. Pairs Championship, 1931.
Won all five Charity Exhibition Matches v. two English Champions.
Winner Muswell Hill Silver Jubilee Cup, 1935.
Captain English International Team v. South Africa, 1935.
Winner Old Coulsdon Mixed Pairs Tournament, 1936.
Runner-up Hastings Open Single-handed Tournament, 1936.
Broadcast on 'Game of Bowls' in 1936 and 1939.
Member Paddington Indoor Team, Runners-up English Club Championship, 1937.
Winner Wimbledon Hospital Mixed Pairs Tournament, 1937.
Winner Paddington Indoor Open Rink Tournament, 1937.
Winner Hastings Open Triples Tournament, 1937.
Captain English Team in International Matches, 1938.
English Indoor International, 1938 and 1939. In this series created a record for Indoor International Matches scoring 62–3 against a Welsh rink and 32–11 against a Scottish rink – a total of 94–14.
Winner Paddington Indoor Singles Championship, 1939 and 1944.
Winner Paddington Open Pairs Tournament, 1943 and 1949.
Winner Paddington Indoor Pairs Championship, 1943 and 1944.
Elected Honorary Life Member of E.B.A., 1945.
Elected Honorary Life Member of Lockerbie Bowling Club, 1945.

Jimmy Carruthers from a pencil drawing – artist unknown. (Courtesy Muswell Hill BC).

Jimmy Carruthers, a caricature by Will Ford. (Courtesy Muswell Hill BC).

David Cutler

Surely only David Bryant can match the overall tournament record of 31-year-old Cornishman David J. Cutler, who entered the record books as the youngest-ever winner of an EBA national title when, with Chris Yelland and skip Bill Oliver, he won the triples at Mortlake in 1972.

Even as an 18-year-old Cutler played with the calm assurance that has become his trade mark, causing Billy Gillis, veteran skip of the defeated trio from York, to remark: 'With young bowlers like that England has nothing to worry about.' Wise and prophetic words from a man with a long international career and Cutler has justified every one of them.

Born at Redruth on 1 August 1954, Master Cutler dispatched his first bowl on its path to the jack at the age of 14 after watching a cousin, recuperating from illness, trying his luck on the green at St Austell's Poltair Park. Two years later, still a novice, he won the singles championships of the St Austell BC, a significant enough achievement for any 16-year-old but a success that touched a responsive nerve and David Cutler had discovered that he not only enjoyed winning, but that he had the raw ability and, above all, the temperament to make it a habit.

A remarkable sequence of results which has seen him outgun Bryant by winning every national singles tournament that the EBA can offer, began in 1974 with victory over another up-and-coming youngster, Tony Allcock, in the Under-25's competition. Outdoor international honours arrived in 1975 and the indoor selectors followed suit one year later. It

Hop to it! An airborne David Cutler wills his bowl to the jack. (Charles Turner, courtesy Plymbowl).

'Gotcha.' The superb delivery action of David Cutler. (S. J. Line).

was in 1979, however, that this quiet young man, endearingly deliberate in his slightly splay-footed stride, pulled off the English bowlers dream, victory in the EBA National Singles and, still enjoying only his 24th summer, was the youngest ever to do so.

Since then the trophies and the titles have mounted at a rate likely to cause a severe shortage of Silvo in the hardware stores of Cornwall. Included among these honours are two victories in the EBA Invitation 128 Singles, regarded by some observers as being the most testing competition of them all. Among the players taking part are the previous year's national singles quarter-finalists, semi-finalists of the Under-25's and finalists from the previous year's 128 and Saga Singles with the remaining 112 bowlers nominated by county associations. In 1983 Cutler registered his first 128 win, beating Bill Hobart in the final, followed that by winning the inaugural DRG-EBA Champion of Champions tournament in 1984, and then became the first man to win the 128 more than once with a final victory over Peter Line in 1985.

Strange to relate the career of this highly successful bowler has had its ups and downs, but the downs rarely had any relationship to his ability. For a three-year period he was dropped from England's outdoor team before regaining his place in 1984 and he has never been included in a representative touring side abroad. This disappointment he accepts with a wry grin and goes off to another tournament or attend to his recent business interest in bowls equipment. David Cutler may not punch the air when he wins or take a lap of honour around the green but the will to win is deeply embedded in him and with sponsors' money weighing heavier each year he may not need to.

Mal Hughes

Mal Hughes, 'the Durham Dancer', is a hugely popular figure in the bowling world and a player of outstanding ability. He plays the game with amazing zest and flair, always on the move as soon as his bowl is delivered, following its progress with an arcing run as though biased himself. A fine tactician, he has the knack of conjuring up the 'impossible' shots when they are required and can read all the possibilities offered by a 'head' quicker than most.

Mal's first major achievement in the game came in 1970 when he won his county singles, in 1973 he won outdoor international honours at Bournemouth and, a regular member of the England team until 1981, captained the side in 1977 and 78. In 1978 Mal was a member of the English Commonwealth Games team at Edmonton, Canada, the first of many representative journeys he was to undertake throughout his career. In 1980 he collected a team gold medal at the World Championships held at Melbourne, Australia and in the same year appeared in the Mazda Masters singles tournament in Melbourne, returning to compete in 1982 and '83.

At home Mal captained the Eldon Grove Club to victory in the Nat West Club Two Top Fours competition in 1979, and four years later played an inspired game at skip to win the EBA pairs title with clubmate George Turley. The man's indoor record is equally impressive. Capped in 1975, he played in all but one of the home international series between '75 and '81. In 1978 he won both the English and British Isles indoor singles competitions, won the fours in 1980 and '81, adding the British Isles title to his 1980 success, and has captained his Hartlepool club to a dominant position in the Denny Cup, winning this much sought-after trophy in 1978, 1984 and 1985. Among the many other honours won by the amiable Hughes are captain of the Durham side which won the Liberty Trophy in 1983, and success in the 1984 Hartlepool Masters pairs with George Turley, but it was his success in the Dundee Masters in 1974 against a strong field which is the one he takes most pleasure in.

Although out of the international teams since 1981, Mal Hughes at 53 years of age is as busy on the green as ever, still looking for success and more often than not finding it; the quest for that little white ball goes on. Recently, however, it is his administrative skills which have become increasingly apparent. In 1984 he took over the management of his beloved Hartlepool IBC and returned to the international scene in 1985 as team manager of the England side which won the *News of the World* Trophy for the third time in succession.

Mal Hughes (left) with George Turley after their success in the 1983 EBA national pairs competition. (Alan North, Gateway Building Society).

Norma Shaw

Until 1981 Norma Shaw was best known for her prowess at the indoor game. A three-time winner of the EWIBA national singles title, she had got no further than runners-up spot in the outdoor singles. A gold medal at the Women's World Championships of 1981 changed that view, however, and won her recognition as the best singles player the English women's game had yet produced.

A native of Norton, Cleveland, Norma Shaw embarked upon her bowling career at her local club in 1963 at the age of 25. It was at the nearby Teesside indoor club however that she took the first steps towards the higher levels of the game with a victory in the annual Teesside International Tournament in 1975. Two years later she made an impact outdoors, as runner-up to Betty Stubbings in the EWBA national singles and skipped the Durham rink to victory in the fours. A growing reputation brought her indoor international honours in the same year and in 1978 she won not only the first of her four national indoor singles titles, but success in the outdoor two-wood singles as well. The women's game, it soon became obvious, had on its hands a player of tremendous potential and an outdoor international debut followed in 1979. Despite victory in the 1980 EWBA pairs, her selection as the singles representative for the 1981 World Championships surprised many in the bowling world, but the result effectively quashed any lingering doubts regarding her ability outdoors.

Norma Shaw's game is built on the firm base of an accurate draw shot. Calm and unruffled under pressure, she won the national triples in 1982 and collected her second two-wood title in the following year. Indoors she followed her 1978 success in the national singles with further victories in 1980–1 and 1983 each time adding the British Isles title to her tally. She has won the pairs four times and the fours once.

Her expertise has in recent years taken her into realms of the game undreamed of only a short time ago – mixed singles, and her record in that tough world is impressive to say the least. Chris Ward, the 1982 EBA singles champion, and David Cutler who won the same title in 1979, were both beaten in televised competition, but it was in the 1984 Granada Superbowl that Mrs Shaw showed her skills against the men to full advantage, clipping the wings of such high flyers as world indoor champion Jim Baker, Richard Corsie, the reigning Scottish and British junior champion, and Commonwealth Games gold

109

medallist Willie Wood – quite a bag! Her record against David Bryant is not so good, she has yet to beat him and sure enough it was Bryant, the eventual winner, who ousted her in the semi-finals.

Heady stuff indeed but Norma Shaw keeps her feet on the ground; certainly she would like to beat the great David but for the moment she'd settle for that elusive outdoor national four-wood singles title.

'One Shot': Norma Shaw signals the good news. (Duncan Cubitt, *Bowls International*).

John Snell

The return of John Snell to top level bowls in 1985 after a two-year break was no doubt good news for Australia's selectors and certainly good for the game. Prior to his retirement from the international scene in 1983, Snell was regarded as the world's number two bowler with silver medals in the 1978 Commonwealth Games and the 1980 World Championships plus the runners-up prize in the 1982 Kodak Masters, competitions all won by David Bryant.

In 1983, the last year of Kodak's involvement with the Masters, Snell, short of practice, played with the worry of a sick wife destroying his concentration and, after a disappointing performance against George Souza Jnr of Hong Kong, the eventual winner, decided to withdraw from international competition. The decision no doubt arrived like a bombshell on the desks of the selectors who must have at least pencilled him in for the 1984 World Championships.

Born in Jerilderie, New South Wales on 9 September 1934, Snell discovered bowls relatively late in the day at the age of 25. As an employee of the Bank of New South Wales, he was posted to the small town of Kaniva in Victoria and chanced on the game while waiting for a tennis partner at the courts adjoining the town's bowling green. Earlier hopes of a career in tennis had been destroyed by coach Harry Hopman's observation that Snell's reflexes were 'abnormally slow' and a sport where this proved no handicap to high ambition was too good to resist.

Snell's first championship win came at Ararat in 1965 and a successful defence one year later encouraged him to enter the Victorian Masters in 1968. Hardly expected to survive the first round, Snell caused a huge upset by registering his first major success and proved he was no flash-in-the-pan by repeating his victory in the following year, the first bowler to do so. State team honours came in 1969 and, although nominated by Victoria for the Commonwealth Games and World Championships continuously from 1970, eight years were to pass before he was chosen to don the green blazer of Australia.

Before his short-lived 'retirement' Snell played 182 matches for Victoria, won the Victorian Masters singles five times, the

Victorian Champion of Champions title, the Ampol Masters in Sydney and represented his country on 63 occasions. A successful coach, his book *Winning Bowls* (Souvenir Books), written in conjunction with Bill Pritchard and first published in 1982, is a well presented step-by-step course which reflects the clear and logical approach to the game adopted with such success by its author.

After many years in Melbourne where he was a member of the Ivanhoe Club, Snell plans a move to Lake Cathie, New South Wales in 1989, and it was in the state of his birth that he posted notice of his return by winning the highly-rated Hub of the Hunter Invitation Singles.

In the early stages of his career, Snell set himself three goals: 1) Best in Victoria; 2) Best in Australia; 3) Best in the World. Two of these have been achieved; it now remains to be seen whether he can fulfil his ambitions.

John Snell lines up a typically Australian thunderbolt. (Duncan Cubitt, *Bowls International*).

Mavis Steele MBE

With the exception of Clara E. Johns it would be difficult to find anyone who has contributed more to the women's game than Mavis Steele, current assistant secretary of the EWBA.

Born at Kenton in Middlesex on 9 September 1928 into a family of bowlers, Miss Steele took up the game at the age of 18 under the tutelage of her father and brother. Since then she has compiled a record unmatched by any other **woman bowler**, winning 31 Middlesex county

Mavis Steele holds the record number of women's world championship medals. (Duncan Cubitt, *Bowls International*).

and 11 national titles. She made her international debut in 1959 and has retained her place without fail for 27 years! English singles champion in 1961, 1962 and 1969, Mavis represented England in the 1973 South African Games winning the gold medal in the singles, a silver in the pairs and the team gold for best overall performance. Later that same year she won a silver medal in the World Championship singles at Wellington, losing only to the eventual winner, Elsie Wilkie. In the pairs Miss Steele, partnered by Phyl Derrick of Surrey, collected her second silver medal with a superb performance which saw them in second place to Australia on shots difference.

After suffering, along with the other home players, a curious loss of form in the 1977 Championships at Worthing, Mavis Steele reached the pinnacle of her distinguished career at Toronto in 1981 when she skipped the England four to a gold medal, collected a silver in the triples and a further gold for team performance. In 1983 Miss Steele was awarded the MBE for her services to the game and rarely can such an honour have been so richly deserved, for her work as an administrator alone has contributed tremendous benefits to the game.

In her 40th year of bowling, Mavis Steele was still among the medals at the highest level. In 1985 she skipped the English four to third place bronze at the Melbourne World Championships and retained her position as top medal winner in the history of the competition.

Mavis Steele (left) keeps an eye on things. (Duncan Cubitt, *Bowls International*).

Terry Sullivan

Terry Sullivan, a 49-year-old electrical works manager from Swansea, born 6 November 1935, made a dramatic entry into the ranks of the world's bowling elite in 1984 by winning the CIS UK Indoor Singles at Preston. A few months later the new status of this pleasant, quietly spoken man was confirmed with his victory in the 1985 Embassy World Indoor Singles at Coatbridge, Scotland.

His previous record was solid enough: an indoor international since 1980, Welsh national champion in 1983 and various local tournament successes including the Swansea IBC singles and triples titles. What had transformed Sullivan's game from Brand X quality to market leader however was no great secret, simply it was dedication to the powers of practice – hours of it, drawing to the jack at his local Swansea club, hours which were to

pay handsome dividends in terms of confidence alone.

Entering the Preston arena as a rank outsider Sullivan swept to the final beating English champion, Andy Ross, George Adrain of Scotland (who, earlier in the year had helped America to win a World Championship gold medal substituting for the injured Jim Candelet), the defending champion David Bryant and his own fellow countryman, Russell Evans. Quite a bag but hardly a prelude to the nine-set final classic against England's World Championship fours gold medallist, Tony Allcock of Gloucestershire, perhaps the finest bowls match ever televised, attracting a record audience of over seven million.

There is little anyone can teach Allcock about tactical play and, having witnessed Sullivan's nagging accuracy, he knew what he was up against. The Welsh champion, slow and deliberate in his action, delivers his bowls with a minimum of body movement but maximum efficiency. He is a tall man, with thinning hair and a toothy grin but on the green he is all concentration, the smile reserved for the post-match handshake. What he seeks, all the time, is accuracy, whether drawing, firing or delivering any shot in between those two extremes, and the first set saw him almost ignoring Allcock's carefully worked ploys to upset his rhythm. Meticulously he found the jack at any length, occasionally snapping a glance at his opponent as though to gauge the effect of such consistency. Whenever he got the mat Allcock rang the changes but to no avail and the first set went to Sullivan 7–1. Opening the second, Allcock took the mat up at the earliest opportunity and experienced success, running out the winner at 7–6, but it was the Welshman back in command in the third with Allcock forced to produce at least one superbowl on every end to stay in the match. He got to 4–5 thanks to a perfect trail into the ditch followed by a precise draw, but that was his last score in the set as Sullivan finished things off in the eighth end with a confident drive to take the jack into the ditch when two down. The fourth went the same way and the two men went off for a 2½-hour interval with Allcock in the surprising position of being 3 sets to 1 down.

The England skip returned refreshed and in a very different frame of mind, his game tight in defence and potent in attack as he scored 2-2-1-2 before Sullivan knew what had hit him. In the sixth Sullivan led 3–0, Allcock was level on the fourth end and then lay set with four perfectly weighted deliveries. An express speed drive from the Welshman killed the end

and the set eventually went to Sullivan 7–4. Although 4 sets to 2 down Allcock's play was then at a higher level than at any previous time in the match; it was now Sullivan who was forced to use weight, and the Englishman posing all the questions. The seventh went quickly to Allcock 7–1 with the Swansea man showing signs of fatigue, his game looking a little frayed around the edges. A 7–0 whitewash in the eighth brought the match level. Allcock, it seemed, had his opponent down but it was soon apparent that Sullivan was by no means out. Physically tired, certainly, but the concentration was still intact and the patience strong enough to be content with the single shots, seven of them, which won him the match and the £4500 first prize.

Terry Sullivan's victory in the World Indoor Championships in February 1985 may have been more important in prestige terms, but it was at Preston that he cracked it and it was there that he took part in a bowls classic which must have done wonders for the game's image.

Terry Sullivan with the 1984 CIS UK Singles trophy, won after an epic nine set battle against Tony Allcock which drew a record television audience. (Scope PA).

Opposite Terry Sullivan framed by the jack on his way to the 1985 Embassy World singles title. (Author).

Willie Wood

While it would be inaccurate to say that William Walker Wood learnt the game of bowls at his father's knee, it is certainly true that he was taught the rudiments at a pretty early age. The gritty little Scot from Gifford, East Lothian was born 26 April 1938 and was on the green just 13 years later with William senior, Scottish singles champion in 1967, providing all the necessary encouragement.

At 14 he won the Gifford Club singles tournament and was picked for his county side in 1956. The next ten years were spent in assimilating the character-building lessons that bowls is so good at handing out and the reward was an international cap in 1966. From that point on the career of 'Willie the Wood' blossomed and although he may not be the most elegant stylist in bowls, one glance at his record will tell you that he is one of the most effective performers in the game.

In 1967 and '69 he was City of Edinburgh Champion of Champions and in 1970 just failed to emulate the feat of Willie Snr, beaten in the final of the Scottish BA singles by Dick Bernard of Gorebridge, although success in both the singles and triples of the East Lothian and District championships brought at least some compensation. Three years later, however, at the South African Games in Pretoria, Wood, brought up on the plodding greens of his homeland, discovered true love in the speedy running surfaces found where the sun shines. A distinct outsider at the start of things, he cruised past the more favoured Dick Folkins (USA), Peter Line (England) and Tommy Harvey (South Africa), edged out Ellis Stanbury of Wales by the odd shot and demolished the favourite, David Bryant, 21–11 in the final. Willie Wood, Scottish champion or not, had arrived on the international scene in some style.

Since then, victories at home peaked when he skipped the Gifford rink to the Scottish fours title in 1980 but, for Willie Wood, the really big ones so far have been won abroad. The 1974 Commonwealth Games in New Zealand brought singles bronze, silver in the pairs came four years later in Canada and in 1980 a fours silver medal at the World Championships in Australia suggested that he had mastered every facet of the game of bowls. Confirmation arrived two years later with a Commonwealth Games singles gold medal in Australia.

In 1983 they dubbed the motor mechanic from Gifford 'William the Conqueror' after his victory in the Australian Mazda Masters at Melbourne and, if his crown slipped during the English equivalent at Worthing, he was destined to play supremely well during the 1984 World Championships at Aberdeen. The match in which he defeated David Bryant 21–18 was described by Clarence Jones in the magazine *Bowls International* as 'The Greatest Match Ever Played', hyperbole perhaps but it was certainly great bowls and one by which even the final against Peter Belliss paled by comparison. The result of that final encounter, decided in favour of the New Zealander on a measure, still causes heads to shake in disbelief in clubs all over Scotland, but I bet Willie would have become the champion if it had taken place in Australia – come to think of it, if they could hold the Scottish BA singles in Melbourne . . .!

Willie Wood, Scotland's Commonwealth Games singles champion. (S. J. Line).

6 Federation Bowls

OPERATING in just 11, mainly eastern, counties of England, Federation bowls, with its own laws, customs and history, finds itself in the eighties with little apparent prospect of expansion and dominated by the sheer magnitude of the EBA. Many of its top bowlers, offered no opportunity to attain international standing through their own code, simply either decamp to the IBB game via the English Bowling Association or divide their time between the two versions.

Federation laws differ from those of the IBB in a number of instances but over the years there has been a consistent lobby in favour of introducing at least some of these into the mainstream of bowls. While the attempts have so far proved largely unsuccessful, it is worth noting that at least one aspect of the Eastern game, mixed bowling, was adopted in 1985 by both the EBA and the EWBA with their joint sanctioning of the McCarthy and Stone mixed pairs championships. Not so successful but winning increasing support among IBB bowlers, are the Federation rules regarding 'touchers' and variations in the order of play. Law XI (1) of the English Bowling Federation states that 'a bowl which runs off the green or is driven into the ditch by the effects of play shall be counted as dead, and must be removed to the bank'. There is no special case made for the bowl that touches, or has touched, the jack – if it ends in the ditch it is out of the game. The jack, however, if suffering the same fate, remains live but the ruling nevertheless effectively removes the 'toucher' from the game, a feature that certainly meets with the approval, on two counts, of David Bryant who wrote in the magazine *Bowls International* (March 1985), 'I have never been happy with a rule which allows for bowls to be handled while they are still in play – and by that I mean the chalking of touchers'. Later he cites a further, if more surprising, reason: 'If a team is playing well on an end with shots on or behind the jack and the opposition merely has bowls short or at best, jack high, is it justice when the opposition skip fires the jack into the ditch and sits on top of it?' And that from the owner of one of the

most feared drive shots in the game! Bryant, in the same article, also advocates, on tactical grounds, the adoption of the Federation Law V (4e) which states, 'players may alter the order in which they play, but only after completion of an end and before the commencement of the next end'. This he sees as a valuable option should any particular member of a team find himself struggling to fulfil the tasks required by his position. '. . . What about the lead who's having an off day and seems unable to draw within a yard. I'm sure the chance to settle down by switching to no. 2 for a few ends would be gratifying to all concerned.'

In Federation bowls a rink consists of three players as against the four in the IBB game and play is to a count of 2 yd – i.e. any bowl more than 6 ft (1.8 m) from the jack does not count. Basically a two-wood game, four-wood singles and three-wood triples have been introduced to help bowlers adapt to the IBB code.

The history of the Federation game, or something close to it, can be traced back to the Northumberland and Durham Bowling Association formed in 1892 by four Newcastle Public Park clubs. Association members played to a set of rules, reputedly emanating from Scotland, which perfectly suited the Midland's workforce of the time. With long working hours to contend with, bowlers in the area were forced to seek a shorter game than that played under prevailing EBA laws and, with no call in their adopted rules for ditches or banks, any suitably grassed and level area provided adequate facilities. In 1925 an Association with a similar code of play was formed in Lincolnshire, while in Norfolk a game featuring a roving cot, or jack, was the favoured variation.

Many of the Norfolk greens were situated in the grounds of public houses and, in many cases, were smaller than the normally required EBA version. To allow for this the jack cast was to a minimum of 21 yd (19.2 m) rather than 25 yd (22.9 m) and even then was often played corner to corner in an effort to gain the required length. In 1926 Lincolnshire, Norfolk and Nottinghamshire joined forces to form the

Midland and East Anglian Bowling Association, a body separate and distinct from the established ruling body of bowls. A. C. Adams of Nottinghamshire was elected to the office of president with A. O. Jones, also a Nottinghamshire man, as secretary and Tom Brown, treasurer. The Lincolnshire town of Spalding was the chosen site of the headquarters of the new Association and a trophy presented by the president incorporated the various coats of arms of the affiliated counties. The Adams Trophy is presented to the winners of the county team championship in which matches are played to 31 ends by teams of 6 rinks (3 players per rink) who compete to area finals with the counties divided into two sections, North and South. Nottinghamshire became the first Midland and East Anglican county champions in 1927 and were to be involved in the final placings for each of the following seven years, chalking up a further four victories and achieving second place on the other three occasions. With the administration now firmly into its stride, strenuous efforts to popularize the new code, to spread the game further afield, met with some success as Northants, Derbyshire and Suffolk who joined in 1929, were followed by Durham in 1935 and Northumberland one year later. A North versus South match was instituted in 1945 and the same year saw the Association adopting its new title, the English Bowling Federation.

All outdoor Federation championships are held at Skegness during August while the indoor section finals are played at Nottingham in April. The Newton Trophy is an additional county team championship instituted in 1960 and run in tandem with the Adams Trophy matches, both events taking place on the same day. For this newer tournament, however, teams are restricted to just six county badged players among their full complement of 18 bowlers. Nottinghamshire were once again first off the mark, winning the inaugural 1960 tournament and repeating that success in the following year. The two-wood singles championship for the Proctor Cup was instituted in 1935 with F. J. Adams of Suffolk registering the first win. In 1938, R. Stoddard, the reigning president, presented an unusual award for the rinks championship. The Stoddard Trophy comprises models of three players, lead, number two and skip. The design of the trophy allows these figures to be separated from the main body and presented to the respective bowlers of the winning rink and are held by them for one year. First to receive these unique awards were the Nottinghamshire trio of J. Hart, W. Swain and A. Flewitt. Other

important Federation championship events include: the Lincolnshire Cup, a four-wood singles tournament, played to 21 shots and first held in 1963; the Jim Pratt Trophy two-wood singles for players under-25, instituted in 1969; the Ludlam Trophy, veteran singles trophy, for bowlers over the age of 65, first played in 1975; the Gratton Trophy, pairs championship played to 21 ends, first contested in 1948; the Ludlam Trophy, mixed pairs, played to 21 ends and instituted in 1968; the Frank Holmes Shield, a three-wood rinks competition played to 18 ends and first played in 1970; the Victor Ludorum Trophy presented to the county aggregating the greatest number of points from EBF events on the basis of two points for a winner and one for a runner-up. This trophy was first presented in 1979 to the victorious county, Norfolk.

A number of bowlers with dual EBF/EBA affiliations have achieved honours under the laws of both codes. Jim Grigor of Boston, Lincs was introduced to the EBF game by his father at the age of 11 and, three years later, was a member of a League team. In 1955 he made the transition to the IBB game via the EBA, representing his county in the Middleton Cup, and was capped as an international in 1965-6 and 1969 to 1972. His career victories include: Lincolnshire singles three times, Midland Counties singles and pairs three times, triples twice and fours once. Harry Kershaw from Jarrow, Co Durham, won Northumberland pairs and fours under the EBF code. Switching to the EBA he was national singles champion in 1970, won an international cap in 1971 and was a regular member of the Northumberland Middleton Cup side in which he made his debut in 1964. Bernard Gedney was an amateur footballer until the age of 40 with Boston United and Grantham. A true dual bowler, Gedney won the *News Chronicle* national EBA fours in 1957 and the EBF All England two-wood singles in 1971. He has represented Lincolnshire in the Middleton Cup and won EBA county titles in singles (1972), pairs (1963), triples (1968). In 1965 he reached the EBF Adams Trophy final as a member of the Lincolnshire side and carried off the Federation two-wood singles in 1969, 1971 and the rinks in 1971. He was an EBA England triallist in 1972. Bob Dickens: took up bowls in 1965, winning the EBF Jim Pratt Under-25's Trophy in 1971. In 1970 he was a member of the Nottinghamshire side which won the Adams Trophy (EBF). Under EBA/IBB laws, Dickens won the Nottinghamshire singles in 1972 and was a regular member of the Nottinghamshire Middleton Cup side.

The English Women's Bowling Federation

controls the women's side of the Federation game as a separate body to the EBF. Formed at Peterborough in 1957 with Mrs K. Bozeat of Lincolnshire as its first president, the EWBF have adopted similar laws and championship regulations to those of the men, although county matches are played to only 25 ends instead of 31. Principal tournaments in the EWBF bowling calendar are: the county competitions for the Donald Steward Trophy dating from the inaugural year of 1957 and the Silver Jubilee Vase which began only in 1983; the Paul Howard Trophy, a two-wood singles championship played to 21 shots; the Wyand Trophy, a four-wood singles, played to 21 shots; the Hilda Carver Trophy, a two-wood, 21 shots singles game for under-25's; the Anne Saint Trophy, a two-wood, 21 shots tournament for 'senior citizens'; the Alice Rice Trophy, a pairs competition played to 21 ends; the G. W. Jones Trophy, a rinks competition played to 21 ends; the Shepperson and Brown Trophy, a rinks, three-wood tournament played to 18 ends; and the Victrix Ludorum Trophy which is conducted on exactly the same lines as the men's Victor Ludorum Trophy competition.

As with the men's game, many EWBF bowlers divide their time between the two codes and the most successful of these was undoubtedly Mrs Doreen Clark of Nottingham, whose amazing career record totals some 30 national and county titles including the EWBF two-wood singles in 1963; the Alice Rice pairs in 1970 and two indoor titles, the Nottinghamshire pairs in 1954 and triples in 1956. She was the first Notts women's player to achieve EWBA international status, representing England every year between 1961 and 1970. It was in 1957 however that she was to write her name large in the records of the game when, by winning the EWBA two-wood singles, she became the first Notts bowler, man or woman, to win a national title.

While the administrators of Federation bowls find their charge in a state akin to limbo, they are far-sighted enough to ensure that stagnation is kept firmly at bay. Following a coaching seminar held at the Crystal Palace Sports Centre in July, 1972, the EBF initiated one of the first planned coaching schemes in bowls, an innovation which continued with notable success until overtaken by the formation of the national coaching scheme in 1984. A further example of the EBF's ability to adapt to changing conditions is revealed by the fact that they were the first of the flat green codes to embrace open bowls.

English Bowling Federation

Affiliated counties
Derbyshire (19 clubs), Durham (45 clubs), Huntingdonshire (16 clubs), Lincolnshire (142 clubs), Norfolk (160 clubs), Northamptonshire (25 clubs), North Cambridgeshire (17 clubs), Northumberland (13 clubs), Nottinghamshire (83 clubs), Suffolk (133 clubs).
No. of bowlers: 25 000 approx.

English Women's Bowling Federation

Affiliated counties
Derbyshire (7 clubs), Durham (7 clubs), Huntingdonshire (15 clubs), Lincolnshire (57 clubs), Norfolk (23 clubs), Northamptonshire (5 clubs), North Cambridgeshire (4 clubs), Northumberland (12 clubs), Nottinghamshire (35 clubs).

Adams Trophy

Year	County	Year	County	Year	County
1927	Nottinghamshire	1950	Norfolk	1969	Northumberland
1928	Nottinghamshire	1951	Northumberland	1970	Nottinghamshire
1929	Nottinghamshire	1952	Durham	1971	Durham
1930	Nottinghamshire	1953	Durham	1972	Durham
1931	Norfolk	1954	Durham	1973	Durham
1932	Nottinghamshire	1955	Nottinghamshire	1974	Durham
1933	Suffolk	1956	Norfolk	1975	Suffolk
1934	Suffolk	1957	Durham	1976	Derbyshire
1935	Durham	1958	Norfolk	1977	Nottinghamshire
1936	Nottinghamshire	1959	Durham	1978	Durham
1937	Durham	1960	Northumberland	1979	Norfolk
1938	Lincolnshire	1961	Suffolk	1980	Lincolnshire
1939	Northumberland	1962	Durham	1981	Lincolnshire
1940–5	Competition Suspended	1963	Durham	1982	Durham
		1964	Durham	1983	Suffolk
1946	Nottinghamshire	1965	Norfolk	1984	Derbyshire
1947	Durham	1966	Norfolk	1985	Suffolk
1948	Northumberland	1967	Durham		
1949	Durham	1968	Nottinghamshire		

Newton Trophy

1960 Nottinghamshire
1961 Nottinghamshire
1962 Norfolk
1963 Nottinghamshire
1964 N. Cambridgeshire
1965 Norfolk
1966 Norfolk
1967 Northants
1968 Suffolk
1969 Lincolnshire
1970 Nottinghamshire
1971 Lincolnshire
1972 Durham
1973 Durham
1974 Lincolnshire
1975 Nottinghamshire
1976 Norfolk
1977 Nottinghamshire
1978 Norfolk
1979 Nottinghamshire
1980 Lincolnshire
1981 Lincolnshire
1982 Norfolk
1983 Lincolnshire
1984 Suffolk
1985 Nottinghamshire

Eversley Trophy

1974–5 Northamptonshire
1975–6 Durham
1976–7 Northamptonshire
1977–8 Nottinghamshire
1978–9 Nottinghamshire
1979–80 Nottinghamshire
1980–1 Derbyshire
1981–2 Durham
1982–3 Durham
1983–4 Derbyshire
1984–5 N. Cambridgeshire

Lincolnshire Cup

1963 B. Clark *Nottinghamshire*
1964 K. Allonby *Northumberland*
1965 C. Ward *Norfolk*
1966 W. Hogg *Northumberland*
1967 T. Handysides *Northumberland*
1968 D. C. Raynes *Northants*
1969 C. Reynolds *Lincolnshire*
1970 A. Burgess *Suffolk*
1971 J. Luck *Huntingdonshire*
1972 G. Bullimore *Norfolk*
1973 R. Earl *Derbyshire*
1974 G. Pugmire, Jnr. *Durham*
1975 D. Hoodless *Lincolnshire*
1976 R. Dickens *Nottinghamshire*
1977 N. Douglas *Durham*
1978 B. Thorpe *Suffolk*
1979 M. Gill *Norfolk*
1980 S. Hubbard *Durham*
1981 R. Vinter *Lincolnshire*
1982 R. Earl *Derbyshire*
1983 J. Wheatley *Nottinghamshire*
1984 G. Buxton *Derbyshire*
1985 R. Staples *Lincolnshire*

Jim Pratt Trophy

1969 O. C. Stanley *Lincolnshire*
1970 J. Tyler *Suffolk*
1971 R. Dickins *Nottinghamshire*
1972 A. Ayre *Nottinghamshire*
1973 M. Barker *Norfolk*
1974 D. Broadhurst *Derbyshire*
1975 D. Broadhurst *Derbyshire*
1976 K. Howlett *Norfolk*
1977 D. Broadhurst *Derbyshire*
1978 G. Mallett *Norfolk*
1979 F. Ely *Lincolnshire*
1980 M. Durber *Huntingdonshire*
1981 J. Wheatley *Nottinghamshire*
1982 C. Rumsby *Suffolk*
1983 I. Wones *Norfolk*
1984 R. Dixon *Lincolnshire*
1985 I. Wones *Norfolk*

Proctor Trophy

1935 F. J. Adams *Suffolk*
1936 W. Ridley *Norfolk*
1937 R. George *Norfolk*
1938 G. Adams *Lincolnshire*
1939 O. Gibson *Northumberland*
1940–5 Competition Suspended

1946 M. Jones *Norfolk*
1947 T. Wilkinson *Northumberland*
1948 C. Parnaby *Durham*
1949 S. L. Spurr *Derbyshire*
1950 C. Forster *Durham*
1951 V. Foxhall *Norfolk*
1952 B. Chambers *Nottinghamshire*
1953 A. Adey *Durham*
1954 C. Holt *Northants*
1955 J. Clark *Durham*
1956 T. Wilkinson *Northumberland*
1957 J. McLeod *Northumberland*
1958 H. Bowler *Northumberland*
1959 L. S. Henshall *Nottinghamshire*
1960 L. Cooper *Derbyshire*
1961 J. R. Wright *Suffolk*
1962 A. Houlton *Lincolnshire*
1963 G. Hall *Durham*
1964 E. Moll *Northumberland*
1965 K. Hardy *Derbyshire*
1966 A. Southern *Durham*
1967 W. J. Hobart *Lincolnshire*
1968 W. J. Hobart *Lincolnshire*
1969 H. Wand *Nottinghamshire*
1970 G. Everitt *Suffolk*
1971 B. Gedney *Lincolnshire*
1972 E. Clarke *N. Cambs.*
1973 R. Dancer *Derbyshire*
1974 C. Reynolds *Lincolnshire*
1975 R. Lacey *Derbyshire*
1976 J. Brookes *Nottinghamshire*
1977 M. Stratton *Northants*
1978 S. Towle *Nottinghamshire*
1979 N. Foxon *Lincolnshire*
1980 P. J. Hammond
　　　Huntingdonshire
1981 D. Frost *Norfolk*
1982 D. Broadhurst
　　　Northamptonshire
1983 M. Douglas *Durham*
1984 G. McElveen *Norfolk*
1985 A. Ayre *Nottinghamshire*

Veterans Singles Trophy

1975 J. Sayer *Suffolk*
1976 E. Stevenson *Nottinghamshire*
1977 E. Stevenson *Nottinghamshire*
1978 E. Leonard *Lincolnshire*
1979 W. Hogg *Northumberland*
1980 A. Flowers *Derbyshire*
1981 W. English *Northumberland*
1982 E. Jenkinson *Nottinghamshire*
1983 T. Greetham *Derbyshire*
1984 N. Hart *Lincolnshire*
1985 G. Lewthwaite *Humberside*

Gratton Trophy

1948 J. Mills and F. Moore *Durham*
1949 W. Routledge and W. Clark *Durham*
1950 B. Williams and J. Crossman *Durham*
1951 A. and G. Wharton *Derbyshire*
1952 G. Ryan and F. Kirk *Lincolnshire*
1953 R. J. Chisholme and J.. Mather
　　　Northumberland
1954 E. Brennan and E. Moll *Durham*
1955 P. Brazier and A. Rose *Northants*
1956 G. Wilkinson and T. Wilkinson
　　　Northumberland
1957 F. Harris and W. Nutter *Durham*
1958 E. Moule and H. Bitton *Huntingdonshire*
1959 S. Judge and W. Clark *Durham*
1960 W. Heslop and J. Hancock
　　　Northumberland
1961 G. Livingstone and P. MacDonald *Durham*
1962 D. Purves and J. Atkinson *Durham*
1963 H. Dell and J. Oliver *Durham*
1964 S. R. Coupe and T. Butlin *Northants*
1965 G. Finlay and J. Bray *Northumberland*
1966 T. Stevenson and E. Bickthall *Durham*
1967 P. Snowdon and J. Hancock
　　　Northumberland

1968 G. Crozier and J. P. Ashurst
　　　Northumberland
1969 L. Wynne and F. Longden *Lincolnshire*
1970 W. Charlton and S. Hancock
　　　Northumberland
1971 K. Tomlinson and W. Hufton
　　　Nottinghamshire
1972 K. Richardson and G. Lambert *Durham*
1973 H. Buxton and T. Wright *Durham*
1974 J. Wright and J. Laud *Lincolnshire*
1975 J. Topple and I. Self *Norfolk*
1976 W. Raine and R. Devon *Northumberland*
1977 J. Briston and W. Green *N. Cambs*
1978 D. Broadhurst and J. Dickenson *Northants*
1979 H. V. Garner and R. Haynes *Northants*
1980 C. Bowers and J. Bowers
　　　Nottinghamshire
1981 D. Charlton and N. Franklin *N. Cambs.*
1982 B. Walsham and G. Plaskitt *Lincolnshire*
1983 R. Staples and N. Sanson *Lincolnshire*
1984 M. Burnett and D. Daniels *Norfolk*
1985 A. Wass and R. Copestake
　　　Nottinghamshire

Ludlam Trophy

1968 Mrs Hassell and D. Ashley *Lincolnshire*
1969 Mrs Weston and J. Weston *Northants*
1970 Mrs. Priestley and J. Priestley *Northumberland*
1971 Mrs Talbert and M. Talbert *Durham*
1972 Mrs Bates and A. Wright *Lincolnshire*
1973 Mrs Newton and W. Newton *Durham*
1974 Miss Cousins and W. Duffield *Norfolk*
1975 Mrs Strickland and R. Mackay *Northants*
1976 Mrs Norris and M. Baker *Norfolk*
1977 Mrs Chapman and L. Chapman *Norfolk*
1978 Mrs P. Gill and M. Gill *Norfolk*
1979 Mrs Montgomery and K. Montgomery *Northants*
1980 Mrs Tomlin and M. Tomlin *Lincolnshire*
1981 Mrs Evans and C. Evans *Durham*
1982 Mrs Bird and J. Bird *Nottinghamshire*
1983 Mrs Bird and J. Bird *Nottinghamshire*
1984 Mrs M. Morrell and F. Harris *Humberside*
1985 Miss A. Walsham and E. Tolville *Lincolnshire*

Stoddard Rinks Trophy

1938 J. W. Hart, W. Swain and A. Flewitt *Nottinghamshire*
1939 W. Bayfield, C. Cottrill and A. T. Dodds *Durham*
1946 B. Williams, W. Easton and J. Crossman *Durham*
1947 J. W. Hart, R. Whitehouse and A. Flewitt *Nottinghamshire*
1948 G. Keenlyside, W. Clark and S. Judge *Durham*
1949 G. Wilkinson, J. Parker and T. Wilkinson *Northumberland*
1950 O. Bartlett, J. Bennett and E. Ord *Northumberland*
1951 O. Bartlett, J. Bennett and E. Ord *Northumberland*
1952 R. Cogle, C. Davidson and R. Morrison *Durham*
1953 R. Howe, J. Galloway and J. Clark *Durham*
1954 E. Brown, W. Topliss and J. Wright *Derbyshire*
1955 C. Clark, S. Bridge and B. Wright *Suffolk*
1956 J. Booth, H. Boddice and C. Ball *Nottinghamshire*
1957 J. Booth, J. Lee and C. Ball *Nottinghamshire*
1958 G. Duffield, C. Summers and A. Norton *Norfolk*
1959 C. Richardson, J. H. Stonehouse and W. Stonehouse *Durham*
1960 G. W. Nicholson, J. Oliver and H. Bell *Durham*
1961 S. Judge, L. Robson and T. R. Urwin *Durham*
1962 J. Allison, W. Charlton and T. Wheeler *Northumberland*
1963 J. Allison, W. Charlton and T. Wheeler *Northumberland*
1964 L. Davey, F. Gilhespy and E. Moll *Northumberland*
1965 P. Farrow, J. Powell and J. Brown *N. Cambs.*
1966 E. Foster, R. Dring and S. Dodson *N. Cambs.*
1967 E. Foster, R. Dring and S. Dodson *N. Cambs.*
1968 T. Dawson, G. Lambert and R. Russell *Durham*
1969 W. Stevenson, G. W. Stevenson and C. Oakton *Nottinghamshire*
1970 H. Froggatt, A. Dove and A. Topliss *Nottinghamshire*
1971 F. Wooltorton, J. Thurtle and H. Coleman *Norfolk*
1972 G. Harvey, K. Harvey and T. Jones *Nottinghamshire*
1973 R. High, E. Harrison and D. Frost *Norfolk*
1974 J. King, A. King and M. Ottaway *Norfolk*
1975 M. Stevenson, H. Collier and E. Cooke *Nottinghamshire*
1976 P. Ormston, J. Grieve and C. Nesbitt *Durham*
1977 W. Garbutt, J. Johnson and A. Sampson *Nottinghamshire*
1978 G. Harvey, W. Houseley and T. Jones *Nottinghamshire*
1979 D. Home, A. Williamson and R. Devon *Northumberland*
1980 T. J. Arnold, J. Barringer and P. V. Green *Huntingdonshire*
1981 T. F. Merrell, J. E. Frost and H. W. Angood *N. Cambs.*
1982 R. Burnham, E. Mitchell and L. Buttery *Northamptonshire*
1983 M. Wood, J. Marples and M. Raines *Derbyshire*
1984 J. Bowers, D. Gibson and W. Gregory *Nottinghamshire*
1985 R. W. Cree, W. Patterson and R. Cree *Durham*

Frank Holmes Shield

1970 R. Green, E. Tacon and S. Bacon *Norfolk*
1971 S. Holden, A. Stickland and H. Goodwin *Northants*
1972 C. Reynolds, D. Boone and F. Kingswood *Lincolnshire*
1973 W. Thompson, J. Burch and G. Mee *Nottinghamshire*
1974 D. Edwards, H. Lovegrove and E. G. Horner *Huntingdonshire*
1975 B. Foxon, N. Foxon and R. Foxon *Lincolnshire*
1976 K. Morris, J. Hardy and O. Gilbert *Northants*
1977 S. Stanley, R. Stanley and J. F. Hall *Lincolnshire*
1978 P. Cossey, R. Stocker and K. Sansom *Huntingdonshire*
1979 H. P. Edgley, E. W. Moule and E. J. Saint *Huntingdonshire*
1980 J. Webb, A. Nelson and E. Clark *N. Cambs.*

1981 W. Kemp, C. Thomas and B. Thorpe *Suffolk*
1982 B. Shepperson, D. Carlin and A. Bunting *Derbyshire*
1983 B. Gaunt, M. Ball and R. Hall *Nottinghamshire*
1984 J. Webb, A. G. Nelson and E. Clark *N. Cambs.*
1985 I. B. Walker, S. Wilson and C. Bircumshaw *Nottinghamshire*

Stoddard Tourist Trophy

1948 C. Bushby, J. Cooke and H. Fairhurst *Derbyshire*
1949 No Competition held
1950 W. Carter, G. Wharton and H. Crofts *Lincolnshire*
1951 A. Wrigley, D. Johnson and J. Hopper *Lincolnshire*
1952 E. Waddington, C. Beacock and C. Blackwood *Durham*
1953 G. Keenlyside, R. Davidson and S. Judge *Durham*
1954 G. Keenlyside, C. Pattison and S. Judge *Durham*
1955 G. Keenlyside, C. Pattison and S. Judge *Durham*
1956 J. Blackwood, J. Hopper and C. Blackwood *Lincolnshire*
1957 S. Melton, L. Pearce and A. H. Cope *Lincolnshire*
1958 A. W. Bareford, F. Fossitt and R. G. Clements *Northants & Lincs.*
1959 F. Richardson, G. Tetther and B. Huls *Lincolnshire*
1960 W. Kirtley, G. Parkinson (Durham) and W. Harding *Northumberland*
1961 J. MacFarlane, J. Armstrong and W. Harding *Northumberland*
1962 C. Neaverson, J. E. Needle and H. V. Goodwin *Northants & Hunts.*
1963 F. Richardson, W. Young and B. Huls *Lincolnshire*
1964 G. Pease, P. Sabberton and E. Sabberton *Norfolk*
1965 R. Danby, L. J. Clarke (Northants) and R. Jackson *Lincolnshire*
1966 G. Pease, P. Sabberton and E. Sabberton *Norfolk*
1967 J. Smith, R. Stanley and F. Smith *Lincolnshire*
1968 G. Pease, P. Sabberton and E. Sabberton *Norfolk*
1969 S. Neale, R. Wyand and R. Summers *Norfolk*
1970 F. Rose, C. Neaverson and R. Johnson *Northants*
1971 C. Wilson, D. Fawbett and S. Short *Hunts.*
1972 B. Kidd, S. Steward and H. Carver *Norfolk*
1973 S. Steward, C. Lee and H. Carver *Norfolk*
1974 J. Smith, R. Jackson and F. Smith *Lincolnshire*
1975 G. Pease, E. Sabberton and P. Sabberton *Norfolk*
1976 R. Burton, B. Wyand and R. Haynes *Norfolk*
1977 G. Pease, E. Sabberton and P. Sabberton *Norfolk*
1978 W. Childerley, J. Bryant and F. W. Hawkins *Hunts.*
1979 K. Woods, R. Lambert and G. Howes *Norfolk*
1980 R. Howell, F. Hardesty and L. Chapman *Norfolk*
1981 K. Woods, G. Howes and M. Lambert *Norfolk*
1982 F. Curtis, E. Henson and A. W. Rickwood *Hunts.*
1983 M. Aldred, A. W. Rickwood and F. Curtis *Huntingdonshire*
1984 B. Windsor, R. Kettle and R. E. Small *Northants*
1985 K. Woods, M. G. Ottaway and R. Lambert *Norfolk*

The Howard Tourist Trophy

1976 Mrs M. Wright, S. Kett, I. Thomas *Suffolk*
1977 Mrs M. Clouting, G. Gooding, Q. Fox *Suffolk*
1978 Miss S. Bryant, Mrs E. Hawkins, L. Bryant *Huntingdonshire*
1979 Mrs C. Blyth, Miss M. Ely, Mrs M. Phillips *Norfolk*
1980 Mrs N. Beattie, I. Anton, J. Chamberlain *Northants*
1981 Mrs J. Haynes, J. Holden, B. Warters *Northants*
1982 Mrs J. Haynes, J. Holden, B. Warters *Northants*
1983 Mrs J. Haynes, J. Holden, B. Warters *Northants*
1984 Mrs J. Haynes, J. Holden, B. Warters *Northants*
1985 Mrs O. Sales, E. Simpson, J. Adams *Lincs*

The Ina Thomas Trophy
1976 Mrs H. Doggett, Mr H. Lambert
1977 Mrs S. Sabberton, Mr F. Phillips
1978 Mrs J. Haynes, Mr H. J. Carver
1979 Mrs G. Henson, Mr John Webb
1980 Mrs N. Beasley, Mr P. Sabberton
1981 Mrs S. Sabberton, Mr R. Snell
1982 Mrs M. Davis, Mr P. Sabberton
1983 Mrs D. Cooper, Mr G. Branch
1984 Mrs I. Meeks, Mr W. Bucknall
1985 Mrs M. Lawes, Mr J. Webb

The Langham Trophy
1975 Mrs Hawkins, Mr J. Coleman
1976 Mrs M. Unwin, Mr F. Curtis
1977 Mrs M. Doggett, Mr M. Ottoway
1978 Mrs M. Duce, Mr R. S. Jackson
1979 Mrs M. Doggett, Mr F. J. Mason
1980 Mrs J. Holden, Mr John Webb
1981 Mrs M. Rickwood, Mr R. S. Jackson
1982 Mrs N. Lilley, Mr J. Ottaway
1983 Mrs N. Branch, Mr R. E. Snell
1984 Mrs I. Younger, Mr E. Wakefield
1985 Mrs R. Tetley, Mr A. Quail

The Donald Steward Team Trophy
1957 Nottinghamshire
1958 Nottinghamshire
1959 Nottinghamshire
1960 Nottinghamshire
1961 Northern
1962 Nottinghamshire
1963 Nottinghamshire
1964 Nottinghamshire
1965 Norfolk
1966 Nottinghamshire
1967 Norfolk
1968 Nottinghamshire
1969 Norfolk
1970 Nottinghamshire
1971 Lincolnshire
1972 Norfolk
1973 Northern
1974 Nottinghamshire
1975 Suffolk
1976 Nottinghamshire
1977 Suffolk
1978 Derbyshire
1979 Suffolk
1980 Suffolk
1981 Suffolk
1982 Suffolk
1983 Suffolk
1984 Suffolk
1985 Northants

The Silver Jubilee Vase
1983 Suffolk
1984 Suffolk
1985 Norfolk

The Paul Howard Two-Wood Singles Trophy
1957 Mrs K. Hassall *Lincolnshire*
1958 Mrs R. Sandle *Norfolk*
1959 Mrs K. Hassall *Lincolnshire*
1960 Mrs Dick *Northern*
1961 Mrs Clough *Northern*
1962 Mrs K. Hassall *Lincolnshire*
1963 Mrs D. Clarke *Nottinghamshire*
1964 Mrs K. Hassall *Lincolnshire*
1965 Mrs I. Usher *Northern*
1966 Mrs K. Perry *Suffolk*
1967 Mrs Ward *Suffolk*
1968 Mrs I. Lewars *Northern*
1969 Mrs M. Podd *Suffolk*
1970 Miss B. Atherton *Nottinghamshire*
1971 Mrs V. Peck *Suffolk*
1972 Mrs B. Annison *Norfolk*
1973 Miss G. Restall *Nottinghamshire*
1974 Mrs M. Edgley *Huntingdonshire*
1975 Mrs G. Hancock *Derbyshire*
1976 Mrs E. Evans *Suffolk*
1977 Mrs P. Glassey *Durham*
1978 Mrs C. Charlton *North Cambridgeshire*
1979 Mrs G. Hofton *Nottinghamshire*
1980 Mrs E. Turner *Northumberland*
1981 Mrs B. Willetts *Nottinghamshire*
1982 Mrs B. Warters *Northants*
1983 Mrs B. Warters *Northants*
1984 Mrs B. Atherton *Nottinghamshire*
1985 Mrs P. Mather *Durham*

The Wyand Four-Wood Singles Trophy
1963 Mrs A. Ellison *Northern*
1964 Mrs B. Miller *Northern*
1965 Mrs A. Ellison *Northern*
1966 Mrs M. Allen *Norfolk*
1967 Mrs Appleby *Lincolnshire*
1968 Mrs R. Lee *Northern*
1969 Mrs A. Ellison *Northern*
1970 Mrs N. Richardson *Nottinghamshire*
1971 Mrs P. Glassey *Northern*
1972 Mrs D. Redgrave *Norfolk*
1973 Miss B. Atherton *Nottinghamshire*
1974 Mrs G. Short *Huntingdonshire*
1975 Mrs G. Parr *Suffolk*
1976 Mrs M. Doggett *Norfolk*
1977 Mrs M. Doggett *Norfolk*
1978 Mrs G. Restall *Nottinghamshire*
1979 Mrs M. Bryant *Suffolk*
1980 Mrs I. Anton *Northants*
1981 Mrs E. Bird *Nottinghamshire*
1982 Mrs M. Croxford *Northants*
1983 Miss J. Moses *Lincolnshire*
1984 Mrs O. Henderson *Durham*
1985 Mrs A. Talbot *Durham*

Hilda Carver Trophy
1982 Mrs F. Baker *Derbyshire*
1983 Miss Laflin *Suffolk*
1984 Miss S. Smith *Norfolk*
1985 Miss M. Brundle *Northamptonshire*

Anne Saint Trophy
1975 Mrs E. Britton *Nottinghamshire*
1976 Mrs E. Beckett *Suffolk*
1977 Mrs R. Stickland *Suffolk*
1978 Mrs D. Smith *Lincolnshire*
1979 Mrs I. Lewars *Northumberland*
1980 Mrs I. Lewars *Northumberland*
1981 Mrs M. Brown *Northumberland*
1982 Mrs S. Holmes *Northumberland*
1983 Mrs E. Lunt *Derbyshire*
1984 Mrs N. Branch *Northamptonshire*
1985 Mrs D. Redgrave *Norfolk*

The Alice Rice Pairs Trophy
1957 Miss Minns, Mrs W. Plummer *Norfolk*
1958 Mrs Waters, Wormald *Nottinghamshire*
1959 Mrs Falkinder, Francis *Northants*
1960 Mrs Dick, Miller *Northern*
1961 Mrs A. Ellison, Brooks *Northern*
1962 Mrs Carter, F. Hawthorne *Nottinghamshire*
1963 Mrs E. Smith, F. Holland *Northern*
1964 Mrs Britten, D. Dickens *Nottinghamshire*
1965 Mrs E. Brooks, A. Ellison *Northern*
1966 Mrs T. Oram, C. Reynolds *Nottinghamshire*
1967 Mrs Warren, Thacker *Nottinghamshire*
1968 Mrs L. Corrall, I. Morris *Nottinghamshire*
1969 Mrs I. Usher, J. Knowles *Northern*
1970 Mrs D. Clark, Y. Radage *Nottinghamshire*
1971 Mrs B. Spencer, K. Hassall *Lincolnshire*
1972 Mrs M. Simmons, D. Lomax *Suffolk*
1973 Mrs J. Sullivan, J. Thompson *Lincolnshire*
1974 Mrs N. Holt, B. Warters *Northants*
1975 Mrs P. Glassey, E. Crook *Northern*
1976 Mrs G. Hancock, B. Dangerfield *Derbyshire*
1977 Mrs J. Coe, V. Peck *Suffolk*
1978 Mrs C. Laskey, S. Symonds *Norfolk*
1979 Mrs E. Stacey, N. Branch *Northants*
1980 Mrs M. Presswood, R. Bannister *Derbyshire*
1981 Mrs N. Holt, B. Warters *Northants*
1982 Mrs S. Sabberton, M. Woods *Norfolk*
1983 Mrs P. Carter, J. Stone *Lincolnshire*
1984 Mrs B. Wortley, O. Frith *Nottinghamshire*
1985 Mrs M. Fisher, Mrs M. Manchett *Huntingdonshire*

The G. W. Jones Two-Wood Rinks Trophy

1957 Mrs Waters, Wormald, Whittaker *Nottinghamshire*
1958 Mrs Roberts, Sullivan, Smith *Lincolnshire*
1959 Mrs Huntsa, Draper, Rollit *Nottinghamshire*
1960 Mrs Lee, Beaumont, Holland *Northern*
1961 Mrs Nichols, Wilton, Miss K. Pope *Suffolk*
1962 Mrs Usher, Johnson, Knowles *Northern*
1963 Mrs E. Britten, D. Dickens, E. Storey *Nottinghamshire*
1964 Mrs G. Holmes, M. Sale, G. Parr *Suffolk*
1965 Mrs C. Reynolds, E. Webb, F. Hawthorne *Nottinghamshire*
1966 Mrs M. Sale, G. Holmes, G. Parr *Suffolk*
1967 Mrs Buttery, Lind, Haycock *Nottinghamshire*
1968 Mrs E. Maples, E. Walters, E. Desborough *Northants*
1969 Mrs M. Rickwood, I. Smith, N. Bailey *Huntingdonshire*
1970 Mrs I. Southwick, G. Pearce, M. Mearns *Lincolnshire*
1971 Mrs E. Cullen, N. Chapman, I. Thompson *Lincolnshire*
1972 Mrs E. Cook, A. Stanley, M. Pell *Lincolnshire*
1973 Mrs E. Howlett, N. Brown, Miss V. Southgate *Suffolk*
1974 Mrs L. Musson, S. Lovett, E. Storey *Nottinghamshire*
1975 Mrs J. Haynes, P. Aldcroft, N. Holt *Northants*
1976 Mrs E. Storey, L. Musson, S. Lovett *Nottinghamshire*
1977 Mrs D. Redgrave, B. Annison, M. Doggett *Norfolk*
1978 Mrs B. Dunkley, E. Blenkinsop, G. Hancock *Derbyshire*
1979 Miss G. Pacey, Mrs R. Hodgson, V. Grooby *Lincolnshire*
1980 Mrs J. Elton, J. Shephard, E. Lunt *Derbyshire*
1981 Mrs J. Ramsbottom, S. Sabberton, M. Woods *Norfolk*
1982 Mrs J. Ramsbottom, S. Sabberton, M. Woods *Norfolk*
1983 Mrs R. Stanley, J. Pacey, V. Grooby *Lincolnshire*
1984 Mrs L. Smith, Mrs C. Dungar, Miss S. Smith *Norfolk*
1985 Mrs J. Head, C. Quinney, J. Savage *N. Cambridgeshire*

The Shepperson and Brown Three-Wood Rinks Trophy

1971 Mrs G. Fox, M. Simmons, D. Lomax *Suffolk*
1972 Mrs I. Lewars, E. Lee, R. Wilson *Northern*
1973 Mrs A. Wyand, C. Laskey, Symonds *Norfolk*
1974 Mrs G. Bryan, M. Middleton, T. Oram *Nottinghamshire*
1975 Mrs O. Harvey, B. Marsden, H. Cook *Lincolnshire*
1976 Mrs L. Hunt, J. Elton, J. Sheppard *Derbyshire*
1977 Mrs I. Lewars, E. Lee, P. Wilson *Northumberland*
1978 Mrs A. Talbot, M. Goldthorpe, L. Miller *Durham*
1979 Mrs J. Pacey, R. Hodgson, V. Grooby *Lincolnshire*
1980 Mrs J. Rix, J. Spooner, Miss J. Couzens *Norfolk*
1981 Miss S. Smith, Mrs H. Smith, L. Smith *Norfolk*
1982 Mrs R. Stanley, J. Pacey, V. Grooby *Lincolnshire*
1983 Mrs E. Blenkinsop, G. Hancock, B. Dunkley *Derbyshire*
1984 Mrs B. Cade, E. Housdon, M. Roberts *Huntingdonshire*
1985 Mrs F. Batchelor, J. Baker, M. Bonsor *Derbyshire*

The Harry Carver Indoor Team Trophy

1977 Northamptonshire
1978 Northamptonshire
1979 Suffolk
1980 Nottinghamshire
1981 Lincolnshire
1982 Norfolk
1983 Norfolk
1984 Huntingdonshire
1985 Lincolnshire

The Reg Wright Trophy (Under-25 Teams)

1983 Lincolnshire
1984 Lincolnshire
1985 Nottinghamshire
Note: Mr. W. G. Denny, Patron of the English Bowling Federation, introduced sponsorship to the Reg Wright Trophy competition in 1985 by offering a seven-day holiday at the the David Bryant Bowling Centre, Almeria, Spain to the winning 12-man team.

7 The Young Bloods

WITH increased television and media exposure making the game a more attractive proposition to companies with sponsorship ambitions, bowls finds itself in the fortunate position of proving equally inviting to a growing legion of youngsters. In 1985 the English Bowling Association was forced to abandon its lower age limit for entry into its competitions, official acceptance of the fact that the old game is undergoing a period of radical change.

England, with the larger proportion of young players already involved at international level, would appear to be in a uniquely favourable position. Already blooded are talented young men such as Steve Halmai (born 26 March 1959), a solid bowler of great assurance and a quiet confidence that belies his age. Steve started bowling at Paddington in 1976, winning his club championship in the same year. In 1979 he reached the semi-finals of the Middlesex singles and repeated that performance in the EBA under-25's competition in 1980 and 1982. He won the Middlesex fours in 1980, the Middlesex pairs and EBA county top fours competition in 1984. An outdoor international since 1983, Steve made his indoor debut for England in 1984.

Brett Morley (born Nottingham 28 May 1960) is a young man with a justifiable confidence in his own ability. He is an exciting bowler, never found wanting when the pressure is on and has the ability to improvise a shot for any situation. At the age of 17 Brett won the Notts Spring Bank Holiday Pairs, he won the Notts county pairs in 1980 and was runner-up in his county's singles and triples in 1982. He came to wider notice in 1984 by winning the Kodak EBA Under-25's

---

Most Titles International (Indoor) England have won the indoor international series (inst. 1936) on 21 occasions (including 6 consecutive wins 1955 to 1960). In 1985 England's indoor team matched the hat-trick of wins achieved by the outdoor team in the same year. Scotland have won the series 17 times and Wales 3 with Ireland yet to break their duck.

---

competition and, with Peter Goulding, the EIBA pairs. The British Isles indoor pairs was added to a mounting collection of titles in 1985 and in June of that year he displayed his adaptability by playing in his first 'sets' tournament, the EBA Glynwed Midlands Masters and winning it, despite the presence of David Bryant, Tony Allcock, Wynne Richards, David Cutler and a host of other star names. Brett made his outdoor international debut in 1983.

Gerry Smyth (born 29 December 1960) is another young Paddington bowler carrying a lot of England hopes on his shoulders. Gerry won his first outdoor international cap in 1981, at 19 years of age, the youngest ever to do so. He started bowling in 1972, won the Middlesex County Unbadged singles five years later, whilst still only 16 and in 1980 was a member of the winning rink in the county fours. In national competitions Gerry reached the semi-finals of the Kodak-EBA Under-25's competition in 1978, the quarter-final in 1981, the final in 1983 and was semi-finalist in the EBA 128 Singles in the same year. Indoor he was EIBA singles semi-finalist in 1983. Gerry made his indoor international debut in 1982.

Garry Smith (born 13 October 1958) is a member of the Old Colfein's BC at Eltham in Kent. He started bowling in 1973 and won the Hastings Open Pairs three years later. In 1977 he was runner-up in the Kodak-EBA Under-25's tournament and won the Kent County singles and pairs in 1980. One year later, at 22 years of age, he was semi-finalist in both the EBA singles and fours, winning the latter title in 1983. Indoors Garry was a member of the successful Cyphers Club which won the Denny Cup in 1983. Outdoor international since 1982, he made his indoor debut in 1984.

Nigel Smith (born 2 February 1965) is perhaps the best known of England's youngsters thanks to his remarkable run in the 1984 World Indoor Championships in which, at just 19, he beat Commonwealth Games gold medallist Willie Wood and the great David Bryant before losing to Jim Baker of Ireland in the final. Nigel began his trip to the top level of bowls by winning the Surrey County Unbadged singles and the Worthing Open in 1982. He plays in Surrey's Liberty Trophy and Middleton Cup teams and in 1983 was chosen as England reserve in the indoor international series played at Ardrossan, winning his first full cap at Folkestone in the following year. In 1983 he was runner-up to Tony Allcock in the Prudential EIBA Under-31's competition.

Waiting their turn for the big-time are a host of other skilled and highly motivated young bowlers: EBA fours winner Russ Morgan (born 1965) from Hampshire made his outdoor international debut in 1985; John Leeman (born 1965), perhaps the brightest prospect of them all, has already won the Lombard Champion of Champions tournament and the Prudential Under-31's titles. The Pull brothers, Peter (born 1964) and Laurie (born 1967) from Hampshire who, with Russ Morgan and Chris Paice won the EBA fours in 1984, are obviously exceptional talents as are Ian Grady (born 1965) from Norfolk who won the EBA and British Isles Under-25's titles in 1982 and 1983 respectively; Kevin Bone (born 1961) from Newcastle, EBA national singles runner-up in 1983; and Garry Harrington (born 1963) of Oxford who lost narrowly to Tony Allcock in the 1985 EIBA singles after handing John Bell a 21–3 hiding in an earlier round.

No other country in the British Isles can match this wealth of talent but in Scotland, Richard Corsie (born 1966) is a bowler of immense promise. Taking the game up at the age of 12, Corsie progressed swiftly, capturing the Ayr Junior title two years later. In 1983 he won the SBA Junior singles competition, collecting the British Isles title one year later. In 1984 he also won the Scottish Indoor Junior singles and, still only 17, made his debut in Scotland's Outdoor International team. To date Corsie's career record includes wins in the Glasgow Lignoid Champion of Champions tournament and the Edinburgh Indoor BC singles championship.

Wales too can boast a precocious talent in Robert Weale (born 1963) from Presteigne. The Weale family could quite comfortably turn out two mixed rinks of high quality bowlers and one of them would comprise father Bill and his sons Robert, Brian and David, the Welsh National fours winners in 1984.

Robert notched up his first important win in 1977 beating his father in the final of the Rhaader Open singles and one year later became, at 15 years of age, the youngest player ever to contest a WBA final when he finished runner-up in the Welsh Under-35's competition. At 18 he won the highly rated Gibson-Watt Cup at Llandrindod Wells for the first time and in 1982 was capped for Wales. It was in 1984 however that the reputation of this highly skilled and immensely mature young man was heard of outside Wales when he represented his country in the World Championships at Aberdeen, the youngest bowler in the tournament. A year which also saw him skipping his father and brothers to the Welsh fours title and scoring his second victory in the Gibson-Watt indicated that in Robert Weale, Wales has something much more than just a bowler of promise.

Ireland meanwhile has a number of bright prospects including Cecil Worthington who won the Irish National and British Isles Junior singles titles in 1980 and '81 respectively, and Rodney McCutcheon (born 1962), who beat Jim Baker to win the 1981 Irish Junior Championship and went on to a famous British Isles victory by defeating Tony Allcock in 1982. Rodney was capped indoor and out in 1985 and gained invaluable experience as a member of the Irish Test team which took on Israel in a series of matches in the same year. Rodney's record also includes success in the Irish National pairs with Keith Herron.

Bowls has progressed a long way since it gained the tag of an 'old man's game'. The semi-final rounds of the 1985 DRG Croxley Script Champion of Champions tournament featured four players with an average age of 27 with Roy Cutts of Suffolk the 'old man' of the party at 32. The winner, Danny Denison of Devon, was 23.

Highest Prize Money The highest prize money in the British game, £25 400, was offered for the Television Superbowl Indoor Bowls Championship, an event conceived and sponsored in its first year by Granada Television and held at their Stage One Studios in Manchester over six days, 15–20 October 1984. The first prize (also the highest) of £10 000 was won by David Bryant who beat John Bell 5–7, 7–6, 7–6 in the final. In 1985 Liverpool Victoria Insurance assumed the role of sponsor raising the prize money to £26 400.

8 Bowls Goes Indoors

The Background

THE ORIGINS of indoor bowls go back in time almost as far as the outdoor version. While the early skittle alleys no doubt spawned the ten pin game of today, it is also likely that devotees of the outdoor flat-green game sought to continue their sport during the winter months protected from the elements. These early efforts, by today's standard, were primitive in the extreme and the first serious attempt to produce an indoor surface at least comparable to an outdoor green came in 1888. William Macrea, then president of the Drumdryan Bowling Club in Scotland, leased a drill hall in which to demonstrate his theory of bringing the game successfully indoors. With a concrete floor to contend with, Macrea fitted bands of

rubber into grooves cut into a set of lignum bowls in the hope that the resulting friction would slow their progress sufficiently to keep them on the playing area. With the initial experiment ending in failure, the determined Scot then covered the floor with sawdust and tried again. While not a total success, bias did begin to take effect and even the sceptics conceded that Macrea had made his point. With a suitable surface, indoor bowls of an acceptable standard was now seen as a definite possibility and experiments with various forms of matting, including bata-weave, coco-matting and baize, led eventually to the jute, felt and other surfaces now in common use.

The first indoor club was the Edinburgh Winter Bowling Association founded in 1905, with its members enjoying the facilities offered by two gas-lit, 27-yard (24.7 m) long rinks situated in the basement of the Synod Hall in the city's Castle Terrace. In England, bowlers used the Kings Hall, Wimbledon around the turn of the century, but it was the vast and inviting interiors of the Crystal and Alexandra Palaces which attracted most interest. Following experiments by W. G. Grace, who laid a carpet in one of the Crystal Palace galleries, the first English club was formed there in 1906 with R. P. Grace, brother of the famous sportsman, as first president.

England

Although at this period the game was usually housed in far from perfect conditions, it proved an instant success. Clubs were formed throughout the country with bowlers often playing in cramped, poorly-lit halls, more often than not on greens some way below regulation length. Inevitably conditions gradually improved with the gas mantle giving way to the electric light bulb and better surfaces beginning to eradicate many of the problems endured by the indoor pioneers. Sadly, many plans for new purpose-built stadia were halted by the First World War although a number did make it through to completion. The thirties saw the continuing rise in the

Belgian-born Edward Ecrepont prepares to deliver the first bowl at his indoor bowling centre at Ayr, the first purpose-built indoor facility in Scotland.

fortunes of the indoor game reflected in the addition of indoor facilities to the superb bowling complex at Paddington's Castellain Road green. Known as the unofficial headquarters of the EBA, the Paddington club was, for some years, the showpiece of bowling, both indoor and out, in England.

The indoor section of the EBA was formed on 8 April 1933 at a meeting of the Association's Emergency Committee at the Hotel York, Berners St, London. Delegates from the Alexandra Palace, Bognor Regis, Bournemouth, Crouch Hill, Crystal Palace, Lyons, Margate, Newport (IOW), South East London, Southend, Temple and West London Bowling Clubs showed just how popular winter bowls had become and how quickly the game was growing. Sir Frank Godstone was elected as first chairman of the new section with Richard B. Hilton, vice chairman and Felix Hotchkiss as secretary and, on the occasion of the first AGM in April 1934, no less than 25 clubs were affiliated. In an effort to instill some kind of order into the indoor game the EBA produced a specification to guide new clubs which gave the essentials required for an indoor green, complete with minimum dimensions and details of available and acceptable floorcoverings. The estimated cost for a 30-yard (24.4 m) green with dressing rooms was £1000 per rink, an interesting sum compared with the £500 000 required to build a modern six-rink stadium today.

The first national indoor competition, an inter-club one-rink knock-out championship was inaugurated in 1935 with matches played on a home and away basis for a trophy donated by the president of the Middlesex County Bowling Association, Leonard Denny. Twenty-two clubs competed in the inaugural tournament which saw Crystal Palace emerge as winners, a feat they were to accomplish for the next two years. Although originally devised as a single rink competition, the Denny Cup has, through several rule changes, finally evolved as a 16-man club-team event. Members play as four fours, two playing at home and two away until the final stages. The Crystal Palace green, by that time housed in the Australia Pavilion, was completely destroyed by the fire which gutted the famous Palace in November 1936. Less than a year later however, club members were in action once more at a new, purpose built stadium, a magnificent seven-rink affair with a 42-yard (38.4 m) green, completed in just ten weeks on a site donated by Frederick Goodliffe, a keen bowler and England International in 1937.

The indoor international series, run on identical lines to the outdoor version, got under way in 1935 but it was not until the 1960/1 season that the first National Indoor Championship, the singles, came into being, with Alan Spooner of Ascot the first winner. Inevitably, it is David Bryant of Somerset who, with a staggering nine victories, has carved his name deep into this championship! Two years later came the pairs, won by Croydon's Vic Oliver and John Carden. The 1966/7 season saw the Ascot Club complete a noteworthy double when the quartet of A. Stubbs, E. Neal, W. Stubbs and J. D. Boothman added the inaugural fours title to the singles crown of their Mr Spooner. The national titles rosta was completed in 1971/2 with the addition of the triples with B. Button, J. Taylor and H. V. Wisdom of White Rock becoming the first holders.

On 1 July 1971, the indoor section broke its ties with the EBA to form the English Indoor Bowling Association, a separate and autonomous body with Stan Dengate voted in as president and George Dominay as secretary. Dominay's successor, Bernard Telfer, took over in 1972 and this year (1985) entered his 14th successive season as secretary. Today a compatible harmony exists between the two associations and the EIBA has wisely retained links with the EBA through representation on the council of the parent body.

One of the more recent additions to the indoor bowling calendar and certainly one of the most popular, is the Prudential Liberty Trophy, an indoor equivalent of the inter-county Middleton Cup. Like the Denny Cup competition, this six fours competition is played on a home and away basis until the quarter-finals. These are played on neutral greens with the home and away rule abandoned for the semi-final and final stages where all matches are played on the same green. Extra ends are played which are only taken into account in the event of a tied result. Middlesex were the first winners of the Liberty Trophy in 1974/5 beating Yorkshire/Durham in the finals.

This year (1985), the Lombard-sponsored Champion of Champions competition, now in its third year, has been officially adopted by the EIBA. The first winner in 1973 was Richard Roylands of the Mansfield Club.

From the 25 clubs affiliated in 1934, membership of the indoor section rose steadily to 50 after four years. Immediately following the Second World War, however, this figure dropped alarmingly to 33 and in 1971 at the formation of the EIBA there were just 49 indoor stadiums in England. Since then, a rapid acceleration has seen the figures jump to 117 clubs with 22 000 bowlers in the early seventies and the 1984 figures reveal that there are now something like 65 000 bowlers affiliated to the

EIBA through 196 clubs.

Indoor Bowls Note
The Indoor Season commences in the October of each year and concludes in the April of the year following. Championship results are indicated by the latter year in each case; i.e. the season 1984/5 is indicated as 1985.

EIBA Championships

Singles
1961 A. Spooner *Ascot*
1962 L. Kirton *Richmond*
1963 P. G. Brimble *Bristol*
1964 D. J. Bryant *Bristol*
1965 D. J. Bryant *Bristol*
1966 G. Attwood *Bristol*
1967 D. J. Bryant *Bristol*
1968 L. Kirton *Richmond*
1969 D. J. Bryant *Bristol*
1970 T. Brown *Ascot*
1971 D. J. Bryant *Bristol*
1972 D. J. Bryant *Bristol*
1973 B. Mattravers
    Ilminster
1974 A. Jackson *Worcester*
1975 M. Hughes *Hartlepool*
1976 A. Windsor *Wey
    Valley*
1977 D. J. Bryant *Clevedon*
1978 A. Dunton
    Wymondham Dell
1979 D. J. Bryant *Clevedon*
1980 D. Bell *Hartlepool*
1981 J. Dunn *Tunbridge
    Wells*
1982 M. Luker *Tunbridge
    Wells*
1983 D. J. Bryant
    Clevedon
1984 A. Ross *Longmeadow*
1985 T. Allcock *Cotswold*

Pairs
1964 V. Oliver, J. J. Carden *Croydon*
1965 F. Harris, J. Brayley *Paddington*
1966 D. Rowlands, L. Traves
    Paddington
1967 A. W. Knowling, A. Spooner
    Worthing
1968 J. Austen, F. Mortimer
    Richmond
1969 I. J. Harvey, J. A. Lewis
    Desborough
1970 C. Everett, M. Wade
    Wymondham Dell
1971 A. Windsor, R. Lamden *Ascot*
1972 R. G. Harris, D. Crocker *Cyphers*
1973 H. R. Woodhouse, R. Wealands
    Teesside
1974 M. Willis, J. Haines
    Whiteknights
1975 D. Cutler, W. E. Oliver *Bodmin*
1976 R. Roylands, W. McIntosh
    Mansfield
1977 J. Gordon, F. Clarke *Isis*
1978 R. Richardson, C. Davidson
    Newcastle
1979 J. Williams, N. Thompson
    Cambridge Park
1980 K. Illingworth, G. Turley
    Hartlepool

Teenager Nigel Smith of King George's Field, Surrey during the match which made him a star overnight. (Duncan Cubitt, *Bowls International*).

1981 J. Barnes, E. P. Hanger
    Sunderland
1982 D. Rhys Jones, D. J. Bryant
    Clevedon
1983 M. Henderson, J. Knox
    Concordia
1984 B. Morley, P. Goulding
    Nottingham
1985 R. Stephens, R. Fairbairn
    Newcastle

Triples
1972 B. Button, J. Taylor, H. V.
    Wisdom *White Rock*
1973 M. Knight, G. Haddon, G. D.
    Knight *Preston*
1974 A. L. Rider, I. Boys, L. Traves
    Century
1975 B. Badgery, A. O'Connell,
    A. Murrell *Richmond*
1976 P. Goyot, S. Hooper, A. Thorpe
    Essex County
1977 W. Davis, A. A. Elson, R. J.
    Smerdon *Exonia*
1978 L. Edwards, J. Robbins, J.
    Wiseman *Atherley*
1979 M. Goddard, S. Wilkes, A.
    Windsor *Wey Valley*
1980 L. Edwards, G. North, J.
    Wiseman *Atherley*
1981 D. Clark, T. Heppel, A. Thomson
    Cyphers
1982 T. Branchett, A. Masters,
    L. Shoobridge *Stour*
1983 D. M. Wilson, A. E. Horobin,
    N. A. Atkinson *Huddersfield*
1984 E. Brookes, R. Hall,
    R. Robertson *Lincoln*
1985 I. Lambert, J. Thirlbeck,
    J. Lambert *Stanley*

Fours
1967 A. Stubbs, E. Neal, W. Stubbs,
    J. D. Boothman *Ascot*

1968 R. Rowe, W. Taylor, W.
    Renshaw, W. Hart *Crouch Hill*
1969 C. Sparkes, I. J. Harvey,
    A. Whitehead, J. A. Lewis
    Desborough
1970 J. Muddle, F. Stansfield,
    R. Biggs, E. H. Burns *Croydon*
1971 C. Bridle, G. Booth, M. Walton,
    P. A. Line *Atherley*
1972 J. Bridle, G. Booth, M. Walton,
    P. A. Line *Atherley*
1973 F. Jeavons, R. Orwell, M.
    Phillipps, F. Sekjer *Greenwich*
1974 W. Walker, H. Siddle, H.
    Armstrong, T. Fleming
    Teesside
1975 G. Pease, P. Sabberton, C.
    Read, W. Burrell *Norfolk &
    Norwich*
1976 J. Gray, K. Storey, D. Dawson,
    T. Buller *Gateshead*
1977 R. Bowden, T. Wright, L.
    Bowden, J. Evans *Torbay*
1978 D. Hall, F. Shell, L. A. Hall,
    F. Cooper *Victory*
1979 R. Howard, K. Shaw, D.
    Bundell, M. Wade
    Wymondham Dell
1980 K. Illingworth, G. W. Newton,
    G. Turley, M. Hughes
    Hartlepool
1981 K. Illingworth, G. W. Newton,
    G. Turley, M. Hughes
    Hartlepool
1982 P. Hooper, R. Aitkin, Ron Aitkin,
    R. Jones *Desborough*
1983 M. Sekjer, G. A. Smith, T.
    Heppell, A. Thomson *Cyphers*
1984 M. Sekjer, G. A. Smith, T.
    Heppell, A. Thomson *Cyphers*
1985 W. Richards, J. Williams, C.
    Yelland, N. Thompson
    Cambridge Park

Denny Cup

1935	Crystal Palace	1957	Bounds Green
1936	Crystal Palace	1958	Croydon
1937	Crystal Palace	1959	Richmond
1938	Richmond	1960	Richmond
1939	Alexandra Palace	1961	Ilford
1948	Temple	1962	Worthing
1949	Calthorpe, Birmingham	1963	Paddington
		1964	Croydon
1950	Cambridge Park	1965	Cyphers
1951	Boston	1966	Worthing
1952	Paddington	1967	Falcon
1953	Portland Nottingham	1968	Paddington
1954	Bournemouth	1969	Richmond
1955	Paddington	1970	Vines Park
1956	Paddington	1971	Bristol

1972	Bristol
1973	Teesside
1974	Worthing
1975	Falcon
1976	Cyphers
1977	Barking
1978	Hartlepool
1979	Cambridge Park
1980	Bristol
1981	Torbay
1982	Richmond
1983	Cyphers
1984	Hartlepool
1985	Hartlepool

Liberty Trophy

1975	Middlesex
1976	Sussex
1977	Hampshire
1978	Surrey
1979	Somerset
1980	Yorkshire
1981	Lincolnshire
1982	Norfolk
1983	Durham
1984	Wiltshire
1985	Durham

Wales

Until the opening of the magnificent Cardiff stadium in 1960, indoor bowls in Wales was confined to the short-mat game. Despite the obvious drawbacks that this imposed, the Welsh Indoor Bowling Association was formed in Cardiff on 19 July 1934. Representatives from the nine short-mat clubs in existence, Dinas Powis, GWR A and B, Pontyclun, Sully, Trinity (Penarth), St Martins (Caerphilly), St Pauls (Penarth) and St Catherines (Caerphilly) elected Sir William James Thomas Bart., JP, as their first president, Arthur C. James as secretary, Emlyn Jones, vice chairman and R. Watts as honorary treasurer. With the main interest concentrated in an area within a 25-mile radius of Cardiff, bowlers utilized any hall of suitable size, playing on mats 45–55 ft (13.7–16.8 m) in length and 6–8 ft (1.8–2.4 m) in width, which were rolled up and stored after each session.

League matches commenced in the October of 1934 and, at the close of the first official season, it was the Trinity club of Penarth which became the first holders of the Sir William James and Lady Thomas League Challenge Cup, presented by the Welsh president. Other essentially short-mat competitions which emerged during this period were the fours championships for the Welsh Sports Ltd Cup, won in 1935 by GWR Central; the pairs (Alf Chapman Cup) won in 1936 by St Pauls; an inter-club tournament (J. Fligelstone Challenge Cup) won for the first time in 1947 by Pontyclun; and the singles (Sir William James Cooper-Thomas Cup) with F. Allen of Porth emerging as the first victor in 1949.

Welsh bowlers have taken part in the Home International indoor series ever since its inception in 1936 but, due to a lack of acceptable facilities, were forced to play their 'home' matches in England. This situation was resolved with the opening, on the 21 January 1960, of a magnificent indoor stadium in Cardiff, the result of much hard work on the part of many bowlers but perhaps especially, Jim Herbert, Reg Davies and Emrys Williams. The availability of a full-sized green after so many years led directly to a gradual raising of standards in the Welsh indoor game and obviously played its part in the first Welsh victory in the indoor international series at Crystal Palace in 1964. One year later, amid scenes of great jubilation, Wales made it two in a row, this time on their home 'turf' at Cardiff, thus winning the first series ever played in the principality.

The Cardiff Stadium championships, generally regarded as the national titles for singles, pairs and fours, were instituted in 1961 but the official Welsh national competitions were to follow in 1966 with the Cardiff Stadium based Llanishen Club making a clean sweep with home advantage. Winners in that inaugural season were: W. J. Mills (singles); L. Webley and J. R. Evans (pairs); R. Mead, H. W. Roan and C. Watkins (triples); J. R. Evans, J. A. Morgan, R. Thomas and G. Humphreys (fours). Further indoor bowling facilities joined the Cardiff Stadium with the opening of the Merthyr Tydfil and Rhondda Indoor Clubs in 1975. Swansea opened one year later and Vale of Glamorgan was founded in 1981. Despite this progress the indoor game in Wales suffered a terrible blow with the collapse of the Cardiff Stadium on 10 January 1982. Under tremendous pressure from heavy snow, the parabola-designed glass roof gave way, completely destroying the green and taking some of the walls with it. Fortunately the disaster happened at night and although the caretaker, Kevin Dart, narrowly escaped serious injury, no one else was present in the stadium at the time of the collapse. In 1985 a new indoor facility was opened at Sophia Gardens in Cardiff bringing the number of indoor clubs in Wales up to six with a combined membership of 2183. New centres at Bridgend, Llanelli and Milford are now nearing completion.

WIBA Champions

Singles

1967 W. J. Mills *Llanishen*
1968 W. J. Mills *Llanishen*
1969 P. Miller *Llanishen*
1970 W. J. Mills *Llanishen*
1971 J. E. Thomas *Treorchy*
1972 C. Watkins *Llanishen*
1973 J. R. Evans *Llanishen*
1974 D. L. Clark *Llanishen*
1975 C. Watkins *Llanishen*
1976 D. C. Osling *Llanishen*
1977 J. L. Stanfield *Merthyr Tydfil*
1978 G. Evans *Rhondda*
1979 G. Hindmarsh *Llanishen*
1980 J. E. Thomas *Rhondda*
1981 J. Price *Swansea*
1982 J. Squires *Swansea*
1983 T. Sullivan *Swansea*
1984 J. R. Evans *Vale of Glamorgan*
1985 P. Evans *Torfaen*

Pairs

1967 L. Webley, J. R. Evans *Llanishen*
1968 E. Stanbury, W. J. Mills *Llanishen*
1969 R. Young, S. Hynam *Llanishen*
1970 P. D. Evans, D. L. Clark *Llanishen*
1971 D. Nicholas, S. Hynam *Llanishen*
1972 E. J. Williams, M. J. Edwards *Llanishen*
1973 L. Webley, J. R. Evans *Llanishen*
1974 J. E. King, D. L. Clark *Llanishen*
1975 W. Fletcher, B. Hawkins *Llanishen*
1976 J. Power, J. Thomson *Llanishen*
1977 C. Beer, J. J. John *Llanishen*
1978 R. Williams, C. Watkins *Llanishen*
1979 A. Thomas, P. Austerberry *Llanishen*
1980 T. King, P. Bailey *Swansea*
1981 R. Williams, L. Webley *Llanishen*
1982 D. Osling, B. Hawkins *Llanishen*
1983 C. Taylor, M. Bishop *Swansea*
1984 S. Rees, J. Price *Swansea*
1985 J. Thomas, D. Evans *Rhondda*

Triples

1967 R. Mead, H. W. Roan, C. Watkins *Llanishen*
1968 R. F. Jones, W. Fletcher, L. C. Williams *Llanishen*
1969 L. Bird, G. Roberts, G. Crowther *Llanishen*
1970 E. Jenkins, R. Watts, C. Watts *Llanishen*
1971 G. Arthur, C. Williams, P. E. Ridd *Llanishen*
1972 D. C. Osling, B. Thompson, L. Rae *Llanishen*
1973 J. R. Evans, J. A. Morgan, G. Humphreys *Llanishen*
1974 J. E. King, J. Calnan, D. L. Clark *Llanishen*
1975 H. Hewitson, J. Hardman, F. Leamon *Llanishen*
1976 M. Bishop, C. Taylor, F. Bishop *Llanishen*
1977 W. J. Mills, D. Conibear, D. Adamson *Llanishen*
1978 P. Webley, G. W. Thomas, L. Webley *Llanishen*
1979 R. Williams, J. A Morgan, C. Watkins *Llanishen*
1980 A. Thomas, R. Williams, C. Watkins *Llanishen*
1981 J. Colwill, R. Thomas, E. Colwill *Swansea*
1982 P. Carpenter, R. Morgan, J. L. Stanfield *Merthyr Tydfil*
1983 J. Price, H. Price, R. Hill *Swansea*
1984 B. Rowley, M. Cox, P. D. Evans *Torfaen*
1985 S. Rees, T. Sullivan, C. Williams *Swansea*

Fours

1967 J. R. Evans, J. A. Morgan, R. Thomas, G. Humphreys *Llanishen*
1968 R. Mead, D. J. Cole, H. W. Roan, C. Watkins *Llanishen*
1969 S. Colston, H. Colston, D. Norman, V. Harris *Llanishen*
1970 H. W. Roan, D. J. Cole, W. Dacey, C. Watkins *Llanishen*
1971 D. J. Cole, R. Pomeroy, W. Dacey, C. Watkins *Llanishen*
1972 L. Fullilove, P. D. Evans, L. Probert, J. Thomson *Llanishen*
1973 F. Groves, R. Evans, L. Probert, J. Osborn *Llanishen*
1974 W. Fletcher, L. Hughes, S. Hull, B. Hawkins *Llanishen*
1975 R. Ashe, R. Pomeroy, P. D. Evans, C. Watkins *Llanishen*
1976 W. R. Pomeroy, T. Nash, P. D. Evans, C. Watkins *Llanishen*
1977 E. Blatt, D. G. James, I. Sutherland, J. Thomson *Llanishen*
1978 T. Mounty, H. Green, G. Roberts, L. Jones *Llanishen*
1979 C. Taylor, E. Colwill, C. Rees, R. Thomas *Swansea*
1980 J. Price, H. Price, J. John, R. Hill *Swansea*
1981 A. Thomas, H. Meddins, P. D. Evans, C. Watkins *Llanishen*
1982 D. Teague, R. Ash, D. Osling, B. Hawkins *Llanishen*
1983 G. Williams, T. Coulthard, B. Hawkins, J. A. Morgan *Vale of Glamorgan*
1984 J. Price, H. Price, C. Williams, R. Hill *Swansea*
1985 M. Thomas, A. Thomas, A. Davies, C. Lewis *Merthyr*

Youngest British Isles senior indoor singles winner Jim Baker (Ireland) aged 22 (born 18 February 1958) beat Steward Douglas (Scotland) 21–16 in final 1981.

Scotland

Although Scotland can justly claim to have had, in the Edinburgh Winter Bowling Association, the first indoor bowling club, the game has lagged behind England in the provision of facilities. For some 30 years, although increased in size to accommodate seven rinks, the Castle Terrace site remained the sole venue for indoor games in Scotland. Fortunately with such men as F. B. Young, who remained in office as president of the Edinburgh club for 20 years and Archie Martin, first president of the Scottish Indoor BA, the game north of the border somehow retained viability. In 1932 Martin played host to a team of London-based bowlers and one year later took a team of Edinburgh bowlers to London. Contact had been established between the indoor bowlers of Scotland and England and the seeds of an international series, similar to that of the outdoor game, had been sown. The first purpose-built indoor bowling stadium in Scotland was constructed at Ayr in 1935 by Edward Ecrepont, a Belgian, who, one year later, added a second in Glasgow and it was on this Glasgow green that the second indoor international series took place in 1937. Other indoor facilities were opened in the thirties including the two-rink Jewel Miners Welfare Club at Edinburgh in 1939 and a green at Kirkcaldy. A four-rink jute surfaced green was in operation at Perth in

Take your partners: Scotland's David Gourlay (left) and Jim Blake celebrate. (Duncan Cubitt, *Bowls International*).

1955, but it was not until the opening in 1960 of the Dundee indoor club that Scotland had a six-rink green of regulation length.

The Scottish Indoor Bowling Association, formed in 1951, is now a vigorous and healthy body with 32 clubs, 25 000 and 12 500 female members playing in leagues sponsored by Schweppes, A. T. Mays and Thistle Metalics. The national competitions began in 1965 with Harry Reston winning the *Daily Mail* Trophy in the singles, Ayr taking the Ecrepont Trophy by defeating Banfield in the pairs, and Blantyre collecting the Carlsberg Trophy as fours champions. The triples championship was added in 1970 with Prestwick the first winners and holder of the J. R. Donald Trophy. All Scottish National Championships are now sponsored by CIS Insurance. Apart from these national trophies there are singles, pairs and fours regional championships sponsored by Cattos Scotch Whisky, and competitions such as the Perth Cities and Counties which, until the advent of the Scottish League Cup in 1964, was the closest thing to a national competition in Scotland with a trophy donated by the Perth Ice Rink Club. This competition is now sponsored by Schweppes.

Regulations for admission to the SIBA are perhaps the most stringent in the game. All clubs seeking admission must, under the constitution of the SIBA, 'control and play on an indoor green with suitable playing surface, containing at least four rinks measuring not less than 38 yd (34.7 m) in length and not less than 15 ft (4.5 m) in width, with regulation banks and ditches at each end and side ditches of $1\frac{1}{2}$ in (38 mm) minimum depth'.

CIS Scottish National Championships

Singles
1966 H. Reston *Bainfield*
1967 H. Reston *Bainfield*
1968 W. Gibb *West of Scotland*
1969 J. Marshall *Blantyre*
1970 A. McIntosh Jnr. *Edinburgh*
1971 W. McQueen *Lanarkshire*
1972 A. McIntosh Jnr. *Edinburgh*
1973 P. McLean *Prestwick*
1974 W. Wilkie *Dundee*
1975 R. Sutherland *Bainfield*
1976 J. Boyle *West of Scotland*
1977 A. Prentice *East Fife*
1978 J. Blake *West of Scotland*
1979 J. Watson *West of Scotland*
1980 R. Burnett *Ardrossan*
1981 S. Douglas *Coatbridge*
1982 J. Fullarton *Ardrossan*
1983 R. Sutherland *West Lothian*
1984 F. McCartney *Irvine*
1985 J. Muir *Irvine*

Junior Singles
1975 J. Watson *West of Scotland*
1976 G. Neil *Ayr*
1977 A. E. Thomson *East Fife*
1978 M. Marshall *Edinburgh*
1979 G. Adrain *Irvine*
1980 J. M. Murray *Glasgow*
1981 A. Smillie *Prestwick*
1982 F. McCartney *Prestwick*
1983 J. Roxburgh *Headwell*
1984 J. Campaigne *Blantyre*
1985 R. Corsie *Edinburgh*

Pairs
1966 Ayr
1967 West of Scotland
1968 Blantyre
1969 Edinburgh
1970 West of Scotland
1971 Edinburgh
1972 Prestwick
1973 Arbroath
1974 Prestwick
1975 Edinburgh
1976 Glasgow
1977 Edinburgh
1978 Perth
1979 Edinburgh
1980 Dundee
1981 Blantyre
1982 West Lothian
1983 Irvine
1984 Ardrossan
1985 Aberdeen

Fours
1966 Blantyre
1967 Ayr
1968 Edinburgh
1969 Prestwick
1970 Lanarkshire
1971 Dundee
1972 Prestwick
1973 Coatbridge
1974 Edinburgh
1975 Coatbridge
1976 Prestwick
1977 Dundee
1978 Dundee
1979 Ardrossan
1980 Aberdeen
1981 Aberdeen
1982 Dundee
1983 Ardrossan
1984 Blantyre
1985 Perth

Triples
1971 Prestwick
1972 Prestwick
1973 Prestwick
1974 Paisley
1975 Aberdeen
1976 Paisley
1977 Irvine
1978 Prestwick
1979 Coatbridge
1980 Prestwick
1981 Arbroath
1982 Cumbernauld
1983 Auckinleck
1984 Midlothian
1985 Coatbridge

Senior Fours
1970 Blantyre
1971 Glasgow
1972 Glasgow
1973 Edinburgh
1974 Dundee
1975 Aberdeen
1976 West of Scotland
1977 Perth
1978 Glasgow
1979 Arbroath
1980 Dundee
1981 Bainfield
1982 Turriff
1983 Irvine
1984 Glasgow
1985 East Fife

Ireland

It is a highly successful short-mat game, organized with tremendous enthusiasm by the Irish Indoor Bowling Association which dominates winter bowling in Ireland. The Association is not affiliated to the Irish BA which has its own indoor section to organize the regulation indoor game.

With only one indoor bowling facility of the required standard, the P. T. Watson Stadium in Belfast, it is hardly surprising that Ireland's bowlers have yet to win an international indoor series. Ireland took no part in the series until, as invited guests, they joined the other home country teams at Dundee in 1963. Since the opening of the Watson Stadium in 1966, however, Ireland have at least made their mark on the indoor game, performing with increasing confidence and success in the British Isles Indoor Championships which serve as an hors d'oeuvre to the main international event each year. In 1969 Peter McConnell skipped his rink to a famous victory in the fours getting Ireland off the mark, while Eddie Gordon (now highly active in bowls journalism) and Brenden McBrien took the pairs in the following year. In 1972 McBrien struck again, this time winning the singles and the trio of Stan Espie, Tom Sutton and Sammy Ashwood made it a complete set in 1975 with victory in the triples.

The P. T. Watson Stadium is soon to be joined by a new indoor facility which will be named after Ireland's most successful bowler of recent times: Jim Baker, 1984 World Indoor Champion and gold medal winner at the World Outdoor Championships in the same year at Aberdeen as skip of the powerful Irish triples combination.

First find your green! The crown green bowlers who frequent Huddersfield's Griffin Inn are a hardy bunch. Spurning the attractions of the local indoor stadia they play their favoured game for 12 months of the year come rain, shine or even snow! It is quite usual on a winter Sunday morning to find men wielding squeegees, shovels and brooms to clear water or snow from the playing area and, on some occasions, an iced-up surface is simply rolled and then used. In 1979 thick snow defeated even the shovel brigade but, not to be thwarted, the bowlers borrowed a JCB and set to clearing an area sufficient for play to take place. Players in the Sunday 16 invitation tournament turn out once every three weeks throughout the year playing for a place in a Champion of Champions final.

Irish Indoor Championships

Singles

1967	Hugh Montgomery
1968	Wm. Pimley
1969	Daniel Laverty
1970	Charlie Stewart
1971	Jim J. Donnelly
1972	Brenden McBrien
1973	Roy Fulton
1974	T. Stanley Espie
1975	John S. Higgins
1976	Tommy Reeves
1977	John Greer
1978	Jim Donnelly
1979	John Greer
1980	Wm. McKelvey
1981	Jim Baker
1982	Wm. McKelvey
1983	Jim Baker
1984	Michael Dunlop
1985	Jim Baker

Pairs

1967	H. Spence, A. McConnell
1968	D. White, A. McConnell
1969	C. Park, J. Carlisle
1970	E. J. Gordon, B. McBrien
1971	T. Reeves, H. Montgomery
1972	H. Caruth, S. J. Thompson
1973	R. Fulton, J. Henry
1974	S. Nash, T. Sutton
1975	J. Greer, B. McBrien
1976	D. Francis, S. Ashwood
1977	S. Espie, J. J. Donnelly
1978	T. Reeves, W. McKelvey
1979	N. McQuay, W. Watson
1980	C. Aiken, E. Steele
1981	J. Greer, B. McBrien
1982	C. Campbell, W. Pimley
1983	J. McMullan, M. Dunlop
1984	N. McQuay, W. Watson
1985	W. Montgomery, J. Branklin

Triples

1972	J. Warden, T. J. Haslem, J. E. Haslem
1973	R. Fulton, J. Henry, J. J. Donnelly
1974	W. McKelvey, J. Brankin, E. McNally
1975	S. Espie, T. Sutton, S. Ashwood
1976	B. McBrien, S. Espie, J. J. Donnelly
1977	J. S. Higgins, D. Heatley, S. Curry
1978	M. Dunlop, S. Ashwood, W. Murray
1979	J. Higgins, D. Heatley, S. Curry
1980	S. Allen, R. Fulton, J. Henry
1981	R. Burns, E. McVeigh, S. Ashwood
1982	M. Dunlop, N. McQuay, W. Watson
1983	C. Craig, M. Dunlop, B. Dunlop
1984	S. Allen, S. Hegan, T. Kennedy
1985	D. Minelly, D. Johnston, S. Ashwood

Fours

1967	T. McKelvey, B. McBrien, W. Pimley, J. J. Donnelly
1968	T. McKelvey, B. McBrien, W. Pimley, J. J. Donnelly
1969	J. Webb, D. White, A. Smith, A. McConnell
1970	T. McKelvey, B. McBrien, W. Pimley, J. J. Donnelly
1971	T. Reeves, C. Stevenson, K. Lynn, H. Montgomery
1972	R. Larmour, S. Leslie, J. Carlisle, R. Crockard
1973	J. Thompson, J. Kendal, T. Neil, L. Churms
1974	M. Murray, J. Greer, E. J. Gordon, B. McBrien
1975	S. Allen, A. Kennedy, R. Fulton, J. Henry
1976	S. Millar, T. Burnett, J. Ralph, E. Cruickshanks
1977	H. Humphries, C. Stevenson, J. Donaldson, H. Stevenson
1978	W. Roberts, W. Chambers, S. N. Coulter, D. L. Cowden
1979	T. Porter, D. Corkill, N. McQuay, W. Watson
1980	J. Rogan, J. Greer, B. Dunlop, B. McBrien
1981	S. Hegan, A. Dornan, S. Espie, W. McKelvey
1982	B. Sloan, B. Higgins, R. Horner, D. Corkill
1983	W. Roberts, S. Millar, M. Beattie, T. S. Brown
1984	W. Montgomery, E. McNally, S. Elliman, J. Brankin
1985	J. McMullan, P. Davey, M. Dunlop, D. Hamilton

When conditions are particularly bad, margarine or coconut oil is often spread on the bowl to prevent snow gathering on the running surface. Perhaps a trophy in the form of a brass monkey would be appropriate.

And it's not even Burns Night! The Scots celebrate another wonder shot by their unseen skip, David Gourlay. England's Bill Hobart (extreme left), Peter Line and Roy Cutts (extreme right) inspect the damage. (Duncan Cubitt, *Bowls International*).

The British Isles Indoor Championships

Singles
1967 D. J. Bryant *England*
1968 W. Mills *Wales*
1969 D. J. Bryant *England*
1970 W. J. Mills *Wales*
1971 W. McQueen *Ireland*
1972 B. McBrien *Ireland*
1973 B. Mattravers *England*
1974 W. Wilkie *Scotland*
1975 M. Hughes *England*
1976 A. Windsor *England*
1977 D. J. Bryant *England*
1978 J. Blake *Scotland*
1979 D. J. Bryant *England*
1980 W. McKelvey *Ireland*
1981 J. Baker *Ireland*
1982 J. Fullarton *Scotland*
1983 R. Sutherland *Scotland*
1984 M. Dunlop *Ireland*
1985 A. Ross *England*

Triples
1972 S. Grant, J. Neven, J. McNair *Scotland*
1973 M. B. Young, J. Walker, S. Grant *Scotland*
1974 A. Rider, I. Boys, L. Travers *England*
1975 S. Espie, T. Sutton, S. Ashwood *Ireland*
1976 B. McBrien, S. Espie, J. J. Donnelly *Ireland*
1977 W. Davis, A. A. Elson, R. J. Smerdon *England*
1978 M. Dunlop, S. Ashwood, W. Murray *Ireland*
1979 M. Goddard, S. Wilkes, A. Windsor *England*
1980 A. O'Hara, R. Campbell, D. Gourlay *Scotland*
1981 G. B. Anderson, J. Henderson, L. Sim *Scotland*
1982 D. Carpenter, R. Morgan, L. Stanfield *Wales*
1983 T. Branchett, W. Masters, L. Shoobridge *England*
1984 D. Rowley, P. D. Evans, C. Watkins *Wales*
1985 D. Johnstone, D. Mineely, S. Ashwood *Ireland*

Pairs
1967 A. W. Knowling, A. Spooner *England*
1969 T. McLean, R. Bernard *Scotland*
1970 E. J. Gordon, B. McBrien *Ireland*
1971 T. Reeves, H. Montgomery *Ireland*
1972 R. Harris, D. J. Crocker *England*
1973 L. Webley, F. Rieple *Wales*
1974 A. O'Hara, D. Gourlay *Scotland*
1975 J. Greer, B. McBrien *Ireland*
1976 J. Power, J. D. H. Thomas *Wales*
1977 C. Beer, J. J. John *Wales*
1978 T. Reeves, W. McKelvie *Ireland*
1979 W. Paul, A. Binnie *Scotland*
1980 K. Illingworth, G. Turley *England*
1981 R. Williams, L. Webley *Wales*
1982 J. Barnes, E. Hanger *England*
1983 D. Rhys-Jones, D. J. Bryant *England*
1984 N. McQuay, W. Watson *Ireland*
1985 B. Morley, P. Goulding *England*

Fours
1967 Wales (G. Humphreys)
1968 Wales (C. Watkins)
1969 Ireland (P. McConnell)
1970 Wales (C. Watkins)
1971 England (P. Line)
1972 Scotland (D. Goulay)
1973 Scotland (J. Freeland)
1974 Ireland (B. McBrien)
1975 Ireland (J. Henry)
1976 Wales (C. Watkins)
1977 Scotland (W. G. Scott)
1978 Scotland (W. G. Scott)
1979 Ireland (W. Watson)
1980 England (M. Hughes)
1981 Wales (C. Watkins)
1982 Ireland (D. Corkill)
1983 Wales (J. A. Morgan)
1984 Scotland (S. McCall)
1985 Scotland (J. Bright)

International Matches

Year	Venue/Winners
1936	Paddington *England*
1937	Glasgow *Scotland*
1938	Bournemouth *Scotland*
1939	Croydon *Scotland*
1949	Paddington *England*
1950	Paddington *Scotland*
1951	Ayr *Scotland*
1952	Croydon *England*
1953	Boston *England*
1954	Ayr *Scotland*
1955	Croydon *England*
1956	Croydon *England*
1957	Perth *England*

1958	Crystal Palace *England*
1959	Boston *England*
1960	Perth *England*
1961	Crystal Palace *Scotland*
1962	Cardiff *England*
1963	Dundee *England*
1964	Crystal Palace *Wales*
1965	Cardiff *Wales*
1966	Glasgow *England*
1967	Belfast *England*
1968	Desborough *Scotland*
1969	Cardiff *England*
1970	Belfast *England*
1971	Aberdeen *Scotland*

1972	Teesside *Scotland*
1973	Cardiff *Scotland*
1974	Prestwick *Scotland*
1975	Rutherglen *Scotland*
1976	Rugby *England*
1977	Cardiff *Scotland*
1978	Teesside *Scotland*
1979	Aberdeen *Scotland*
1980	Hartlepool *England*
1981	Cardiff *Wales*
1982	Teesside *Scotland*
1983	Ardrossan *England*
1984	Folkestone *England*
1985	Swansea *England*

World Indoor Championship

The Embassy World Indoor Championships began in 1979 at the Coatbridge IBC near Glasgow. Now one of the most prestigious events in the bowling calendar, this tournament evolved from a one-day 'International Invitation' event jointly organized by the Coatbridge Club and the Monklands District Council in 1976. The success of this competition, featuring the champions of the four home countries and screened by BBC Scottish Television, encouraged thoughts of a World Championship at the same venue. Three years later plans reached fruition with bowlers from nine countries (David Bryant appeared as Commonwealth champion) taking part in the inaugural championship, with Bryant defeating Jim Donnelly of Ireland in the final to become the first indoor world champion.

Embassy World Indoor Championships

1979	David Bryant *Commonwealth*
1980	David Bryant *England*
1981	David Bryant *England*
1982	John Watson *Scotland*
1983	Bob Sutherland *Scotland*
1984	Jim Baker *Ireland*
1985	Terry Sullivan *Wales*
1986	Tony Allcock *England*

Israel's Cecil Bransky at play in the 1985 Embassy World indoor singles – he finished runner-up to Terry Sullivan of Wales. (Author).

Darts player Jocky Wilson in an unaccustomed role watched by a fascinated Ian Botham (left) and Bob Willis (centre) – all taking part in a 'celebrity' match during the Granada Television Superbowl tournament at Manchester in 1984. (Duncan Cubitt, *Bowls International*).

The UK Indoor Singles

A new kind of tournament was born on 31 October 1983 with the inaugural CIS Insurance sponsored UK Indoor Singles Championship, at Preston's Guildhall. Apart from a rather mixed bag of flat green bowlers, the line-up included four men from the crown green code, Noel Burrows, Tony Poole, Michael Robinson and Alan Thompson. Play, which took place on a revolutionary styled portable wooden rink, was scored on the best of three sets of seven-up system and promotion was in the capable hands of Mike Watterson Ltd, making a calculated forray into the new television sport of bowls from his snooker-based headquarters. The venue was Watterson's favourite, Preston Guildhall, and the only blot on the proceedings came when television technicians downed tools and relegated to the sports pages a tournament wholly geared to a viewing public.

With a total prize money of £16 800 (£4 000 to the winner) to aim at, only Thompson and Burrows of the crown greeners made the

second round, Thompson eventually falling to the Welshman J. R. Evans, while Burrows went down in straight sets to the young Irish star, Michael Dunlop. Bob Sutherland, an ex-Glasgow Rangers and Stirling Albion footballer, entered the tournament on the crest of a very big wave indeed as World, British Isles and Scottish indoor champion and his path to the final was trouble-free, just one set dropped to John Bell of Cumbria. The form of David Bryant, however, was ominously impressive with straight sets victories all the way. In the five-set final, the English star from Clevedon played what many observers described as the finest match of his career, completely dominating the bewildered Scot to win 7–4, 7–3, 7–1.

The CIS UK Singles

1983 David Bryant *England*
1984 Terry Sullivan *Wales*
1985 Jim Baker *Ireland*

Windsor BC.

A Royal Tradition Bowls was first played at Windsor Castle in 1663 by Charles II. Today the Royal Household Bowling Club carries on that tradition on a green opened on 18 June 1921 by King George V. Members wear ties of purple, gold and crimson, the Queen's racing colours. Always high on the list of touring sides from abroad, the club has played host to visiting sides from South Africa, New Zealand and Australia. The men's singles competition is played for the King George VI Championship Cup while the small but highly successful ladies section compete for the Duchess of Kent Cup. In 1984 Betty Crisp, Doreen Parker, Kathleen Williams and Mary Crisp added the Berkshire County Women's fours trophy to the nine county titles won in previous years by the men of the RHBC.

The Granada Television Superbowl Championships

In 1984 the Watterson portable rink was used for yet another new tournament, the Granada Television Superbowl. This television-inspired and financed competition took place on 15–20 October 1984, at the stage one studio of Granada Television in Manchester, and featured a fresh innovation by including not only crown green exponents – 17 this time – but six of the top bowlers from the women's game. Burrows, the Manchester publican showed that he had digested the lessons of Preston by gaining revenge over Michael Dunlop, beating the Irishman 7–6, 7–3, but went out in the quarter-finals to John Bell, the 1983 outdoor singles champion of England. As the score of 7–4, 4–7, 7–3 might indicate this was no easy passage for John Bell who was forced at one stage to unleash a rocket-like drive to save the match.

Shocks also came from the ladies with women's world outdoor queen, Norma Shaw, beating Ireland's 1984 world indoor champion, Jim Baker, in two sets before going on to ruin the day for the young Scottish hopeful Richard Corsie in the quarter-finals, beating him also in two sets. Shaw's superb run came to an end in the semi-finals where she came up against an old adversary, David Bryant, a man she seems unable to match and this occasion proved no different as Bryant swept her challenge aside to enter the final with a 7–3, 7–5 victory. In what turned out to be a classic confrontation, Bryant found himself matched in the final with John Bell who had shown great skill and grit to defeat Willie Wood in their semi. It was however two mistakes, one a short bowl, the other a too short jack on the final end, which cost the big Cumbrian the match and the £10 000 first prize, with David Bryant collecting yet another title by virtue of a 5–7, 7–6, 7–6 victory.

The 1985 Superbowl saw the entry of the Liverpool Victoria Insurance Friendly Society into bowls sponsorship heralded by record prize money totalling £26 400. Included in this amount was £1000 for the bowler winning a match in the least number of ends.

The Granada Television Superbowl Championships

1984 David Bryant *England*

Liverpool Victoria Insurance Superbowl Championships

1985 N. Burrows *Crown Green*

9 The Game Worldwide

National Associations in Membership with the International Bowling Board

FULL MEMBERS (1985)

English Bowling Association
Secretary: J. F. Elms, 2a Iddesleigh Road, Bournemouth BH3 7JR. UK.

Irish Bowling Association
Secretary: J. Barnes, 212 Sicily Park, Belfast BT10 0AQ. Ireland.

Scottish Bowling Association
Secretary: P. Smith, 50 Wellington Street, Glasgow G2 6EF. UK.

Welsh Bowling Association
Secretary: G. Roberts, 54 Neath Road, Tonna, nr. Neath, W. Glam. UK.

American Lawn Bowls Association
Secretary: W. C. Shonborn, 5200 Irvine Blvd., 52 Irvine, California 92714. USA.

Australian Bowling Council
Secretary: J. M. Dobbie, A.M., 245 Warrigal Road, Burwood 3125, Victoria, Australia.

Canadian Lawn Bowling Council
Secretary: J. Angell, 785 Alder Avenue, Sherwood Park, Alberta T8A 1V1. Canada.

New Zealand Bowling Association
Secretary: G. Mackay, P.O. Box 65–172, Mairangi Bay, Auckland 10. New Zealand.

South African Bowling Association
Secretary: A. H. R. West, PO Box 64113, Highlands North, Johannesburg 2037. South Africa.

Zimbabwe Rhodesia Bowling Association
Secretary: V. Atkinson, PO Box 1336, Bulawayo, Zimbabwe.

ASSOCIATE MEMBERS (1985)

Argentina Bowling Association
Secretary: P. Kay, Zabala 2477 (1426), Buenos Aires, Argentina.

Botswana Bowling Association
Secretary: D. C. W. Rose, PO Box 1704, Gaborone, Botswana.

Fiji Bowling Association
Secretary: A. M. Christian, PO Box 119, Suva, Fiji.

Guernsey Bowling Association
Secretary: J. Farncombe, 27 Hauteville, St Peter Port, Guernsey, CI.

Hong Kong Bowling Association
Secretary: R. D. Hayes, c/o Hong Kong BA, GPO Box 1823. Hong Kong.

Israel Bowling Association
Secretary: C. Cooper, PO Box 2331, Tel Aviv, Israel.

Japanese Bowling Association
Secretary: Tadao Nishi, 2–46, 3 Chome Takaai, Higashisumiyoshi-Ku, Osaka. Japan

Jersey Bowling Association
Secretary: D. E. Foster, 19 Richelieu Park, Tower Road, St Helier, Jersey, CI.

Kenya Bowling Association
Secretary: I. S. Keen, PO Box 43259, Nairobi, Kenya.

Malawi Bowling Association
Secretary: R. F. D. Dunn, PO Box 555, Blantyre, Malawi.

Papua New Guinea Bowling Association
Secretary: W. R. Marchant, PO Box 1227, LAE, Papua New Guinea.

Swaziland Bowling Association
Secretary: L. James, PO Box 8, Malkerns, Swaziland.

Transkeian Bowling Association
Secretary: B. Dineen, 24 Willow Drive, Fort Gale Umtate, Transkei.

Western Samoa Bowling Association
Secretary: F. A. Kirisome, PO Box 53, Apia, Western Samoa.

Zambia Bowling Association
Secretary: J. Keeling, PO Box 708, Mufulira, Zambia.

Argentina

While the appearance of the Argentine team at the 1984 World Bowls Championships at Aberdeen, so soon after the Falklands conflict, caused some surprise in sporting circles, there was almost equal wonder among spectators that the game was played in that country at all. Lawn bowls however has been played in Argentina since around the turn of the century, introduced into the country by employees of the British-owned railway companies and, although never reaching the status of a major sport, has nevertheless survived.

In the early years, elderly but determined bowlers utilized the cricket pitches in Buenos Aires and the towns of Rosario and Campana, both lying to the north of the capital and possessing a strong British presence thanks to the combination of various thriving industries and rail termini. At the close of play, heavy rollers would be trundled onto the pitch, closely followed by a number of ancient bowlers, eager to get in as many ends as possible before nightfall. As the popularity of the game increased, purpose built greens were constructed at the various athletic clubs in and around Buenos Aires and, in 1934, three of the railway clubs, the Western, the Central Argentina and the Pacific joined with the Belgrano AC to form the British Bowls Association. T. Patterson (Western) was elected first president of the Association with C. W. Carlisle (Belgrano) secretary, and the new body represented a membership of around 80 bowlers plus a ladies section of 40.

In 1939 the title of the association was changed to the Asociacion Britanica de Bowls de la Republica Argentina, no doubt reflecting a growing interest in the game among the Argentine nationals. At the height of its popularity, however, there were only ten clubs numbering bowls among their sporting attractions and the sale of the railway companies to the Argentine Government in 1949 was severely to deplete even that small membership. At present there are but five clubs, the Belgrano AC, the Lomas AC (one of the two sporting clubs organized by the Great Southern Railway), San Isidro, the Mitre (formerly Central Argentine Railway) and San Martin (formerly the Pacific Railway), with many of the older greens converted to other uses.

In 1970 the Argentine governing bowls body underwent yet another change of title adopting the current Argentine Bowls Association (Asociacion Argentina de Bowls), and two year's later the San Martin club was instrumental in arranging the association's first 'international tour', a modest weekend trip to Brazil, to compete against bowlers of the Paissandu Atletico Club of Rio de Janeiro. The Paissandu, founded by British residents of Rio, and another at Sao Paulo, are the only two bowling clubs of any size in Brazil and are both honorary members of the Argentine Bowls Association.

In 1980 Argentina became an Associate Member of the International Bowling Board and adoption of IBB laws led to a change from the traditional Argentine two-wood game to the more widely practised four-wood mode of play.

Ballentine Cup

Trophy donated in the early Thirties by F. G. Ballentine. Originally competed for by teams of Argentine residents representing England, Ireland, Scotland and Wales. This was changed, first to 'Foreigners versus Argentines' and eventually to North versus South and played on an annual basis. Teams comprise 12 players with the North chosen from the Belgrano, Mitre and San Isidro Clubs and South from the Lomas and San Martin ACs. Play is governed now by IBB laws and features singles, pairs, triples and fours events.

The Clover Cup (The Irish Cup)

A four-wood singles knock-out competition.

The Cunningham Cup

Championship club tournament of six players per team. IBB laws.

The Daddy Williams

Knock-out singles for players over 60 years of age.

The Dowson Cup

Dating from the 1920s, this essentially Masonic tournament is a knock-out singles competition organized on a private basis.

Tom Blades: for many years one of Argentina's top bowlers.

Mixed pairs at the San Martin Athletic Club, Buenos Aires.

The Freeland Cup
Round robin (Australian-style) mixed four-wood doubles.
The Hollyman Cup
Championship club tournament.
The Percy Clark Cup
A married couples round robin tournament.
The Presidents Cup
Knock-out four-wood pairs.
The Smart Cup
Knock-out four-wood singles.
The Stocks Tray
Knock-out triples.
The Ted Hemmery Trophy
Fours.

There are also a number of charity tournaments played annually including those for the British Hospital, a mixed triples event with all proceeds and donations going to the hospital, and another for the Diego Thompson Hospital.

Julian Dannevig, Carlos Gonzalez and Enri Merli of the San Martin Club, Clemente Bausili from the Lomas AC and Albert Geddes from the Belgrano AC represented Argentina in the Fifth World Bowls Championships at Aberdeen in 1984 with Derby-born Dennis Watson as team manager. Invited to take part as last-minute replacements for Japan, the Argentines can look back on their first World Championships with some pride. Julian Dannevig experienced a superb singles opening match victory beating John Jones of Jersey 21–3 but could only add one more win to his total, a 21–18 defeat of George Croft of Papua New Guinea. In the pairs, Carlos Gonzalez and Clemente Bausili showed determination by climbing back from 19–1 down to Malawi, to lose by a respectable 21 shots to 17, and managed one victory, oddly

enough against Jersey's John Jones and Arthur McKernan by 25–17.

In the triples, skip Albert Geddes kept up the record against Jersey with a 21–19 victory but the team's finest hour arrived in the fours when, skipped once more by Geddes, the Argentine rink inflicted a completely unforeseen 24–15 defeat on the mighty Australians, skipped by Keith Poole. A highly creditable performance by a country with just 300 male bowlers.

Australia

With over 500 000 registered players (1 in 14 of the population), Australia is in the forefront of a world-wide boom in the fortunes of bowls which has followed increased exposure in all forms of the media. Between 1983 and 1984 male membership alone experienced a 10 per cent surge, climbing from a total of 314 678 to a staggering 351 434! While over the same period the women's totals rose from 148 699 to a less spectacular, but nevertheless satisfactory 152 781.

The seeds for this vigorous growth were sown in 1844 by Frederick Lipscombe, an English immigrant and owner of the Beach Tavern at Sandy Bay, Hobart, Tasmania. In an effort to maintain his skills in what was obviously a favourite pastime, Lipscombe constructed a green behind his tavern and advertised the fact to all comers. That this pioneer was to come out second best in the first bowls match to take place in his adopted country in no way dims his contribution to the game. The *Hobart Town's Courier and Van Diemens Land Gazette* published a report on the match on 4 January 1845 which read 'Old English recreations – The first game of bowls ever played in Van Diemen's Land, or perhaps in the Southern Hemisphere, was played at Mr Lipscombe's Sandy Bay on Wednesday last, 1st January 1845, between Mr T. Burgess and Mr F. Lipscombe (both old English players) for a small sum which was decided in favour of the former by the odd game out of 25. We were glad to see this manly and gentlemanly exercise introduced into our adopted country as an exercise.'

The enterprise displayed at Sandy Bay, Tasmania was followed by the laying of greens at Parramatta, Sydney and Melbourne where John Campbell, an expatriate Scot, formed the Melbourne Bowling Club, Australia's first, in 1864. Campbell, having spent the lion's share of his bowling career in Scotland, applied the laws as codified by W. W. Mitchell and adopted by the Scottish Bowling Association, and these, albeit with a number of modifications, remain the basis of the Australian code to this day.

With Melbourne as the example, further bowling clubs were formed including Ballarat (1864), Fitzroy (1865), St Kilda (1865), Prahan (1865) and West Melbourne (1866), many operating with their own 'local variations' of the SBA Laws. In 1867 ten Australian clubs met at the Bull and Mouth Hotel in Melbourne with the object of ironing out these differences and the resulting set of laws were soon dubbed the 'Bull and Mouth laws of the game'.

During the period of development in Victoria, bowls was undergoing a parallel expansion in New South Wales, particularly in the Sydney area where a three-rink green was laid out at the Woolpack Hotel in 1869. Membership soon outgrew these somewhat cramped facilities, however, and new greens laid down at a site in Parramatta's Government Gardens became the base of the Rosehill Club, subsequently renamed the Parramatta Bowling Club. Inter-colonial games (interstate) were inaugurated with a match between New South Wales and Victoria held at the Annandale Club, Sydney on 14 April 1880. The success of this venture led John Young of the host club to arrange a meeting, attended by representatives of Annandale, Balmain, Parramatta and Sydney Bowling Clubs, at which the world's first bowling association, the New South Wales BA, was founded on 22 May 1880, with John Young as president, a position he retained until his death in 1906. Victoria formed its own association in the July of 1880 with Charles Wood elected to the office of president and the means of agreeing common rules of play for interstate matches was clearly established. The influence of Young and Wood was to extend far beyond their state boundaries and it was at their prompting that the first English body, the Imperial Bowling Association, was formed in 1899.

The first overseas tour by an Australian-based team came in 1883 when the Victorian Bowling Association visited New Zealand. A return visit was made by New Zealand five years later during which the visitors won two of the four matches played. A more ambitious tour was arranged in 1895 with an itinerary of 11 matches which included the New Zealand debut in the inter-colonial games, a decision which was to cloud once more the issue of laws in the series. A two-leg match with Victoria found the visitors winning the opening round by 83 shots to 70 with the second ending in a tie. Victorian laws decreed that a further deciding end should be played but the New Zealanders invoked their own rulings which demanded that the tie should stand, eventually winning

the day and, incidentally, the match.

The Western Australian BA was formed in 1898 and the expansion of organized bowls was continued with associations in South Australia (1902) and Queensland (1903). Following a meeting at the 1900 inter-colonial matches an attempt to form a national association in the November of that year proved unsuccessful when New South Wales refused to join such a body. What did emerge however was agreement to send a combined Australia–New Zealand touring party to Great Britain in the following year, an historic decision which resulted in the first series of matches played by a touring side under the authority of the Imperial Bowling Association.

National tournaments in Australia experienced rather hesitant birth with the Melbourne Cricket Club's decision to stage an 'Australian Singles Bowls Championships' in 1900. The Waverley Bowling Club of New South Wales inaugurated the grander-sounding Australasian Singles in 1904 and two years later the South Australian BA introduced its own version with an open Easter tournament. These three essentially national tournaments ran in direct competition until Clarence Moody of the South Australian BA successfully proposed that each state should stage the championships in turn in the form of a bowls carnival week.

The New South Wales BA, perhaps in recognition of its historical significance, was the first to play host in 1908, and it was at this meeting that a conference was held to thrash out an agreed interpretation of the laws. Further progress towards unification surfaced at the 1910 championships held in Adelaide when Clarence Moody, fast emerging as the foremost administrator in Australian bowling circles, proposed the formation of an Australian Bowling Council. Unanimous approval for

John Dobbie (Australia), one of the most influential and able administrators in bowls.

Darby Ross (Australia).
(S. J. Line).

Moody's plans led to a conference at Melbourne in the following year where a constitution was formally adopted and the Australian Bowling Council was formed on 22 September 1911 with Simeon Nathan of Victoria appointed chairman and George M. Munro, also of Victoria, hon. secretary. The first Australian National Championships held under the control of the Australian Bowls Council took place at Melbourne, Victoria in 1912. In recent time these championships have received record entries with the singles normally attracting in excess of 2500 bowlers. Glyn Bosisto of Victoria has earned a unique place in Australian bowls winning the National Singles on four occasions – 1949, 1951, 1952 and 1953.

On the wider stage of international tournaments the performance of Australia's bowlers has left something to be desired and in no way compares with those of the their close neighbours, New Zealand, a country with only one-sixth of the number of bowlers to choose from. Australian teams have competed in the British Empire and Commonwealth Games since 1934, but it was not until 1982 that their efforts were rewarded with a gold medal when Ron Dobbins, Bert Sharp, Don Sherman and skip Keith Poole broke the duck by winning the fours at Brisbane. The World Championships have produced slightly better results for Australia, who began well by winning the pairs with Geoff Kelly and Bert Palm and the triples with Don Collins, Athol Johnson and John

Dobbie at the First World Bowls Championships held at Sydney in 1966. Since then, though, Australia's world championship gold medal collection has increased by just one, received for the pairs success of Alf Sandercock and Peter Rheuben at Frankston in 1980. This meagre tally of gold medals, however, hardly reflects the worldwide popularity of Australian bowlers, or the general admiration for the skills of such men as Glyn Bosisto, Bob Middleton, Keith Poole, Kenny Williams, John Dobbie and John Snell and a host of other superb bowlers who have represented Australia in other countries, often in conditions which bear little similarity to those found at home.

In 1983 the first International Test series was inaugurated between Australia and England and held at the Tweeds Head BC, Victoria. Representing the hosts were Dennis Dalton (Victoria), Peter Lawson (Tasmania), Dennis Katuna-Rich and Geoff Oakley (Western Australia). The series, two tests of five matches each were played and the Australians, up against Andy Thomson (Kent), Julian Haines (Berkshire), Pip Branfield and David Bryant (Somerset), emerged the victors with three wins in each test.

Television is playing an increasingly important role in spreading the popularity of the game in Australia and the *Jack High* series, with eight international bowlers competing for the Mazda Trophy, has proved an immense success with the viewing public since its inception in 1980 following the Frankston World Championships.

Australia's women bowlers have their own council, operating in much the same manner as the men's governing body. The first women's club, the Rainsford Bowling Club at Melbourne, was formed in December 1898, but it was not until 1907 that the first competition for Australia's women bowlers was held in Melbourne when six clubs, Auburn, Brighton Beach, Fitzroy, Middle Park, South Melbourne and SMCC competed for the Clauscen Trophy and the *Sporting and Dramatic News* Trophy. Encouraged by the success of their enterprise these same six clubs formed the Victorian Ladies Bowling Association, the first Women's Association in the world, on 19 September 1907 under the presidency of Mrs Bleazby. The first ladies' club in New South Wales came into being in 1912, but it was another 17 years before five clubs, Bulmain, Leichhart, Rose Bay, Torpey Place and Western Suburb, were able to form the New South Wales Women's BA on 21 November 1929. Queensland followed suit on 7 March 1930 with seven clubs, and South Australia organized one month later with three. The largest of

the new Associations was the Western Australia Ladies BA, founded with 11 clubs on 29
May 1935 and the final gap was closed with the
formation of the Tasmania WBA on 23
September 1936. The Australian Women's
Bowling Council was formed on 27 August
1947 at the instigation of Mrs Wolinski, president of the New South Wales WBA, who invited delegates from all the ladies' associations
to a meeting at which a constitution was
adopted and the governing body duly formed.

The international record of Australia's
women bowlers has a more impressive ring to it
than that of their male counterparts. Over the
five occasions that the Women's World Championships have taken place, Australia has collected five gold medals, winning the pairs in
1973, the fours in 1977, and singles, pairs and
triples in 1985 plus, of course, the team award.
In Merle Richardson, Australia has perhaps
the outstanding woman bowler in the world at
present.

Botswana

With just six clubs and around 300 players
Botswana, an associate member of the
International Bowling Board, is one of the
smaller bowling nations. Greens and clubhouses have been built largely by self-help,
constructed more often than not by club
members with the assistance of labour and
equipment loaned by local business and mining
companies.

The Francistown BC formed in 1957 was the
first club in Botswana to open in 1962 with
John Carver as president. Land for the green
was donated by The Tati Company of
Francistown and their 'elephant' logo was
incorporated into the club badge in
appreciation. Plans for construction were
obtained from South Africa and work, which
began in 1961, was carried out under the
supervision of club member John Kernon. In a
country with such a dry climate, Francistown is
in the fortunate position of having a regular
and plentiful water supply together with
excellent drainage. Not so lucky however are
the greens at Garborone and Orapa which
have been completely devastated by a
protracted drought. At Orapa, though, the
recent discovery of a supply of borehole water
has at least made the construction of a new
green a worthwhile venture. These and other
clubs at Lobatse and Selibe-Phikwe were
joined in 1982 by Jwaneng, with two greens the
largest club in Botswana.

Singles championships were inaugurated in
1972 when Keith Cummings (Francistown)
became the first champion of Botswana.

Bowling standards, considering the small pool
of players, is surprisingly high with the fours
semi-final placing achieved by the Francistown
quartet of Tom Shankland, Alec Cohen, Paul
Stubbs and Lofty de Beer in the 1965 South
African Championships justifiably viewed with
considerable pride.

The Botswana Bowling Association was
formed in 1976 and in 1982 a team was entered
in the Commonwealth Games for the first
time. One victory in the singles (21–18 against
Fiji), two in the pairs (25–21 against Fiji and
23–14 against Zambia) and three in the fours
(29–16 against Papua New Guinea, 21–19
against Hong Kong and 25–16 against Zambia)
was a decent enough record for a debut
performance but it was the ladies of Botswana,
with seven wins in the triples which included a
one-shot victory over Ireland, who stole the
limelight.

The Selibe-Phikwe Club was the venue for
the 1984 African Six Nations Tournament,
contested by Botswana, Kenya, Malawi,
Swaziland, Zambia and Zimbabwe. Botswana
won the triples in this event but, more
important, with the World Championships
scheduled for later in the same year, was the
rare opportunity for team practice, always a
difficult proposition with some Botswana clubs
separated by as much as 300 miles of very tough
country. At Aberdeen the Botswana team of
Stuart Logan (team manager), Johnny
Kakakis, Bill Haresnip (all Gaberone), Albert
Noel, Ray Mascarenhas (Selibe-Phikwe) and
Ron Anderson (Lobatse) put together a
creditable total of 13 wins over the four events,
and the experience will be sure to promote a
further raising of standards even if the shortage
of facilities may lead to a fairly static
membership.

Canada

Although Canada's first bowling green, at Port
Royal (later Annopolis), Nova Scotia, was laid
in 1734, interest in the game languished until
1832 when the Caer Howell Club was
established in Toronto, Ontario. Once having
reached the predominantly British centre of
population, however, progress began to gather
pace. The Ontario BA was formed in 1888 and
four years later a body with wider powers, The
Dominion Lawn Bowling Association, came
into being. Western Ontario organized in 1896
and British Columbia followed in 1908 with a
green at Beacon Hill Park, Victoria. Growing
interest in the province was reflected by the
founding of the Vancouver BC, and, in 1916,
the formation of the Terminal City Club with
two greens was to spark the establishment of

the British Columbia LBA in the same year. By 1924 there were no less than six provinces affiliated to the Dominion LBA, Alberta, British Columbia, Manitoba, Ontario, Quebec and Saskatchewan, and that same year saw the title changed to the present Canadian Lawn Bowling Council, with membership of the International Bowling Board following in 1928.

Canada introduced bowls into the First Empire Games at Hamilton, Ontario in 1930 and their method of team selection was later to form the basis of the Canadian National Championships first played in 1955. Today, a national team selection committee, administered by a chairman and four committee members, oversee a training week held each June in which 14 players are assessed before selection is made. National championships are held annually with affiliated provinces hosting in turn. Men's events comprise singles, pairs and fours while the ladies play singles, pairs and triples.

Weather conditions experienced in Canada make the maintenance of greens a difficult proposition. Short, hot summers combined with the low temperatures of winter months also mean a relatively brief season, and this has restricted the success of Canadian bowlers in international tournaments. The administration of bowls in the country, however, is an extremely active one receiving support and encouragement from the Canadian Federal Government. A highly organized coaching scheme with a certification programme comprising three component parts, theory, technical and practical, and a National Lawn Bowls Coaching Committee publishing technical manuals for lawn bowlers. Also established is a National Officiating Committee and through this have emerged qualified officials at club, provincial and national levels. Perhaps of most importance to the future progress of bowls in Canada however is the recently established Greens Advisory Committee which has recommended that new greens be constructed on the 'all sand principle', advice based on the success of the four-green complex built on sand for the 1978 Commonwealth Games at Edmonton, Alberta.

At present the majority of clubs have one full green, the exceptions being Willowdale in Toronto which has three and Regina, Saskatchewan and Edmonton which have four each. Latest figures released by the IBB show that women bowlers are in the majority in Canada with a membership of over 10 000 while that of the men just tops the 9000 mark.

Canadian touring sides have visited Great Britain on several occasions, the first, under the auspices of the Imperial Bowling Association in 1904, when a side captained by George Anderson (Prospect Park, Toronto) won five out of its 33 match programme. In 1929–30 the Canadians ventured to New Zealand and Australia winning 5 out of a total of 21 matches played. In more recent times Ronnie Jones of London, Ontario and Burnie Gill from Port Elgin, Ontario have won world-wide recognition with a number of outstanding performances. Gill, competing in the 1983 World Indoor Championships at Coatbridge, Scotland as a 50–1 outsider caused a series of major upsets defeating Tony Allcock, 1982 champion John Watson and Australian Clive White before losing to Bob Sutherland of Scotland in the final. The diminutive Ronnie Jones is another popular Canadian in Great Britain where he has put together some useful results, defeating Willie Wood in the 1984 World Championships and acquitting himself with some honour in the 1985 Gateway Masters tournament at Worthing, England.

Barrie McFadden (Port Credit, Ontario), Glen Patton (Brampton, Ontario), Bill Boettger (Kitchener, Ontario), Dave Hoatby (Niagara Falls, Ontario) and Bill Watkin (London, Ontario) are others who have established themselves in the top class of Canadian bowls over the last decade.

Fiji

The Fiji Bowling Association is an associate member of the IBB with nine clubs, the largest of which is situated in the capital, Suva. Suva BC was formed in 1924 and the clubhouse and

Sean Patton (Fiji). (S. J. Line).

green were constructed on reclaimed land. Exactly one year after the formation of the steering committee Suva BC was officially opened with two greens and a membership of 100.

In 1926 Suva bowlers promoted the first South Pacific Bowling Carnival which, originally conceived as a social-cum-bowling occasion running over ten days, has developed into an event featuring fierce competitive games between representatives from Australia, New Zealand, Hong Kong, Papua New Guinea, Samoa and other island territories. The success of the Suva BC led to further clubs at Levuka, the old capital, and Ba, a centre of the sugar industry, and in 1928 these three clubs became founder members of the Fiji BA. The premier tournament in Fiji is the Pineapple Cup, a competition open to all Pacific Island bowlers. Donated by the Pacific Biscuit Company, the trophy is moulded from sterling silver in the shape of a pineapple and stands 15 in (38 cm) high. This singles tournament was first played in 1928 with the winner, C. C. Clark, registering his second victory in the event in 1939. Inter-club competitions are played for the Governor's Cup, presented by Sir Eyre Hutson KCMG in 1929.

In the early days of bowls in Fiji, the game was restricted to Europeans but for many years now bowlers of all races have been free to play the game and, indeed, many of the country's current top players are of non-European extraction. The standard of bowls is amazingly high for such a small nation and Fiji's teams have a good record in Commonwealth Games and World Championship competitions. A contributory factor to their consistent performances is perhaps a mild climate which allows play throughout the year, and greens which appear to require only minimal maintenance. Fiji representatives at the 1984 World Championships were Sean Patton, a past president of the Fiji BA and a gold medalist at two South Pacific Games; Peter Fong, rated the country's finest player; Geoff O'Meagher, winner of four South Pacific fours titles; Oscar Reymond, Jav Naidu and team manager Edgar Apted. The latest IBB figures show that there are around 600 bowlers in Fiji at present with the men having a small majority.

Guernsey

Of the eight clubs which founded the Guernsey Bowling Association in 1928 only one remains active, the Guernsey BC formed in 1927. Currently the Association has ten clubs and

Above The site of Suva BC prior to development, 1924.
Below Suva BC – one year later.

Levuka Bowling Club, Opening Day 1937. With the Club's compliments. President.

Opening day at Levuka BC Fiji – 1937.

250 bowlers playing on greens situated at the Beau Sejour Leisure Centre, Delancy Park and the newest facility, the Vale Recreation Club, founded in 1973.

Although competitive opportunities are mainly restricted to the Island, an annual match between the Guernsey BA and the Jersey BC was instituted in 1929 and the Northern Club played an annual match against Weymouth until 1940.

In 1958 Walter Woodhard became the first Guernsey bowler to win international recognition with his victory in the World Bowls Vitalite Trophy competition over competitors from 14 other countries. Guernsey entered the British Commonwealth Games for the first time at Edinburgh in 1980, and two years later bowlers from the island made their debut in the World Championships at Worthing. An indoor club was formed in St Peter Port in 1976 but lack of quality opposition leads inevitably to standards some way below the best and, competing in the Embassy World Indoor singles at Coatbridge, Guernsey bowlers Mike Pike in 1982 and Tom Beattie in 1984 were simply outclassed.

Guernsey's women bowlers were represented in the World Bowls of 1977 held at Worthing and, with only 36 players from which to choose their team, performed with credit, none more so than Mrs Dot Foley who finished fourth in the singles.

At the 1984 World Championships, Guernsey's representatives were Derek Hurford, Mike Nicolle, Bill Crawford, Clary Blondel, Cyril Smith and team manager John Farncombe. Although finishing in 15th place in the WM Leonard Trophy, Guernsey bowlers will no doubt savour their 18–15 defeat of England in the triples and a fine result in the fours, when they beat Jim Baker's Irish rink by 15 shots to 12.

Hong Kong

The address 9 Knutsford Terrace, Kowloon is of particular significance to bowls in Hong Kong, the first game ever played in the colony taking place on the lawn of that residence in 1897. Predictably the players, Archie Ritchie, James Macdonald, W. Ramsey and W. C. Jack were Scots to a man and in 1900 they joined with A. Ewing, E. C. Wilkes, H. Schoolbred and J. Allen to form the Kowloon Bowling Green Club.

As enthusiasm grew and new clubs were formed the need for an organization became apparent, and in 1908 an association was formed with a code of play based on the rules of the Scottish Bowling Association but affiliated to the English BA. A singles competition won by S. Bell was held in the following year and league play was instituted in 1910 on an official basis. The present Hong Kong Lawn Bowls Association was incorporated on 11 March 1961 and accepted into the IBB as an associate member.

During the Second World War even occupation by the Japanese failed to prevent the colony's enthusiastic bowlers from pursuing their favourite sport despite their desperate plight and shocking physical condition. This amazing spirit and fortitude is reflected in the results achieved at international level by a colony with only 600 men, 290 women bowlers and 16 clubs, less than many English counties. Over 12 Commonwealth Games and World Championship competitions Hong Kong bowlers have won five gold, one silver and one bronze medals. Eric Liddell holds the record number of appearances for the colony at top level, playing in every Commonwealth Games and World Championship tournament from 1954 to 1980. The most successful bowler in recent years, however, is George Souza junior,

Urban Councillor F. K. Hu, presents the Hong Kong Classic pairs trophy to 1983 champions, Philip Chok (left) and George Souza Jnr (centre).

Left Noel Kennedy, Hong Kong's 1984 national knock-out singles champion.

winner of 11 national titles and a representative player since 1978. In 1983 Souza won the Kodak (now Gateway) International Masters at Worthing, England, beating David Bryant in a rain-soaked final.

The Hong Kong International Bowls Classic began life as a pairs event in 1981 when Australians Darby Ross and Robbie Dobbins were victorious. This prestige tournament however now includes singles with Peter Belliss of New Zealand the inaugural winner in 1983. George Souza Jnr and Phillip Chok won the pairs in that year and repeated their victory in '84 with Souza collecting a double by also winning the singles competition.

Hong Kong finished 9th in the W. M. Leonard Trophy table at the 1984 World Championships with a team comprising Omar Dallah, Mohammed Hassan Jnr, George Souza Jnr, Philip Chok, Edwin Chok and team manager Ken Willis.

Cecil Bransky (Israel). (S. J. Line).

Israel

Bowls was introduced into Israel at the Fourth Maccabiah Games held in September 1953 when a competition took place at Ramat Gan on a green laid at the expense of the South African Zionist Organization. Taking part in these matches, the first ever played in Israel, were Rhodesia, who won the event with 14 points, South Africa and players from the home country, mainly immigrants from the Republic.

Leading light in this and future development of the game in Israel was Max Spitz who, after emigrating to the country from South Africa in 1950, was largely responsible for the founding of the Ramat Gan BC and the Israel Bowling Association.

With only five clubs representing 200 men and 250 women bowlers, Israel has earned the respect of other bowling nations since their entry into the World Championships in 1972.

Cecil Bransky, a 43-year-old who emigrated to Israel from South Africa in 1980, is unquestionably their most successful player. He won the South African singles championship in 1972, adding the fours title to his record in 1976 and the pairs in 1980 just prior to his move. Since taking up residence in Israel he has won the national singles twice as well as the Israeli Masters Singles and national triples. In the 1984 World Championships at Aberdeen, Bransky, as his country's singles representative, came third in his section with seven victories and sixth overall after losing by one shot to Dan Coetzee of Zambia in the play-offs. Bransky was teamed with Cecil Cooper in the pairs finishing in eighth place

overall. The Israeli team in 1984 was completed by Sam Skudowitz, Nathan Lazarus, Jack Trappler and team manager Norman Spiro.

Competing in the 1985 Embassy World Indoor singles championships at Coatbridge, Scotland, Bransky was beaten 21–18 by Terry Sullivan of Wales in the final after accounting for Hong Kong's George Souza, Russell Evans of Wales, and defending champion Jim Baker of Ireland. His performance at Coatbridge no doubt led to an appearance in the 1985 Gateway Masters tournament at Worthing and victories over Dennis Katunarich of Australia, Hong Kong's George Souza and John Bell of England, took him to the final of a second international major competition, and although losing to David Bryant by 21–12, firmly established himself and Israel at the top level of international bowls.

Japan

Formed in 1965, the Japan Lawn Bowls Association owes much to the efforts of John Dobbie, hon. secretary of the Australian Bowls Council until his retirement in 1985. On his recommendation the Japan LBA was admitted to associate membership of the IBB in 1966, and his advice on green construction and other aspects of the game has been invaluable to the fledgling bowling nation.

At present the association has an affiliated membership of 1200 and 16 clubs but, with an estimated 6000 bowlers in the country, some 4000 of these affiliated to the Nagasaki BA and the Akashi BA, the potential at this stage of development is enormous.

At present there are 60 greens in operation

in Japan situated in the Osaka, Hyogo, Nagasaki, Fukuoka, Mie, Shizuoka, Ibaragi and Ishikawa Prefectures. Many of these greens however have three or five rinks and only four are of full size. The Nagasaki Prefecture with 50 greens and 4000 bowlers is the strongest bowling area in Japan but only six of the clubs with 320 bowlers are affiliated to the Japan LBA. Lack of space is an inhibiting factor in the development of the game but indoor bowls is a growing and popular pastime, although to date no indoor club exists.

Tadao Nishi, secretary of the Japan LBA, is a tireless worker on behalf of bowls in Japan but keeps his feet firmly planted on the ground. 'Bowls is still in its infancy here in Japan', he said recently, 'and we have to learn from other countries'. That learning process began at Johannesburg in 1976 when, taking part in their first World Championships, the Japanese team totalled just four points, suffering heavy losses in almost every match. At Frankston, Australia in 1980, the story was a similar one with the sole exception being a 21–19 victory by the Japanese triple over Papua NG, their first, and to date, only success against bowlers from another country. The Japan LBA declined to take part in the Fourth World Bowls Championships in 1984, their eyes, and hopes, firmly set on New Zealand in 1988 and who would bet against at least an improvement in their results.

Jersey

Founded in 1937, the Jersey BA has five clubs in affiliation and a membership of 300 bowlers. The Island's first club, the Jersey BC, was formed in 1912 and for many years its administrators acted as unofficial representatives of Jersey's bowlers in matters involving other countries. The annual match against Guernsey was actually arranged in 1929 between the Guernsey Bowling Association and the Jersey Bowling Club. Of the Island's five clubs only three, the Jersey BC, Sun BC and St Saviours, have their own greens which are shared with bowlers from the remaining two, the Police and Post Office BCs.

While experiencing similar problems to close neighbours Guernsey, in terms of quality competition, Jersey bowlers have pulled off a number of unexpected, if isolated, results at the highest level. Yorkshire-born Arthur McKernan has met the great David Bryant only twice, as Jersey representative in the 1978 Commonwealth Games at Edmonton, Canada and in the World Championships in 1980 at Melbourne, Australia, beating him on both occasions.

At Aberdeen in 1984, the Jersey team of Tim Mallett, John Jones, Arthur McKernan, David Le Marquand, Ken Lowery and manager David Foster maintained the knack of providing the unexpected, with Jones inflicting the sole defeat of the tournament on the eventual champion, Peter Belliss of New Zealand, while the Jersey four skipped by 29-year-old Tim Mallett did a similar job on their English counterparts skipped by Tony Allcock, beating them 24–15.

Kenya

With only five clubs and 100 bowling members the Kenya Bowling Association is a relative newcomer to the sport. The first green was laid by British settlers in Nairobi's City Park during the mid-thirties but it was not until the formation of a bowling section at the Karen Country Club in 1949 that any form of organized bowls emerged. The City Council Bowls Club, using the old green in City Park, was formed shortly afterwards and this was followed by Vet Lab Kabete with a green named after its founder, Dick Skinner.

The Kenya BA was formed on 24 March 1954 at a meeting held under the chairmanship of Colonel 'Daddy' Modera. R. A. Hammond CBE was elected to the position of president with H. S. Haldane, hon. secretary/treasurer. Four years after its formation the Kenya BA entered a team in the British Commonwealth Games for the first time, finishing in tenth place in each of the four events.

Although participating in the inaugural World Championships held at Sydney in 1966, Kenya withdrew from the 1972 Championships in protest at the inclusion of South Africa and were again absent in 1976, returning in 1980 at Frankston.

A fours competition for the Russel Cockburn Bowl was instituted in 1954 but it was not until the completion of a green at the Royal Nairobi Golf Club in 1955 that recognized national championships in singles (the Ray Whittet Cup), pairs (the Isherwood Cup) and triples (the Mayers Trophy) were added over a two year period. There are also competitions featuring double fours, ladies' singles, mixed pairs and invitation fours for both men and women as well as two league competitions for the Gilbey Bowl and the John Weir Shield. Weir, who presented the shield in 1956, is the son of England international, A. Weir (1920–5, 1928), grandson of John Weir, Scotland's first international captain in 1903, and was himself president of the Kenya Bowling Association from 1956 to 1959.

With dwindling memberships, clubs in

Kenya are facing a lean period. In 1971 the Nairobi City Park green was closed and the club amalgamated with the Royal Nairobi Golf Club Bowls Section, itself reduced at the time to seven members. Bowling sections of the Mombasa Sports Club founded in 1958, the Nairobi Club founded in 1959 and the Limuru Country Club founded in 1956 would appear to have the best chances of survival while the fortunes of the Karen Country Club and Royal Nairobi GC could best be described as fluid.

At the 1984 World Championships Kenya was represented by Charles Radbone, Peter Jeens, William Watson, Brian Jennings, James Haggerty and team manager Les Cattermole. Sadly the results achieved by the team at Aberdeen reflected the present state of the game in Kenya as their bowlers filled the last places in singles, pairs and fours, came in 20th out of 22 in the triples and, with a total of six points, were bottom of the Leonard Trophy table.

Malawi

Bowls in Malawi (previously Nyasaland) has experienced a fall in popularity since independence in 1964. At present there are just three clubs operating with a total of around 160 bowlers. Malawi was represented at the 1984 World Championships at Aberdeen by John Chalmers, David Broad, Peter Crossan, Sandy Ross, Bill Haining and team manager Ron Griffiths, finishing 16th in the Leonard Trophy Table. The country did not compete in the 1985 Women's World Championships at Melbourne, Australia.

Versatile David Broad, a University lecturer from Chirchiri Malawi, represented Malawi in the 1984 World Championships at Aberdeen. Apart from bowls David has also represented his country at golf and holds the world record for scoring most trebles in darts, a feat ratified by the Guinness Book of Records.

New Zealand

With 57 000 men and 28 000 women players New Zealand lies mid-table among the larger bowling nations. Its greens number among the finest in the world and the country has produced a constant stream of high-class bowlers from William McLaren, winner of the Australian singles in 1906, to Peter Belliss, World Championship singles gold medalist in 1984.

The modern game arrived in New Zealand in the 19th century when a group of Scottish settlers constructed the country's first green at Auckland, North Island in 1861. By the late 1860s it had reached the South Island, introduced there by George Turnbull who, attracted by the gold fields of Otago, moved house and home southwards from Wellington. From an essentially unorganized pastime, bowls in the South took on an altogether more authoritative stance with the formation of the Dunedin Club in 1871 and the following five years were to show rapid development. North and South Islands combined to form the original New Zealand Bowling Association in 1886 but by that time the South, with eight clubs – Dunedin, Invercargill, Caledonian, Balclutha, Lawrence, Milton, Oamaru and Canterbury – was by far the dominant partner with the North represented by just New Plymouth and Auckland. Headquarters for the association were established in Dunedin with Thomas Callendar installed as president and James Curle as secretary.

In the North, although progress still lagged behind that of the South, nine clubs were operating by 1890 when a second body, the Northern Bowling Association was founded by James Paul and Andrew Campbell at Wellington. Founder members of the new association were the clubs of Wellington, New Plymouth, Napier, Wanganui, Auckland, Palmerston North, Waiau, Blenheim and Gisborne, and by 1905 the North Island, with 43 clubs, had overtaken the South who could muster only 40. A third association was formed in 1895 representing bowlers situated in the Auckland area and playing to their own 'local' version of the rules of bowls. The unsatisfactory situation of three separate administrations continued until 1913 when, at a meeting held in Dunedin, a single body, the Dominion of New Zealand Bowling Association, was formed with a Council elected by the various affiliated centres, and national championships were established in the following year. Victors in the inaugural championships were J. S. Kilgour (Carlton) in the singles, J. Johnson and E. Harraway of Dunedin in the pairs while the fours title went to the Wellington rink comprising W. Grenfell, A. Erskine, W. Thompson and J. Porteous. In 1931 the word Dominion was dropped from the title of the governing body and it is the New Zealand Bowling Association which administers the game to this day with the country divided into 23 centres, 12 in the North and 11 in the South.

Apart from the national championships, played in turn at Auckland, Christchurch, Wellington and Dunedin, there is a champion of champions tournament, a North Island versus South Island match, Inter-Centre Championships featuring teams of seven bowlers playing singles, pairs and fours, and various other invitation 'Classic' and 'Masters' events. Always enthusiastic tourists, New Zealand bowlers visited Australia in 1888 playing four matches with two wins, one draw and one loss. In 1901 they ventured to Great Britain in a combined party with Australia but, eventually, were to play a separate programme. New Zealand–Australia Test Matches were instituted in the course of a 26 match tour undertaken by the Kiwis in 1906–7 and although New Zealand won 19 matches, the Tests, believed to be the first such confrontations outside of the British Isles, went to Australia two matches to one. For the occasion the New Zealand team appeared in white shoes, socks, trousers, coats, ties and hats with black blazer badges and hat-bands decorated with a silver fern. This startling apparel was to earn the team the title of the 'All Whites', a contrast to the famous 'All Blacks' rugger team. On the wider stage of international competition New Zealand's bowlers have earned an enviable reputation, collecting seven gold medals, six silver and four bronze over ten British Empire and Commonwealth Games meetings held, while the World Championships have netted them two gold, one silver and four bronze medals.

New Zealand's successes in recent times have often centred around the stocky figure of Phil Skoglund (Palmerston, North), whose aggressive play has sometimes obscured the more delicate side of his game. Skoglund has won the New Zealand singles five times, the pairs twice and fours once. He has represented his country in World Championship and Commonwealth Games competition, collecting three bronze and two silver medals for his efforts including a silver as runner up in the 1984 World Championship fours. In recognition of an outstanding record Skoglund was awarded the Gold Five Star Medallion of the NZBA. Nick Unkovich (Auckland), also a holder of the Gold Medallion with six victories in the NZBA fours and a singles winner in 1979, played in a successful Test series against England in 1984, substituted for Skoglund who, with Peter Belliss, was engaged in the Hong Kong pairs. Completing the New Zealand Test squad were Rowan Brassey, Jim Scott and Scots-born Morgan Moffat, all members of the World Championship party for that year. Unkovich played singles, with one win and one loss, pairs with Brassey, one win, one loss and fours with Brassey, Scott and Moffat, two wins. A creditable performance against the England Test line-up of David Bryant, Julian Haines, Pip Branfield and Andy Thomson. With the likes of Scott, Brassey, Ian Dickison, 1983 singles champion Danny O'Connor, and the 1984 winner Robin Milne to back up the world class of Peter Belliss, the New Zealand reputation looks safe for a long time to come. With the 1986 Commonwealth Games firmly in mind, the NZBA used the 1985 Pacific Bowls Championships to 'blood' new internationals Jim Christian, Maurice Symes, Terry Scott and Wayne Nairn. As a professional Peter Belliss is not eligible to take part in the 1986 Commonwealth Games at Edinburgh.

New Zealand women bowlers have their own association formed in 1930 although the first women's national championship was not held until 1951. Elsie Wilkie, twice winner of the World Championship singles (1973 and 1977), is undoubtedly the outstanding example of the quality present in the women's game in New Zealand. Joyce Osbourne (Palmerston, North) won the NZWBA singles in 1972, '76 and '83 and a triples silver medal in the 1982 Commonwealth Games. In the 1985 Women's World Championships the NZ team of Osbourne, Rhoda Ryan (Matamata), Daphne Le Breton (Wellington), Barbara Kunicich, and Jean Moffat (Avondale) were placed third overall behind Australia and England, with Ryan winning a bronze medal in the singles. Although unable to collect any further medals, New Zealand chalked up an astonishing 33–8 victory in the fours over the eventual winners, Scotland.

Following past experiments with surfaces of sawdust and a bitumen emulsion, it is the Cotula weed which has proved most popular with New Zealand bowlers. It provides a fast, accurate surface and boasts a durability which will be put to the test in 1988 when the World Championships are staged at Auckland.

Papua New Guinea

After experiencing a fall in the number of bowlers during the late seventies, the game has staged a remarkable recovery in Papua NG. Current membership stands at an all-time high of 700 male and 200 female participants with 12 clubs affiliated to the national association.

However any form of regular competition in an area exceeding 120 000 square miles is, at best, a difficult proposition for Papua's bowlers but their spirit and enthusiasm remains undimmed. They have taken part in all of the World Championships with the exception of those held in Johannesburg in 1976 and, although never in the medals, occasionally spring a surprise result. At

Aberdeen in 1984 the 27–9 triples defeat of New Zealand's Rowan Brassey, Jim Scott and Morgan Moffatt by Rolf Meyer, Lawrence Tamurua and Tau Nancie must have been some compensation for finishing in 19th place in the W. M. Leonard Trophy table.

South Africa

Although a full member of the IBB, South Africa is virtually isolated from the sport at international level. Facilities for the country's 40 000 men and 28 000 women bowlers, however, are excellent and playing standards remain high.

The first bowling club in South Africa was formed at Port Elizabeth in 1882, followed by Kimberley seven years later, Gardens (Cape Town) in 1895 and Victoria Park in 1898, and these four clubs became the founder members of the South African Bowling Association in 1904. The first competitive inter-club match between Kimberley and Port Elizabeth dates from 1894 and this annual fixture, soon embracing other clubs, was to become the forerunner of all national championship competition in the Republic. Although currently showing a slight decline, the popularity of bowls in South Africa grew at a remarkable rate with the number of clubs rising from seven in 1904 to 250 by 1940 and peaking at 817 in 1972. There are at present 796 clubs affiliated to the South African BA.

For administrative purposes, the country is divided into districts and an inter-district tournament was inaugurated in 1957. The national singles championships date from 1897 when F. Whightman (Kimberley) became the first South African national champion on his home green and, apart from breaks between 1900 and 1902 and the war years the event has been held annually ever since. Other tournaments of note are the SA Masters singles first held in 1969 and a rinks team event for the Pyott Cup. This tournament evolved from the two pairs-a-side Port Elizabeth–Kimberley confrontation of 1894 and in its new form was won for the first time by Kimberley in 1906.

The high quality of play in South Africa is reflected by the performance of its players in the British Empire and Commonwealth Games. Up to the time of its withdrawal from the Commonwealth on 31 May 1961, South African bowlers had won four gold, six silver and two bronze medals from a total of 18 events. As a member of the IBB, the country participated in the World Championships until excluded in 1980. In 1976 a clean sweep of all four titles plus the team event showed a continuing urge for success. Doug Watson,

singles and pairs gold medalist in 1976, has been one of South Africa's most consistently brilliant players over the years and in 1972 was, at 29, the youngest bowler ever to represent that country at international level. Bill Moseley, Watson's pairs partner in 1976, is another outstanding bowler, winning the highly rated Kodak Masters tournament in England in 1980 and 1981 before his exclusion in 1983.

An attempt to retain sporting links with a fast-shrinking world led the South African Olympic and National Games Association to host an open international bowls tournament in Pretoria during 1973. The event attracted top men and women bowlers from 13 countries and resulted in an overall victory for players from the British Isles. Scotland's Willie Wood won the singles from David Bryant in second place while Mavis Steele of Middlesex took the women's singles prize. The men's pairs went to the host country's Tommy Harvey and Doug Watson but all of the team awards ended up with England's Peter Line, David Bryant, Mavis Steel, Phyl Derrick and Joan Sparkes.

In January 1982 the worsening relationships between South Africa and the rest of the world were to touch the very roots of bowls in England. An ill-timed 'unofficial' tour of the Republic by an England party was led by EBA president Hylton Armstrong, against the advice of his own association. Returning to an obviously hostile reception by an embarrassed EBA executive, Armstrong resigned his position on 28 October 1982.

Swaziland

In contrast to the situation in many of the independent African nations, bowls in Swaziland is actually gaining ground with the 1983 figures of 82 men and 120 women bowlers rising to 121 and 150 respectively in the following year. Although only finishing 17th in the W. M. Leonard Trophy Table in the 1984 World Championships, the Swaziland team of Tom Green, Tom Sheasby, John Kemp, Richard Cockram and Derek James chalked up one or two notable victories at Aberdeen, including the defeat of Israel and the USA in the fours and Hong Kong in the triples. In the 1985 Women's World Championships held at Melbourne, Swaziland, represented by Liz Jams, Pat MacDonagh, Cynthia Thompson, Jenny Viegas and Dido Loretz, finished 15th in

---

Highest score Outdoor Swaziland defeated Japan by an astounding 63 shots to 1 during the World Championships held at Melbourne, Australia on 16 January 1980.

the overall team table out of 19 participating nations.

Transskei

The Umtata BC, established in 1934, is the oldest, biggest and most active of Transkei's bowling clubs. Until 1976 all clubs in Transkei were affiliated to the Border Bowling Association, a district of the South African BA but, with independence, the Transkeian Bowling Association was formed with His Excellency, The State President, Paramount Chief, the Honourable Dr K. D. Matanzima acting as patron. Mr Rubin Knopf was first president of the new association of which he is a life member.

From nine clubs formed at the height of the game's popularity in the country, the roll call has fallen to six, the Umtata, Butterworth, Coffee Bay, Transkei Prisons, Engcobo and Idutywa BCs. Although without national championships of their own, clubs affiliated to the Transkeian BA are invited to participate in the annual South African National Championships.

United States

Despite a pedigree of a green laid in 1732 by the father of George Washington at the family estate in Mount Vernon, Virginia, bowls has never figured large among American sporting pastimes. Introduced into the country in the 17th century, the game gained a foothold in Boston, Washington, Virginia and New Amsterdam (New York). A green constructed at Battery Park was in use until 1820 and this area of New York is still known as Bowling Green, a name given to several towns across America.

After some 50 years of steady growth, however, the popularity of bowls suffered a dramatic reversal following the War of Independence when all things British proved offensive to the patriotic American. The game's revival dates from 1879 when Christian Shepplin organized the Dunnellen Bowling Club of New Jersey and, after a period of expansion along the eastern seaboard to Boston, spread cross-country to California with the founding of the San Francisco Scottish Bowling Club in 1901, where a green was laid in the Golden Gate Park. Disaster, however, struck in 1906 when the city together with the club were destroyed by the famous earthquake, although by the end of the year a new green was in use and survives to this day. The California Lawn Bowling Club, operating in Los Angeles, was formed in 1908 and the spread continued, reaching Florida with the establishment of the St Petersburg Club in 1908. Climatic conditions in Florida have led to the use of various alternative bowling surfaces including Rubico, a fine slate substance mixed with a binding agent spread over a porous base, and Marl, in which a fine layer of sand is spread onto a base mix of sand, soil and cement. One club, however, at Pebble Beach, Sun City Centre, seems to have solved the problems boasting no less than four grass greens and a total of 32 rinks, all of which are in first class condition.

The American Lawn Bowling Association was formed in Buffalo, NY in 1915 but membership of the IBB was denied until 1938. Displaying its ability to organize and control the game, however, the ALBA staged a

The Clearwater Lawn Bowling Club, Florida, USA 1927.

Clearwater L.B.C.

national tournament at Boston in 1918 with 14 teams from eight clubs in attendance and, with the exception of the war years, this tournament has continued ever since. Bowlers from New Zealand visited the US en route to the Empire Games in 1928 and one year later an American team toured Great Britain. In 1932 America staged a world tournament at Los Angeles during the Olympic Games and held similar contests at San Francisco during the Golden Gate Exposition of 1939, and in Seattle in 1962 on the occasion of the World's Fair. The ALBA rules over six geographical divisions, Eastern, Southeast, Central, Northwest, Pacific Inter-Mountain and the Southwest, and arranges all official international tournaments, assists new clubs to organize and furnishes information on green construction. Each of the six divisions end the season with division play-offs in singles and pairs, divisional winners playing for the American Championships.

The ALBA National Open Tournament, inaugurated in 1928, is open to players from other countries and David White of Boston was the first ALBA open champion. Canadian bowlers have built a good record in this tournament with ten victories while Barrie Swannie of Surrey, England pulled off perhaps the most surprising victory in 1982. With only six days experience of the Rubico surface at the Clearwater BC near Tampa, Florida, Swannie defeated Kenny Dagenhardt, US closed pairs champion, 21–14 in the final having disposed of Dick Folkins on the previous day. The ALBA Open Pairs dates from 1920, the first winner being Thomas Grieve and Thomas Turnbull of Boston, while the earliest US open tournament, the fours, dates from 1918 when the victors from Roselawn BC, Pawtucket, RI were skipped by Thomas Hampson. The American Women's LBA was formed at the Santa Anita LBC, Arcadia, California in 1970 and currently represents around 1300 members.

For such a small bowling nation the United States has performed with amazing success in the World Championships. Bill Miller, Clive Forrester and Dick Folkins combined to win the triples gold medal at Worthing in 1972 with Folkins, a superb draw bowler and skip, also taking silver in the pairs with Jim Candelet. In 1984 Candelet, forced to pull out of the pairs through injury, must have had mixed feelings as his partner, Skippy Arculli won the gold medal for America in partnership with Scottish sub, George Adrain, but no doubt his medal, as official representative, helped ease the pain.

Recent figures show that, with 115 clubs and around 7000 bowlers, the game has remained static in the United States for the past 30 years.

Western Samoa

Bowls in Western Samoa dates from 1919 when a club was formed at Apia. While never catching the imagination of the populace the game nevertheless provided a pastime for the administrators of Samoa and business men in the capital. From 1942, with the threat of war never far away in the Pacific, interest in the game lapsed completely and it was not until a new green was laid by enthusiasts in Apia in 1952 that bowls began to attract the attention of the indigenous population.

In 1962 Western Samoa gained its independence and interest in the game among Samoans was increased by the fact that the country's first Prime Minister, Mataafu Fiamē Faumuinā Mulinu-ū II, was also president of the newly formed Western Samoa Bowling Association.

Entry to the British Commonwealth followed in 1974 and that year a team was entered in the Commonwealth Games for the first time. One year later the Western Samoa BA was accepted as an associate member of the IBB, making its debut in world championship competition at Johannesburg in 1976. In 1983 Western Samoa was host for the South Pacific Games which were held at Apia. Taking part in the bowling events, administered by the home association, were men's and women's teams from Papua New Guinea, Fiji, the Norfolk Islands, Tonga, the Cook Islands and Western Samoa.

With seven clubs the current state of the game in Western Samoa shows a slight but healthy rise in bowling members, from 439 in 1983 to 508 in 1984.

At the 1984 World Championships in Aberdeen, Western Samoa's Maurice Fenn had the distinction, at 73 years of age, of being the oldest competitor on view. Fetalaiga Kirisome, unable to take part in the championships, was replaced by Felavi Petana who, teaming up with Ioapo Iosia, caused one of the shock results of the whole fortnight by beating the much-fancied Scottish duo Willie Wood and David Gourlay by one shot in the opening round of the pairs, a defeat which certainly cost the Scots a medal.

Zambia

With 13 clubs, 268 men and 155 women bowlers, Zambia has established a fine reputation on the world bowls scene. Until independence in 1964 the country, then known as Northern Rhodesia, was rather overshadowed by its neighbour to the south but since then, despite falling numbers, standards appear to have risen.

Zambia did not compete in the 1972 World Championships due to the presence of South Africa but at Frankston, Australia in 1980 Zambian bowlers achieved a creditable 12th place. At Aberdeen in 1984 representatives Japie van Deventer, Daniel Coetzee, Russell Hankey, Tommy Powell, Duncan Naysmith and team manager John Bruce improved on the 1980 position, ending in eighth position. Coetzee took 5th place in the singles, beating Cecil Bransky of Israel by one shot in the play-off, while the triple of Powell, Naysmith and Van der Venkers were beaten into sixth place by the strong Australian trio of Peter Rheuben, Don Sherman and Keith Poole who won by a single shot.

Zimbabwe

Bowls took root in Zimbabwe in 1899 when Cecil Rhodes turned the first sod on the green of the Bulawayo BC, the fifth bowling club to be formed in Southern Africa. For many years the Rhodesian game was closely linked with that of the South Africa BA, forming a district administered by that Association. Rhodesians competed regularly in the South African National Championships as well as their own nine-day annual tournament which dates from 1924. In 1953 Rhodesia joined with Nyasaland to form a Federation comprising Southern Rhodesia, Northern Rhodesia and Nyasaland – the present independent states of Zimbabwe, Zambia and Malawi – and, in the 1954 Commonwealth Games held at Vancouver, Canada, R. Hodges won the singles gold medal for Southern Rhodesia. In 1958 at Cardiff, Wales, a team entered as Rhodesia and, combining bowlers from the Federation, won bronze medals in the singles, pairs and fours events, repeating the feat in 1962 in Perth, Australia.

The unilateral declaration of independence by Ian Smith in 1965 saw a Rhodesian team entered in the 1st World Championships held in Sydney, Australia in the following year, but found them excluded in 1972 from the Championships at Worthing, England. With Johannesburg the venue four years later it is perhaps not surprising that they made their return to the world stage but a poor performance by the Rhodesian team ensured a low profile re-entry. In 1980 the country became truly independent and, as Zimbabwe, took part in the 1984 Championships at Aberdeen, when they were represented by Allan Bernstein (Wingate Park BC), Garin Beare (Avondale BC), Trevor Vincent (Raylton BC), Mannie Vollgraaff (Avondale

BC) and Jack Shiel (Avondale BC) with Louis Nel of Bulawayo as manager. Singles representative Garin Beare, an experienced bowler at international level and a competitor in the 1983 Kodak Masters, garnered six wins out of ten singles matches with a 21–12 victory over Hong Kong's George Souza the most noteworthy. In the pairs, triples and fours events the Zimbabwe team hovered around mid-table and finished the Championships in a creditable sixth place with a total of 59 points, a fine performance from a country with only 1600 male bowlers, the lowest figure among the ten full members of the IBB.

Future Development

The Bowling Association d'Espana, with seven clubs affiliated, was granted temporary membership of the IBB on July 1985, a sign that what had started merely as a holiday attraction was at last firmly established in its own right. Development of bowls in Spain dates from the mid-seventies when John and Sally Jacks opened the aptly named First Lawn Bowls Club at Fuengirola on the Costa del Sol. Since then clubs and facilities have sprung up all along the sunshine coast and across to the island of Majorca where the San Pedro Club was formed in 1984. With climatic conditions in mind several clubs have invested heavily in synthetic surfaces for their greens but at the David Bryant Bowls Centre at Cabrera in the province of Almeria, four grass greens have been constructed in a spectacular setting 1000 ft (304.8 m) up a mountain. Fortunately there is no shortage of water on the site and the greens appear in excellent condition. The Hacienda Miraflores at Marbella is a beautifully appointed time-share complex which provides tennis and squash as well as bowling on two synthetic-surfaced greens while the Bena Vista, at Estepona, has excellent accommodation facilities plus one grass and one synthetic green.

Since its introduction, bowls has proved just as attractive to Spain's English residents as it does to the holidaymaker and their interest, plus a growing awareness of the sport on the part of many Spanish nationals, has given the game a firm base on which to build.

Further expansion of bowls is fast gathering pace. Requests for membership of the IBB have already been received from India and Pakistan and under consideration are others from Singapore, the Cook Islands and Norfolk Islands while information on administrative matters have been requested from the IBB by bowlers in Holland, Belgium, Germany, Egypt and Brazil.

10 Profiles of Leading Players

Past and Present

Tony Allcock

See special feature

Sammy Allen IRELAND

Born: 6 July 1938. Club: Ballymena. Occupation: Civil servant. Bowling since 1966. A brilliant tactician, with a good range of shots and tremendous resilience, Allen is a bowler of wide experience. He represented Ireland at the 1982 Commonwealth Games winning a bronze medal in the fours. He won the Irish BA singles in 1979, the British Isles singles in 1980 and was runner-up in the Irish singles (indoor and out) 1983. He won the triples gold medal at the 1984 World Championships, and beat David Bryant 21–20 in the first round of the 1985 World Indoor Singles at Coatbridge, Scotland over 26 ends despite being behind 17–7 at one stage. Allen has been an outdoor international since 1973, and indoor since 1976.

Jim Baker
E. Percy Baker
John Bell
Peter Bellis

See special features

Cecil Bransky ISRAEL

Born: 15 May 1942 Johannesburg. Club: Ra'anana. Occupation: Gift Store owner
Cecil Bransky, who emigrated to Israel in 1980, first played in the Kodak Masters in 1982 but has only recently made an impact in the UK. A good singles performance in the 1984 World Championships at Aberdeen enabled him to finish in 6th place. He was runner-up to Terry Sullivan in the World Indoor Singles Championships in 1985 and runner-up to David Bryant in Gateway Masters 1985.

Bransky won the South African singles in 1972, the fours in 1976, and the pairs in 1980. He won the SA Inter District tournament four times. He won a gold medal at the 1973 Maccabiah Games, the Australian fours in 1977, the final of the Southern Transvaal Champion of Champions in 1979 (21–0 in 11 ends), the Israel Masters in 1980, the national singles in 1981 and 1983, and the triples in 1981, and in 1985 he won the Irish CIS Jack High tournament.

David Bryant OBE
Jimmy Carruthers

See special features

David Corkill IRELAND

Born: 15 February 1960 Belfast. Clubs: Knock (outdoor), P. T. Watson Stadium (indoor). Occupation: Civil Servant. Bowling since 1970. David Corkill is one of the younger stars in the game, a superb draw bowler and a fine tactician. He won the Irish national fours in 1977 and 1978, the British Isles fours 1978, the Irish national singles 1980, the British Isles singles 1981, the Irish national pairs 1983 and 1984, and the Irish Under-25s in 1983. His indoor honours include: the Irish fours 1979 and 1981, and the British Isles fours 1979 and 1982. He represented Ireland at the 1982 Commonwealth Games, and at the Australian Mazda Masters in 1983 and 1984, and finished in tenth place in the 1984 World Championships singles.

David Cutler

See special feature

Michael Dunlop IRELAND

Born 8 January 1960 Belfast. Club: Ormeau. Occupation: Photoprinter. Bowling since 1971. An experienced and tremendously exciting player with all the shots and the confidence to play them, Dunlop represented Ireland in the fours at the 1978 Commonwealth Games at the age of 18 and was semi-finalist in the national indoor fours in 1980. He won the national indoor pairs and triples in 1983, the national indoor singles and British Isles indoor singles in 1984, and the national indoor fours 1985. He has been an international since 1978.

Eddie Elson CROWN GREEN

Born: 4 March 1922 Warwickshire. Club: Alvis. Occupation: Toolroom Universal Miller (retd.). Bowling since 1937.

Introduced to bowls by his father at the age of 15, Eddie Elson played his first league game for Newdigate Colliery in 1937. He was a founder member of Alvis BC 1950, chairman 1951–61 and 1976–83, secretary 1961–6, and a member of North Midlands CBA Management Committee 1963, secretary 1965–72. He played five times for the county 1970–1, was a county referee and was elected secretary/treasurer of the BCGBA in February 1972 where he remained in office until retirement in 1985. He is a life member North Midlands CBA since 1977, and a life member of the BCGBA since 1985.

Eddie Elson has made a major contribution to the administration of the crown green game and his influence on players and officials has been considerable. His role in obtaining sponsorship at all levels of the game and coverage by television form only a small part of his activities on behalf of crown green bowlers. Prior to his retirement from office he was involved in the formation of the British Crown Green Referees Society and the affiliation of the BCGBA to the National Coaching Scheme. A popular and superb administrator and, when time permits, a more than useful bowler.

John Russell Evans WALES

Born: 29 May 1935. Club: Barry Athletic. Occupation: Bank Cashier. Bowling since 1949. Russell Evans has enjoyed a long and distinguished career. He is an elegant stylist, a good tactician and a superb draw bowler. Welsh captain 1977 international series, represented Wales in the World Championships 1972 (won triples bronze medal) 1976 and 1980. He took part in the Commonwealth Games in 1974 and 1978 (won singles bronze medal). He won the Welsh fours in 1963 and 1969, the singles in 1976 and 1977, and the under-35 singles in 1965.

He won the national indoor singles 1973, 1984, the pairs 1967, 1973, the triples 1973 and the fours in 1967. He won the British Isles fours in 1967, and the indoor international in 1961, 1965–84.

John Fullarton SCOTLAND

Born: 2 July 1940. Clubs: Ardeer (outdoor), Ardrossan (indoor). Occupation: Trades Co-Ordinator. Bowling since 1956.

Always a tough competitor, John Fullarton won the Scottish national indoor fours title in 1978–9 and 1982–3. He won the Scottish national and British Isles indoor singles championships 1981–2, the Scottish indoor pairs in 1984, and was indoor international for four years, 1980–3.

Mal Hughes

See special feature

Margaret Johnston IRELAND

Born: 2 May 1943. Club: Ballymoney. Occupation: Nursing Auxiliary. Bowling since 1964 (short mat); 1979 (outdoor).

After 15 years in the short-mat game Margaret Johnston appeared on the outdoor Irish scene like a breath of fresh air in 1979. In her first year she reached the final of the Irish singles and was semi-finalist in 1981 and 1982 when she also reached the same stage in the national fours. One year later she won her first national title, the Irish fours, and in 1984 embarked upon a remarkable sequence of victories which brought her the national pairs and singles and the British Isles titles in these events in 1985. The extraordinary talents of this attractive woman brought her international honours in 1981, since when her rink status has risen from number two in 1981 and 1982, to number three in 1983 and skip in 1984 and '85. In the year of her British Isles triumphs she also went through the international series undefeated. In 1985, Margaret represented Ireland playing in the triples and fours events. Her remaining ambition is to play for her country in the Commonwealth Games.

David Rhys Jones ENGLAND

Born: 28 June 1942, Gorseinon, Wales. Club: Cleveland. Occupation: Freelance Broadcaster/Journalist. Bowling since 1953. Born at Gorseinon, Glamorgan, David Rhys Jones moved house, home and Henselites to England in 1963 to take up the post of Head of Drama at a comprehensive school at Portishead, a position he relinquished in 1985 to pursue his present career.

Rhys Jones played his first full season for Clevedon in 1964 and one year later was invited by David Bryant to join him in pairs competition. This potent partnership won the Somerset, EBA and British Isles Championships in its first season, with Rhys Jones becoming the youngest title-holder in the history of the EBA, a distinction he held until 1972 when he was superseded by David

Cutler who won the triples at the age of 18.

Further successes came with the British Isles fours in 1969 and 1972, EBA pairs 1969, triples in 1966, 1977, 1985, fours 1968, 1969. Captained Clevedon 1968. Indoor, again with Bryant, he won the EIBA pairs in 1982. Outdoor international debut in 1970, indoor 1974.

Since 1979 Rhys Jones has made a significant contribution to the game by his perceptive, knowledgeable and highly entertaining commentaries for the BBC Television's *Jack High* programmes.

Albert Allison (Bert) Keech
ENGLAND

Born: 13 November 1906, deceased late 50s. At 23 st (146 kg) Bert Keech was truly a larger-than-life figure on the green. He took up bowls at the age of ten and five years later was number two in a rink which reached the final of the Yorkshire and District Championships. At 19 he skipped the winning rink in that competition. He won the Yorkshire and District singles in 1932–3 and 1934, the Brighton open singles in 1939, the Yorkshire county singles in 1938 and 1945, EBA national singles in 1945, and was England international for six years 1946–7, 1949, 1951–3.

An all-round sportsman, Keech was table-tennis champion of York for three years, won ten rowing and sculling trophies at Northern Regattas as a member of the York Rowing Club, represented the city at soccer and kicked the only goal in the rugby union match between York and the touring All Blacks in 1926. The Bert Keech Bowls Club in York is situated on ground that once formed part of his garden and his wife, Edith is president of the ladies secion.

Peter Line ENGLAND

Born: 13 October 1930 Southampton. Club: Banister Park. Occupation: Cartographical Draughtsman. Bowling since 1947.

An outstanding and exacting skip and a superb singles player, Peter Line is the most experienced of England's top bowlers. He won the EBA singles 1961 and 1964, the pairs gold medal at the 1970 Commonwealth Games, and the fours gold medal at the 1972 World Championships. He won Nat West EBA Top Two fours competition in 1981, the Toshiba singles 1984, and was runner-up in the Martini-EBA Invitation 128 singles in 1985. His open tournament successes include Littlehampton, Southampton, Worthing, Bognor Regis, Brighton and, the most difficult,

Bournemouth. Indoors he won the EIBA fours 1970, the British Isles fours 1971, and the EIBA mixed fours 1982. He is a regular in Hampshire Middleton Cup side. He made his outdoor international debut in 1955, and his indoor 1970.

Wynne Richards ENGLAND

Born: 10 June 1950. Clubs: Mid Surrey (outdoor), Cambridge Park (indoor). Occupation: Accountant. Bowling since 1960. Hardly one's idea of the typical accountant from Surrey, Wynne Richards hails from the somewhat earthier environment of Troedyrhiw, Merthyr Tydfil, and is blessed with a sunny disposition off the green which never blossoms into charity once he dons his whites. Wynne's first achievement of note, apart from a degree in geology, was to win his club championship at the age of 18. He was Welsh national fours finalist in 1968 and 1974. He moved to London in 1974, and reached the semi-finals EIBA pairs in 1977. He won the Surrey county triples in 1978, 1982, was fours finalist in 1980, won the pairs and reached the semi-finals EBA triples in 1982. Wynne's greatest moment in bowls came at Worthing in August 1984 when he defeated John Kilyon of Loughborough to win the EBA national singles title. He went on to add the British Isles singles championship to his tally of outdoor successes in 1985. He skipped John Williams, Chris Yelland and Neil Thompson to victory in the 1985 EIBA fours title at Hartlepool.

Norma Shaw
John Snell
See special features

George Souza HONG KONG

Born: 19 August 1942. Club: Craigengower Cricket Club. Occupation: Admin Manager. Bowling since 1965.
George Souza is Hong Kong's most successful bowler having won every national tournament at least once and was first recipient of the H. K. Bowler of the Year Award in 1982. His father, George Snr won Hong Kong's first Commonwealth Games gold medal as skip of the 1970 winning fours. Eight years later George Jnr emulated his father's appearance if not quite his performance by representing Hong Kong in the singles at the XI Commonwealth Games held at Edmonton, Canada, but in 1980 he won a fours gold medal at the World Bowls championships in Melbourne. He took part in the pairs at the 1982 Commonwealth Games in Brisbane and

in 1983 made an auspicious debut in the English game by winning the Kodak Masters at Worthing, England, beating David Bryant both in the qualifying rounds and in a final interrupted by torrential rain. George Jnr won the Hong Kong international pairs classic tournament in 1983 and pulled off the double in 1985 by repeating his win in the pairs and adding the singles title to his tally. He was semi-finalist in the Gateway Masters in 1984, and represented Hong Kong in the 1984 World Championships at Aberdeen and at the Gateway Masters again in 1985.

Mavis Steele
Terry Sullivan
See special features

Bob Sutherland SCOTLAND

Born: 21 May 1942. Clubs: Bathgate (outdoor), West Lothian (indoor). Occupation: Sales Representative. Bowling since 1968.
The slow, deliberate bowling style of ex-Glasgow Rangers centre-half Bob Sutherland, won him many admirers and the title 'the dancing elephant'. He has won various tournaments including the Teesside singles, Hartlepool pairs, Cardiff pairs, and was runner-up in the SIBA pairs in 1981. He won the Scottish national indoor singles, the British Isles indoor singles and the World indoor singles in 1983. He was runner-up to David Bryant CIS UK singles in 1983. He has been a Scottish indoor international 1974–6, 1979–84, and outdoor 1974 and 1983.

Andy Thomson ENGLAND

Born: 26 November 1955. Clubs: Blackheath and Greenwich (outdoor), Cyphers (indoor). Occupation: Indexer. Bowling since 1969.
Scots-born Andy Thomson won Buckhaven Club Championship at the age of 16 and one year later was Fife Under-30 Champion. He won the Scottish junior indoor title in 1978, and gained an indoor cap in 1979 at Aberdeen. He moved to Kent, England where he won the Kent singles, the EBA national singles, the EIBA triples in 1981, the EIBA fours in 1983, 1984 and the Denny Cup in 1983. He has been an English indoor international since 1981 and outdoor since 1982.

Christopher Ward ENGLAND

Born: 25 December 1941. Club: Cromer and District. Occupation: Printer. Bowling since 1951.
Elder brother of David, Chris Ward describes his stance and delivery as 'upright with a double twist'. While not the most elegant, it has nevertheless proved remarkably effective for this ex-Federation bowler. Left-handed at everything but bowls Ward won the Federation

The Island Green The Island Bohemian BC is situated on de Montfort Island in the middle of the River Thames at Reading, a unique and historic setting reached only by the club's own ferry. The club badge depicts a duel which took place in the presence of King Henry II on the island in 1163 between Robert de Montfort and Henry of Essex which lasted 'from sunrise to sunset', and at its conclusion Henry lay badly wounded and close to death. The King charged the monks at Reading Abbey with the task of removing and burying the body but Henry lived and spent the remainder of his days at the abbey.

The duels fought on the island today are not quite so bloody and the bowlers enjoy a comfortable clubhouse and a green laid in 1908. Until the 1940s the boundary line between Oxfordshire and Berkshire ran through the centre of the green which gave club bowlers the unusual distinction of bowling, at times, from one county into another. The present boundary, however, places the island in the county of Berkshire.

Island Bohemian, affiliated to the Berkshire County BA since 1926, has produced several county champions including Eric Marsh, who became president of the EBA in 1974 and, in that same year, acted as team manager to the English Commonwealth Games squad at Christchurch, New Zealand.

The Island Bohemian BC.

four-wood singles in 1965, the EBA fours in 1975 and 1980, the EBA singles in 1977 and 1982, and the British Isles singles in 1982. He was international outdoor 1978–9, 1981 and 1983.

David Ward ENGLAND

Born: 26 October 1945. Club: Cromer and District. Occupation: Industrial Civil Servant. Bowling since 1959.

Although lacking the singles flair of elder brother Chris, David Ward is a superb skip with a finely-tuned tactical awareness and the ability to play any shot with complete confidence. He won Norfolk county fours in 1966, the Bournemouth singles and the East Dorset pairs in 1981. He has been an outdoor international since 1982, indoor since 1983.

Kenny Williams AUSTRALIA

Born: 23 August 1933, Queanbeyan NSW. Club: Culburra New South Wales. Occupation: Cleaning Contractor.

Kenny Williams won the Australian fours in 1978 playing number two in the rink skipped by Tisha McIntosh. He won the Canberra South singles four times, seven Masters pairs titles, and was runner-up to Clive White in the 1974 Australian singles. He played twice in Test

Matches against New Zealand, and took part in the 1981 Kodak Masters and 1984 Mazda Masters. He finished in fourth place in 1984 World Championship singles, but won the 1985 Mazda Masters beating England's Tony Allcock 21–20.

Spencer Wilshire WALES

Born: 7 May 1945. Club: Tonypandy. Occupation: Electrician. Bowling since 1959.

An excellent tactician with a smooth and consistent delivery and wide range of shots, Spencer Wilshire is a pairs specialist but can rise to the occasion in the singles game. His first achievement was winning the Wattstown BC pairs in 1963. He won the Welsh pairs in 1975, 1978 and 1980, the British Isles pairs 1976, 1979 and 1981 with L. Perkins. He was Welsh singles champion in 1978, won the silver medal pairs at the Commonwealth Games, Brisbane 1982, and was runner-up Welsh indoor pairs (with L. Perkins) in 1977, runner-up fours (with L. Perkins, C. Diamond, G. Williams) in 1977 and 1978 (with P. Morgan replacing Williams). He replaced Ray Hill in the 1984 World Championships playing singles and pairs. He has been outdoor international 1977–9, 1981–5, and indoor 1977–8, 1983–4.

Willie Wood
See special feature

International appearances 'Big Syd' Thompson (born 29 August 1912) played 78 times for the Irish outdoor team and also won 51 indoor caps. Nigel Smith (born 2 February 1965) became the youngest bowler to represent England in the Home International series at Folkestone IBC on 7 March 1984 aged 19 years 34 days. Outdoor: Gerard Anthony Smyth (born 29 December 1960) at 20 years 196 days on 13 July 1981.

Syd Thompson (Ireland), the bowler with the most international honours. (*Belfast Telegraph*).

11 Miscellany

Bias and the Bowl

Bias

IN A GAME which abounds in legend, there is the widely canvassed story which tells of how Charles Brandon, the Duke of Suffolk, discovered the advantages of bias in 1522 during a game at Goole in Yorkshire. With one of his own woods split in half by a Bryant-like drive from one of his opponents, we are asked to believe that Brandon sawed off the spherical top of a bannister post and, with the sawn portion creating bias, resumed the game winning the next four ends in succession with his new bowl rounding those of his opponents on its way to the jack or target. A nice, cosy story but, I suspect, no more than that. A more likely theory is that bias can be traced back to the game of half-bowl, a pastime popular in the 15th century in which the object was to knock down 13 pins set in a circle, after first rounding two further pins set, one behind the other, at the rear of the circle. This feat was accomplished by use of the half-bowl described by Fitstephan in 1477 as 'a perfect hemisphere'.

It is also known that bowls used by the Maoris of New Zealand and some Canadian Red Indian tribes were, by accident or design, blessed with a certain amount of bias. Whatever the lineage, bias was certainly an accepted part of the game by the 16th century. In his *Castle of Knowledge* (1556), mathematician Robert Recorde wrote: 'A little altering to the one side maketh the bowle to run biasse waisse', and later Charles Cotton

Don Peoples (Australia) seems unconcerned as Terry Sullivan (Wales) lines up his shot during their semi-final encounter in the 1985 Embassy World indoor singles at Coatbridge, Scotland. (*World Bowls*).

spoke of 'flat bowls, round byassed bowls and bowls as round as a ball' in his book *The Complete Gamester* (1674).

A form of standardization emerged with *Mitchells Laws* published in 1848, which referred to varying degrees of bias numbered from 1 to 3. The first testing table on which bias could be accurately gauged was designed and used by Thomas Taylor Ltd of Glasgow in 1876. At that time bowls of increasing bias were manufactured as standards and numbered 1 to 7, number 1 being straight and number 7 swinging very wide. In the early 1890s the Scottish BA chose the Thomas Taylor number 3 as their minimum bias bowl, but in 1903 the Northumberland and Durham Public Parks BA favoured a bowl with a slightly wider trajectory from the same company as their master bowl. The EBA patriotically plumped for a number 3 bowl manufactured by John Jaques Ltd, an English company established in 1795.

On the formation of the IBB in 1905 it was the Northumberland and Durham Master Bowl, with a bias somewhere between that of the SBA and EBA choices, that was finally selected as the official minimum bias bowl. With the game becoming increasingly formalized, however, the early methods of inserting lead, brass, iron or pewter into one side of the bowl to create bias were found to be open to abuse and when the rules of the famous Scottish tournament for the Eglinton 'Jug' expressly forbade the use of weighted bowls, a new era in the game appeared on the horizon. In 1970 with the dominating composition bowl firmly established, the IBB's master lignum vitae was replaced by one of the plastic variety of the same bias. Testers, appointed through national bodies by the IBB, are each issued with a standard bowl which is checked for accuracy every ten years against the master bowl held by the IBB. Lignum vitae bowls were subject to a permitted weight for size rule, the larger the bowl, the heavier it proved to be. Composition bowls however can be moulded from materials of varying density thus, if required, can be of minimum size yet maximum weight. In 1980 the weight for size rule was dropped in favour of one which regulates only maximum and minimum weights and sizes. Bowl testing is carried out under stringent rules laid down by the IBB. Minimum permitted diameter of a bowl under IBB laws is 4 5/8 in (117·4 mm) and the maximum $5\frac{1}{8}$ in (130·2 mm). Maximum weight allowed is 3 lb 8 oz (1·59 kg).

Official Bowl Sizes

Size in inches	Size No.	Actual metric (mm)	May be rounded off metric (mm)
$4\frac{5}{8}$	0	117.4	117
$4\frac{3}{4}$	1	120.7	121
$4\frac{13}{16}$	2	122.2	122
$4\frac{7}{8}$	3	123.8	124
$4\frac{15}{16}$	4	125.4	125
5	5	127.0	127
$5\frac{1}{16}$	6	128.6	129
$5\frac{1}{8}$	7	130.2	130

On 2 November 1985 the EBA Council dispensed with the restamping laws for composition bowls.

The Bowl

Lignum vitae (*Guaiacum Officiale*), a wood so dense that it sinks in water, had, since its discovery in the West Indies by Columbus in 1492, become the prime material for the manufacture of bowls. Beautifully grained and enhanced with the initials of the owner inset on discs of ivory, lignums, although a distinct improvement on the various stone, earthenware and iron bowls that had preceded them, were nevertheless prone to warping and even cracking if neglected. Companies such as John Jaques (established 1795) and Thomas Taylor (1796) were among the first in Britain to produce lignum bowls in quantity, turning them by hand and comparing the results to a master template. Bias was controlled by

Jim Baker, 1984 Embassy World indoor champion. The moment of triumph! (Bowls International).

shaping rather than by the old method of loading one side of the bowl with lead, but the bias was, at best, variable and bowls were numbered 1 to 4 to help the owner choose the most favourably biased bowl for his purpose. In 1876 the Glasgow-based firm of Thomas Taylors pushed the art of bowl making forward by producing the first copy machine-turned bowls, from a template and a testing table by which bias could be accurately measured.

The development of the all-wood Mosquito aircraft in the Second World War, which succeeded against all odds, caused a revolution in the game of bowls. The extreme hardness and density of lignum vitae, which made it ideal for hurling up and down the bowling greens of the world, also proved an attraction to the designer of the 'wooden wonder', Sir Geoffrey de Havilland. The quantities of hardwood, including lignum vitae, required to build and maintain the Mosquito however

were such that by the end of the war very little of the West Indian hardwood remained and, with the tree taking some 150 years to reach a harvestable maturity, the search for a new bowl-making material became a priority.

The answer to the bowl-makers' post-war problem lay in a series of experiments carried out by W. D. Hensell in Australia as far back as 1910. Climatic conditions 'down under' had been doing strange things to the imported, traditional wooden bowl for a number of years. Hensell, working at the time for a company of official bowl-testers in New South Wales, had designed a machine to reshape the sun-battered lignums but had reached the conclusion that the real solution was to replace them altogether. In 1918, with the Dunlop Rubber Company, he produced a rubber bowl, the Ebonite, but made the vital breakthrough in 1930 by moulding a plastic bowl from a compound called phenolformaldehyde.

The testing table and shute. (*Staffordshire Sentinel*).

Measuring 5 in (12.7 cm) in diameter and weighing 3½ lb (1.6 kg), Hensell's prototype was the largest solid mass of the material then in existence and, christened the Henselite, proved an almost instant success on Australian greens, its reputation spreading worldwide once hostilities had ceased.

The long reign of the lignum vitae bowl was over, the rubber version bounced into oblivion and bowl makers grabbed for the plastic lifebelt to a man. Hensell's company, with its clear advantage of being first away, turned out its millionth bowl in 1956 and hit the four million (one million sets) mark in 1980, collecting three awards for Outstanding Export Achievement from the Australian Government on the way.

The Henselite still retains the lion's share of sales in the UK. British companies, however, taking advantage of the opportunities offered by 'open bowls', are mounting a serious challenge by signing up the game's leading players and manufacturing bowls to their specifications. Thomas Taylor, still going strong after almost 200 years, got in the first and most telling blow by collaborating with David Bryant to produce the Drakelite. A. E. Clare, the long established Liverpool sporting goods company, almost matched that with their Willie Wood-endorsed Drakes Pride while Concorde, the bowl made from Araldite by Wisden Edwards, has the young star Tony Allcock saying nice things about its performance.

Henselite, marketed in the UK by the Sussex-based Douglas Kenn Ltd, has kept out of the endorsement game but, with the prospect of witnessing the top bowlers switching allegiance to other makes, craftily worked a flanker by altering its point of attack to the lower end of the market. Taking over the factory of a new, but failed, bowl maker in Cumbernauld, Scotland, Henselite launched in 1984 the Almark Clubmaster, a bowl aimed through price at the average club player. The Almark is not particularly cheap but it appears that the magic of the Henselite name may tip the scales in its favour. The fight for the favours of a growing bowls market is well and truly on and in 1985 the Henselite Company upped the stakes by signing Tony Allcock to an exclusive endorsement contract, a move which could well ensure that their market lead remains healthy for the foreseeable future.

Prior to the introduction of the Australian-made Henselite composition bowl, the lignums widely in use in the British Isles were manufactured with a broad base in an attempt to obtain maximum weight without a resulting increase in overall size. Composition bowls, constructed from a denser material, required no such special consideration and were noticeably elliptical in shape, producing a wider swing at the end of their run than the old lignums. Henselite apart, the Drakes Pride, made by E. A. Clare and Sons Ltd, Thomas Taylors' Drakelite and John Jaques' Jackfinders and Eclipse bowls fall into the elliptical category, while Gray's Concorde and Tyrolite ranges, Taylors' Lignoids and the Vitalite bowl are manufactured with a base somewhere between that of the lignums and the elliptical variety.

Common sense dictates that the newcomer carries out a full investigation into the different properties of the various makes of bowl and attempts to choose the one best suited to the characteristics of his home green. A slow, heavy green generally calls for the broader-based bowl while on the faster greens and indoor surfaces the elliptical shape can certainly be played to advantage. As to weight and size there is a school of thought that advocates that the largest and heaviest bowl one can comfortably handle will prove the most suitable. There are special measuring devices to assist in determining the correct sized bowl for the hand but, if these are not available, a useful check can be made by spanning the running edge of the bowl with thumb and middle fingers and, when these touch, the correct size bowl has been found.

The Shots
The drawing shot
This is the basic shot in bowls and one which must be mastered before any other. Vital factors in playing the drawing shot are a fine judgment of line and length plus an appreciation and understanding of green conditions. The object is to deliver a bowl, played to the jack, with sufficient weight and accuracy of direction to allow the bias to take full effect before coming to rest in close proximity to the target. Expertise at the drawing shot comes only with constant and intelligent practice, including variation in jack length.

The Wrest
The wrest shot is simply a drawing shot played to rest on another bowl in the head or, played with more weight, to remove (or wrest) an opposing bowl from a scoring position.

The Trail
The trail is one of the most difficult shots in bowls and the faster the green the harder it becomes to employ successfully. Similar to the

Steve Halmai. (*Bowls International*).

Ireland's experienced young star Michael Dunlop. (*Bowls International*).

drawing shot, the trail is used to carry the jack a short distance and, therefore, judgment of the extra weight required is crucial. The objects of the trail are to move the jack either to one's own waiting bowl, to a position of safety or, in the case of a full length head, into the ditch. A trail shot delivered with poor judgment may have the opposite result to that required by flicking the jack to an opponent's bowls or leaving it in an exposed position.

The Wick

The wick is often regarded as a flukey shot but is used by top-ranking bowlers as the 'percentage shot' and played with great skill. The bowl is played to glance off another situated in the head into a position closer to the jack. Weight required will be determined by the speed of the green but the wick is best employed on one of medium pace.

The Cannon

Another 'percentage shot', the cannon is similar to the wick except that it is played with more weight, and with the possibility of using more than one bowl as a means of arriving at its destination.

The Yard-On Shot

A firm delivery, yard-on shot is played with less 'land' than the draw and is used to open up a head, to take out an opposing bowl or to position a 'back bowl'. Once again, the faster the green the more difficult this shot becomes to employ with regular precision, and concentration on weight and line is essential.

The Drive

The most spectacular if hardly the most attractive shot, the drive should be used with economy. It is important to know when to use this shot and inexperienced players, probably influenced by watching top bowlers on television, often drive when a firm or yard-on would suffice, and having done so, find it difficult to rediscover their drawing touch.

The Block

Used as a safeguard, the block, if correctly positioned, can prove a most effective shot. The ideal position for a successful blocker will be determined by the state of the head but it should be short of the head, preferably joining other short bowls to protect a winning position. A block can be employed as a deflector when delivered well short or, when just short of the jack, be in a position to be promoted. Bowled into the draw, a block can have a nuisance value and, the shot deserves more practice time than many bowlers allow, as a poorly delivered block is, more often than not, merely a wasted bowl.

The Positions

The duties associated with the various positions in rinks (fours), triples and pairs matches are detailed in the laws of the game. What will be required from lead, number 2, number 3 and skip, however, could hardly be a subject for legislation.

The most widely played type of game in bowls is the rinks or fours and an essential ingredient of a successful rink is, like many other games, teamwork.

The Lead

The good lead needs to be something of a philosopher. He is expected to produce consistently accurate bowls in the certain knowledge that, if one of his two efforts remains in the vicinity of the jack throughout the course of an 'end', he will be fortunate indeed. The lead's role, however, is a vital one because his bowl, if delivered correctly, can provide teammates with a psychological boost and something quite the reverse to opponents. A penchant for drawing to the jack is the most important tool in a lead's armoury. His length must be consistently good as a short bowl will prove an annoyance to his teammates. Ideally, his line should be such that his bowls finish either just in front or just behind the jack, so making as small a target as possible for the opposing side. Most coaches will counsel a lead to choose the best hand and stick with it come what may. Usually the skip is content to allow the lead to exercise his own judgment but, if called upon to change his hand by the skip, he should do so without vocal dissent. Leads should avoid bowling wing woods where possible and never bowl short.

Number 2

In many clubs, usually those without too much success, the no. 2 slot is reserved for the least experienced bowler in the rink. This is an error which will often spell disaster; a strong second bowler is essential to any combination. If the lead should fail in his task then the no. 2 will be expected to draw to the jack in an effort to establish a good position. Two accurate bowls from the lead will mean that the more difficult task of pure positional play is called for and here a fine judgment of length is especially valuable. The no. 2 may be called upon by his skip to execute any shot required to repair an adverse head or to consolidate a favourable situation. The quality of play by the no. 2 is of vital importance and to saddle an

Dan Milligan (Canada). (S. J. Line).
John Bell practises his 'Eros' shot. (*Bowls International*).

inexperienced bowler with such responsibility is not merely guaranteed adversely to affect his confidence, but will almost certainly put his rink at a disadvantage.

Number 3

Alertness, knowledge and experience of the game, an ability to play a wide variety of shots and a good temperament are the prime requisites of a no. 3. He will be expected to advise his skip of the game position at any time and be aware of the tactical requirements of building a good head. While ready to offer advice, he should never resort to argument once the man in charge has made up his mind. He is the skip's second-in-command and support is the keyword. His support should not just be extended to his skip, however; the lead and no. 2 will also benefit from his encouragement and example.

The Skip

To fill the position of skip, perhaps the most demanding role in bowls, is no simple task. It is not enough to be simply a good or even experienced bowler. While the position calls for the obvious, tactical nous, an ability to play any shot a given situation demands and the courage to do so, skips at the top level usually have more to offer. A sense of diplomacy and a willingness to shoulder the responsibilities inherent in the role are other qualities present in the make-up of a good skip. Added to these, an unflappable temperament, which will find him offering encouragement to his men rather than brickbats, can transform out-of-form bowlers into winners during the course of a match. A good skip will listen to advice from his no. 3, but the final decision will be his alone.

Glossary of Bowls Terminology

Absolute a bowl that draws the shot when other bowls are close to the jack.

Amateur a player who has not competed for a monetary consideration or declared wager. Prizes won must have been taken in kind and not in cash.

Back bowl a bowl some distance behind the jack.

Backhand the delivery of a right-handed bowler towards the jack in a left-handed direction from the mat with bias inwards; or by a left-handed bowler in a right-handed direction with bias inwards.

Badge a metal lapel badge or cloth blazer badge issued by a club, association, council or board and bearing an appropriate design and lettering.

Badged player one who has represented his county or country or other equivalent association; or one who has played in an international trial game and is entitled to wear the appropriate cloth badge on his blazer.

Bank the outer wall of the ditch above the level of the surface of the green.

Be up to reach jack length with your bowls and not be short.

Bias the tendency of a bowl or other spheroid to divert from a straight line in movement because of an imbalance built in by shaping.

Block or Guard a bowl resting in the draw or near the centre-line to hinder an opponent in drawing the shot on a particular hand or 'firing' at the jack or at a bowl or bowls in the head.

Bumper a bowler allowing his bowl to drop on to the green, thereby causing damage to the surface.

Huntingdonshire's Janet Chapman (right), EBF 4-wood singles champion 1983, and runner up J. Spooner of Norfolk. (*Bowls International*).

Burned a term used when the jack or a bowl has been interfered with or displaced other than by a bowl in play.

Cannon a bowl which glances off one bowl on to another.

Chalked when a 'toucher' has been chalked with a cross.

Clean sheet a player who fails to score is said to have a clean plate or clean sheet.

Cot colloquial term for the jack.

Count the total of all the scoring bowls at the completion of an end.

Counter a bowl conceded as a shot.

Covered when the jack or a bowl is guarded by another bowl in front.

Dead bowl a bowl which is no longer part of the head. A bowl illegally played.

Dead draw a precise draw to the jack.

Dead end an end which is deemed not to have been played. It can be caused by the jack being driven out of bounds and by certain accidental happenings.

Dead jack an expression used when the jack has been driven by a bowl in play wholly beyond the boundary of the rink.

Dead length an exact length drawn by a bowl to the jack or level with it.

Delivery the releasing of the bowl from the hand on to the green.

Disc the round piece of plastic, ivory or other material fitted into each side of the bowl, the smaller disc indicating the bias side.

Ditch the channel no less than 2 in deep (nor more than 8 in) surrounding a flat green having as its inner boundary the face of the plinth and as its outer boundary the outer wall up to the surface level of the green.

Ditcher a bowl which runs into the ditch without touching the jack.

Draw the effect of bias upon the bowl. The path which the bowl should take when approaching the jack allowing for the effect of the bias.

Drive a bowl delivered forcefully with the object of breaking up the head, taking out the jack or a bowl or bowls, running the jack into the ditch, or causing a dead end.

Easy-running green a medium-paced green.

Either hand the choice given to a bowler by his

skip of playing the shot on either the backhand or the forehand.

End playing to the jack all the bowls of all players once in the same direction on a rink.

End rink the nearest rink to the ditch on each side of the green.

Extra end an extra end is played by each rink in a tied match where a definite winner is required. A match of 21 ends finishing as a tie would thus be decided on the points scored in the 22nd end. If the match is still tied, further extra ends are played until a result is achieved.

Fast green a green made fast by the sun, cutting close and rolling. A bowl takes a wider curve and longer course to the jack on a fast green.

Firing delivering a bowl powerfully with the object of displacing the jack or a bowl or bowls.

Firm shot a bowl played with more strength than is required for a dead draw, but with less than is required for the drive or firing shot.

Follow-on a bowl played with enough force to move out of the way bowls in front of the jack and then continue on to the jack or other position desired.

Follow through fully completing the action of delivering the bowl along the line of delivery.

Foot-faulting under IBB rules a bowler foot-faults unless he has at least one foot entirely within or over the confines of the mat at the moment of delivery.

Forcing shot a strong delivery midway between a running bowl and firing shot in strength.

Forehand the delivery of a right-handed

Well-known broadcaster Paddy Feeny goes to Top of the Form for his novel delivery action. (S. J. Line).

bowler towards the jack in a right-hand direction from the mat; or by a left-handed bowler in a left-hand direction.

Four a team of four players each with two bowls. In a match the leaders play their two bowls alternately, then the seconds, the thirds and finally the skips.

Good length a bowl resting at the desired length.

Hand a path from mat to jack – forehand on the right and backhand on the left for right-handed bowlers; vice versa for left-handed bowlers.

Hatful the maximum possible score in any one end – four in singles, eight in pairs or fours, and nine in triples.

Head the jack and so many of the bowls, whether on the rink or in the ditch, as have been played at any particular stage of any end.

Heavy a bowl delivered with too much force for the shot required.

Heavy green a slow green caused by rain, lack of rolling or the grass not being cut closely.

Jack the small ball used as a mark to play to. In crown green bowls the jack is biased.

Jack-high when the bowl is level with the jack.

Kill an end to cause a dead end by driving the jack out of the rink.

Kiss a bowl just touching the jack.

Kitty colloquial term for the jack.

Land the amount of green to take to allow the biased bowl to finish near the position desired.

Lead the first player in a pairs, triples or rink who should lay the mat, roll the jack and draw the shot. In crown green bowls called the leader.

Lignum vitae the name of the timber used for the manufacture of wooden bowls.

Live bowl any bowl played and forming part of the head within the confines of the rink or any bowl in the ditch that has been chalked as a toucher.

Marker the scorer in a singles match. The second player should record the score in a rink game.

Mat the rectangular piece of material, usually rubber or canvas, used at each end to bowl

from. The dimensions differ in various countries.

Measure device employed to measure the distance from bowls to the jack to determine the shot.

Merry describes a bowl which is running too fast.

Narrow use of a bowl which is played with too little green to allow for the effect of the bias and which finishes running away from the jack.

No score a term used when the nearest bowl of each player in a singles, or the nearest bowl of each team in pairs, triples or rinks, is equidistant from the jack.

Open hand the side of the jack which has no bowls on it, or few compared with the other side.

Open jack a jack in full view from the mat and not obstructed by bowls.

Opening the head scattering bowls grouped in front of the jack so opening a channel to give an opportunity to draw the shot.

Pairing when one of your bowls and one of your opponent's bowls are resting together at the head.

Pairs two players constitute a team. They are the lead and the skip. A pairs match is played in various ways, each player having two, three or four bowls – the lead playing his bowls alternately before the skips play theirs.

Peels a Scottish expression to indicate that the scores are equal.

Pinching a bowl bowling narrow.

Possession of the rink applies from the time a player steps on to the mat until his bowl comes to rest.

Protective sheets large canvas sheets used to protect the ends of the rinks when the ground is wet. They are secured to the green and the bowl is delivered from a mat placed on the protective sheet or touching the back end of it.

Pulling a bowl delivering a narrow bowl by pulling the hand across the body instead of following through.

Resting on a bowl a bowl lying against an opposition bowl.

Rink the rectangular space on a flat green between the boundary rods upon which play is confined.

Round robin a competition in which each player meets all others. Also known as 'American Tournament'.

'Togetherness': Mr and Mrs Martyn Sekjer, losing semi-finalists in the inaugural McCarthy and Stone national mixed pairs at Hove 1985. (S. J. Line).

Rub a term used when a bowl is diverted from its line of passage by some obstacle on or in the green.

Running wood a bowl delivered with sufficient power to remove a target bowl before running on to a predetermined position.

Second the second player in a rink, who has the duty of recording the scores each end on the score-card, and each alternate end on the score-board.

Short a bowl not up to the jack.

Short end a throw of the jack to a minimum distance of 75 ft (22.8 m).

Shot the nearest bowl to the jack.

Shots the number of bowls of one singles player or team nearest to the jack.

Singles a game between two players, usually with four bowls each, but sometimes with two bowls each.

Skip the captain of a team.

Springing the jack playing a bowl gently on to a 'shot' bowl which is touching the jack at the back of it, so that the contact will spring the jack forward a short distance.

Strong, too when a bowl overruns the jack.

Take-out a bowl which takes out an opponent's scoring bowl, normally to capture the shot or shots.

Taking the green allowing the bias to operate to the full extent so that the bowl on a correct length finishes on the correct line.

Third man the third man in a rink who should do the measuring, determine the number of shots and take charge at the head when his skip is at the mat.

Toucher a bowl in play which touches the jack (but not a bowl onto which the jack is played) or which, having ceased to run, falls over and touches the jack before the next bowl has been delivered. It remains in play throughout the end even when in the ditch. A toucher bowl is indicated by chalking a cross on it. If the chalk mark is not on the bowl before the next bowl comes to rest, the bowl which touched the jack is no longer a toucher.

Trailing an expression used when a bowl moves the jack from an opposing bowl or on to a new position, the bowl keeping with the jack.

Trial end in the IBB Laws of the Game, one trial (practice) end in each direction is allowed.

Triples a team of three players each with three bowls. The leads play their three bowls alternately, then the number two players and finally the skips.

Tuck in an expression used when the jack is behind bowls and not visible from the mat.

Umpire a person appointed by the controlling body or by the opponents to adjudicate on any question or dispute which may arise in the course of a game or on the question of whether the elements permit a game to start or continue.

Weight of the green the force necessary to deliver a bowl of normal length having regard to the pace of the green.

Wick an expression derived from curling, meaning a shot played on to another bowl and being thus deflected towards the jack.

Wide when too much allowance for the bias has been made, and the bowl finishes wide of the jack.

Woods a term used for bowls derived from the fact that bowls were always made of wood before the advent of the composition bowl. The *lignum vitae* (wooden) bowl was extensively used in the British Isles, where bowlers still tend to call all types of bowl 'woods'.

Wrong bias a bowl delivered with the bias side opposite to that intended.

Yard on shot delivered with the object of pushing out an opponent's bowl resting near the jack.

RAF pilots maintain the Drake tradition. (Imperial War Museum).

GUINNESS TIME

SUMMER 1953

I wish that I could bowl a wood
To any length required,
And keep it up till sun goes down,
Without my getting tired.

But for a length, you need the strength
To put behind your wood,
Could Guinness do that trick for me?
My woodness . . . yes it good!

Index

Figures in italics refer to illustrations; *col* refers to colour plates.
The abbreviations BA (Bowling Association) and BC (Bowling Club) have been used.
Names found *only* in tables will not be found in the index.